Groups in Schools

Edited by
Peter Kutnick and
Colin Rogers

CASSELL

To Carole and Fiona

Cassell
Villiers House   387 Park Avenue South
41/47 Strand   New York
London WC2N 5JE   NY 10016-8810

First published 1994

British Library Cataloguing-in-Publication Data
A catalogue record for this book is available from the
British Library.

ISBN 0-304-32732-8 (hardback)
     0-304-32733-6 (paperback)

Typeset by Litho Link Ltd, Welshpool, Powys.
Printed and bound in Great Britain by Redwood Books,
Trowbridge, Wiltshire.

Contents

Contributors

Neville Bennett
School of Education
University of Exeter

Lucia Berdondini
Department of Psychology
University of Sheffield

Helen Cowie
Bretton Hall College
University of Leeds

Anne Edwards
St Martin's College
Lancaster

Eric Hall
Centre for the Study of Human Relations
School of Education
University of Nottingham

David W. Johnson
University of Minnesota
Minneapolis, Minnesota, USA

Roger T. Johnson
University of Minnesota
Minneapolis, Minnesota, USA

Peter Kutnick
Education Faculty
Roehampton Institute

Paul Light
Department of Psychology
University of Southampton

Karen Littleton
Department of Psychology
University of Nottingham

Frank Merrett
School of Education
University of Birmingham

Colin Rogers
Department of Educational Research
University of Lancaster

Peter K. Smith
Department of Psychology
University of Sheffield

Keith Topping
Centre for Paired Learning
Department of Psychology
University of Dundee

Acknowledgements

We would like to take this opportunity of thanking colleagues and friends whose help has been invaluable throughout the gestation of this book. We would especially like to thank the contributors of the original work contained in this book.

Peter Kutnick
Colin Rogers

Part 1

Theories

Chapter 1

Groups in Classrooms

Peter Kutnick and Colin Rogers

INTRODUCTION

Placing pupils into various groups is a feature of all classrooms. That children can and do effectively learn in classroom groups is not really a matter for debate. We must clarify, though, what is meant by groups (as found in classroom practice) and how these groups may be used to the maximum in promoting effective learning.

Chapters in this edited volume have been brought together to identify and demonstrate how classroom groups may be used for pedagogical purposes, creating a more effective learning context within the classroom. We hope to show that consideration of groups and grouping techniques should be at the forefront of teachers' minds when planning their lessons and topics; a consideration which ranks equal to planning of resources, lesson content and pupil tasks. Any general discussion concerning the use of groups in school is necessarily fraught with constraints that governments impose on the resources available in school and classroom, expectations of the effectiveness of schooling, conflicts between the ideologies of government and teachers, and conflicts between ideologies of teachers and their actual practices. These constraints are not a new phenomenon; evidence of them has been with us since the earliest educational writings – certainly from the time of the Greeks.

This opening chapter will focus on current practices and possibilities within primary and secondary school classrooms and provide a brief historic overview of the use of groups in schools, identifying some of the political debates that surround the use of various groupings in classrooms. There is a glossary of various definitions used with regard to groups. A thorough reading of the volume should provide the classroom practitioner and those involved with grouping theory with the means to review, analyse and develop support for the educational practice of grouping in classrooms. The editors have sequenced the chapters so that the book may be read as a coherent volume (for those seeking a theoretical basis for the range of groupings considered) or as individual chapters giving practical insights into specific grouping techniques. The book explores successes and inadequacies of current grouping practices and draws on a range of psychological theories to help explain how groupings of pupils may be structured by the teacher to maximize the learning of a variety of classroom tasks. Thus it can be seen as a continuation of previous work by the editors (see Rogers and Kutnick, 1990), and provides the groundwork for the establishment of a pedagogy of groups in the classroom.

AN OVERVIEW

A chapter on groups in classrooms must begin with agreement on a few basic assumptions. First, we must agree that schools have the ability to enhance learning amongst their pupils, but the effectiveness with which they are able to do so will vary between schools and classrooms. To a large extent, the effectiveness in promoting learning within any school or classroom will depend on the 'ethos' or general structure of action of the classroom, and a large component of the ethos will be the teacher's structuring and use of groups. The second point of agreement is that all pupils in classes are grouped in some form or another. Minimally, as Dean (1992) in the UK and Dreeben (1984) in the US point out, local education authorities (LEAs) and school boards make general organizational decisions regarding the age grouping and social mix (by regional placement of schools) of classes as well as whether school intake is selective or not. Beyond government organization of class groupings, teachers decide whether to use grouping strategies and which groups to employ, from whole class to small groups, to dyads, to individuals. Thus, every pupil in a class can be seen as being involved in a range of pupil groups that may (to a greater or lesser extent) affect her/ his learning potentials. The third point of agreement states that grouping pupils coincides with current theories of learning and development (especially as espoused by Vygotsky, 1978; Newman et al., 1989); that children learn in a social context and as a member of a relationship. The learning relationship may be between the child and teacher, the child within a small classroom group or as a member of the whole class.

The existence of groups in the classroom is not a new phenomenon, although the variety of grouping types and their uses has changed over the years. From the earliest recorded writings about education (certainly from Plato and Socrates) we see that learning takes place in a group context. This group context has, minimally, two elements vital to support the social process of learning – a number of individual pupils and a 'teacher' (one who has knowledge or information that others wish to obtain). The dynamic of individuals who wish to gain some information and a knowledgeable other allows for a number of variations for an effective learning group. The particular grouping which will be most effective in support of that learning will depend on the learning task assigned to the 'pupils' and how the teacher and others support the learning context. Socrates provided problem-solving tasks for his students and supported his learning context through 'dialogue' between expert (the knower) and novice. The dialogues also allowed the novices to generate and discuss ideas amongst themselves. The Socratic dialogue allows two types of learning dynamic, that appropriate answers may be confirmed by the expert and that mutually naive novices may speculate amongst themselves and thus generate new ideas to be tested.

As the privilege of education expanded from a small elite to the general masses (seen in the expansion of education in the late nineteenth century) a variety of new groupings were called upon. The question of who are to be educated and what curriculum they are exposed to has been discussed elsewhere (a useful insight within the English context is provided by Thompson, 1963). Obviously the expansion of numbers being educated meant that teaching could not be maintained in a small group, Socratic method. Expanding the number being educated required more teachers and physical space for education to take place. One of the most effective new groupings for expansion in education was the 'monitorial' method. In this method, teachers could 'teach' a small number of elite students and these students would then take the responsibility to 'teach' larger groupings of pupils. Knowledge and learning tasks under the monitorial method could not support the Socratic-type problem-solving discussions between teacher and pupil or generative discussions amongst pupils themselves; rather the learning task of this grouping was to transmit (rote) knowledge from the expert to others. Because the monitorial method did not allow for a two-way flow of communication the educator had to be satisfied if some of the pupils were able to 'learn' the new information while others were deemed incapable.

Over the last forty years, classrooms in developed countries have changed from large classes (50+ pupils) using 'whole-class' teaching methods to an average class size of 30 with children sitting around tables (as described by Galton and Williamson, 1992). Reports on classroom groupings in the UK and the US (e.g. Tann, 1981; Galton, 1990; Good and Marshall, 1984; Dreeben, 1984) indicate that groupings are often chosen to meet the needs of classroom organization and physical structure rather than being designed to promote the instructional/learning capabilities of children – number and size of groups often being set by the number of tables and chairs around each table. Simply because pupils are seated around tables does not mean that they will or can work as a small group. Galton and Williamson's (1992) review of studies concerning classroom groups found that there are four distinct types of classroom groupings: small groups, pairs, individual and whole class (see Chapter 2). The existence of these four types does not necessarily mean that teachers co-ordinate their assignment of learning tasks to these groupings. Galton and Williamson show that small groups are the predominant seating pattern but class work is often assigned to the individual (see Table 1.1).

Table 1.1   *Galton and Patrick's (1990) seating and working arrangements in small primary schools.*

Grouping	Seating arrangement	Work arrangement
small group	56%	5%
pairs	16%	4%
individual	7.5%	81%
whole class	20.5%	10%

This conflict between seating arrangement and work assignment has also been found in other studies of infant and junior classrooms such as Mortimore *et al.* (1988) and Tizard *et al.* (1988).

Any choice of grouping in the classroom sets the background for classroom control, socialization and administration of tasks, often in preference to instructional capabilities of the groups according to Bossert *et al.* (1984). Realization of the socialization and control features of classroom grouping is not a recent consideration. Within this century there have been debates concerning the role of schools as they relate to society and how schools actually represent existing relationships within society (Bowles and Gintes, 1976). As a gross feature of socialization we can see that whole-class grouping allows the teacher more didactic control while the mutuality of co-operative groups frees the pupil from too much dependence on the teacher and provides a background for classroom autonomy (Kutnick, 1990b). The socialization potential of grouping has been considered over many years; John Dewey discussed the role of co-operative school work as opposed to traditional didactic teaching in *Democracy and Education* (1916); Floyd Allport researched the potential collective nature of co-operative groups as opposed to leader-led groups in his *Social Psychology* (1924); the Hadow Reports on education in England and Wales (1926, 1931, 1933) acknowledged the socialization potential of schools and encouraged small-group work and social education. The debate concerning pupils' groupings and socialization is still being undertaken in the UK and US and other countries – most recently seen in the UK in *Curriculum Organization and Classroom Practice in the Primary School* (Alexander *et al.*, 1992). Applied to the classroom level, control and socialization features of grouping can be seen in the composition of large and small groups, such that: 1) mixing the range of pupil ability within each small group, a key factor in studies of co-operative learning, is not often employed by teachers except in non-traditional curriculum subjects such as art and craft; and 2) size of groups is often related to the amount of apparatus available to the class, especially with regard to classroom computers and materials for science experiments, rather than guided by pedagogic considerations.

That pupil groupings have many instructional/learning capabilities cannot be denied. The educational use of groupings is not a recent idea, and has been found in recommendations for effective education in the Hadow Reports (1926, 1931) and integrated into educational practices in the US of the 1920s (as described by Pepitone, 1980). Current use of groupings in the UK is often tied to the publication of the Plowden Report (1967). Plowden recommended: small groups should be used to increase teacher efficiency – pupils working in autonomous small groups would free the teacher to help individual pupils with problems; group work would allow pupils to recognize and work with the strengths of others; pupils within a group could help each other; explanations that pupils provide for one another would help to increase their learning; and group discussion would help pupils in their planning and discussion skills.

Group size, as already stressed, should not be thought of as limited to the small group (4-8 pupils) but should be seen as a continuum from individuals to the whole class. However large or small a group there will be some common principles that allow pupils to work and learn effectively. Social psychologists have shown that shared perspective-taking within groups increases the likelihood of cognitive understanding; the effective use of small groups promotes greater achievement through co-operation than do comparative whole-class and individualized grouping approaches; co-operative groups also enhance pro-school norms and within-class friendships across ability, gender and racial divides; and effective groups engender a sense of security, trust and identity amongst members (for educational examples see Dean, 1992; and a social psychological explanation see Brown *et al.*, 1988).

Grouping has also become a consideration in developmental psychology. The child is no longer epitomized as an isolated individual 'scientist', growing through a series of cognitive stages. It is acknowledged instead that development takes place as a result of interactions with other people. Interaction with others provides alternate perspectives that challenge and shape children's understanding. In one example of this research, Perret-Clermont (1980) found that pairs of children solved 'conservation' problems more effectively than children working as individuals; children were able to co-ordinate differences between their individual perspectives through conflict resolution. Doise and Mugny (1984) described this process as 'socio-cognitive conflict' and Bearison (1982) stated that interactors make reciprocal sense between themselves. This 'Piagetian' view of grouping asks children to work as equals and compare their limited experience; development takes place between 'mutual' peers (these points are made in greater detail in Chapter 6). An alternative developmental view is described by Vygotsky (1978) as the zone of proximal development (ZPD). The zone is defined as 'the distance between the actual developmental level as determined by independent problem-solving and the level of potential development as determined through problem-solving with adult guidance or in collaboration with more capable peers'. The development taking place between adult and child (or expert and novice) is best exemplified in successful teacher–pupil relationships. The quality interaction between expert and novice may also be found in peer tutoring situations (see Chapter 7).

To be effective, groups cannot be used simply as organizational features of the classroom. In the same way, curriculum presentation is unlikely to be effective if the role and involvement of groupings is not clearly identified. With regard to primary schools, Bennett *et al.* (1984) found that the curriculum practice based on the individual often hindered effective development of learning from taking place amongst pupils. When assigned individual cognitive tasks, pupils had to rely on the teacher when problems were encountered or when they complete an assignment. Reliance on the teacher often leads to management and control problems with many pupils vying for teacher attention and help at the same time. Similarly, at the secondary-school level during the 1970s, the establishment of curricula such as Nuffield Science (based on individualized and experiential principles) was found difficult to implement. Pupils needed to discuss problems amongst themselves. Limited amount of apparatus meant pupils could not experiment individually. In response to these problems, teachers often asked their pupils to work in small groups to ensure the effectiveness of their learning experience; a practical pedagogic response that ran counter to the individualized recommendations of the curriculum writers (Eggleston *et al.*, 1976). The conclusion derived from these critiques is that individualized and experiential curricula must take account of pupils' need to work with others for effective learning (Kutnick, 1990a).

The effective role of groupings in pedagogy is taken up, in part, with the onset of the National Curriculum in England and Wales. While wishing to stay away from evaluative judgements on the general need for and likely outcomes of a National Curriculum, we should note that virtually all of the curriculum guides (particularly in the core curriculum subjects) require children to work together, discuss and jointly solve problems. Pupils, in fact, will be assessed on group skills (for example English Attainment Target 1 is about speaking and listening, and virtually all of the Attainment Targets in science require pupils to collaboratively plan, discuss and communicate results of experiments). Teachers are required to assess and monitor group performance (SEAC, 1990). According to Bennett and Dunne (1990), the targets and skills identified within the National Curriculum can only be attained if teachers are fully aware of the social nature of the Attainment Targets, and use effective grouping practices for the classroom.

WHO LIKES WORKING IN GROUPS?

Teachers

The preceding discussion may be concluded by agreeing that teachers must organize classroom groupings if they are to work effectively. This conclusion suggests that all teachers will 'see the light' and instantly move to effective planning and implementation of group work in their classrooms. We should not be so naive as to expect that all teachers will wish to use groups effectively for learning. Potentially, group work challenges the traditional role of the teacher, i.e. as the one who is in control of knowledge and organization of the classroom (Bruner, 1986). And, the use of particular groupings will be affected by teachers' own education, ideology and preferences (Alexander, 1984).

Most research on teacher preferences focuses on small groupings (4–8 pupils) and rarely considers the use of a grouping continuum. Research findings show teachers may be identified as non-users, occasional users (who are unsure about the merits and effectiveness of groupings), divisive users (who use some groups while the rest of the class undertakes individualized or other assignments), and committed users (Cowie and Rudduck, 1988). Even in grouped classrooms Galton and Williamson (1992) found a vast majority of teacher time (80 per cent) focused on working with individuals as opposed to working with the whole class (12 per cent) and groups (9 per cent). Teachers who use groups in class often identify social reasons for their groupings (such as aiding the shy child who is afraid to speak in front of the whole class, development of relationships amongst pupils and learning to respect the opinions of others) in preference to supporting any type of learning (Crombie *et al.*, 1989). Working with various groups places teachers under particular constraints when it comes to assessment. It is a simple and familiar task to assess a pupil's work when the child is asked to complete an individualized task or make contributions in whole-class discussion. Within small groups, though, the teacher must be aware of within-group processes and should be able to provide whole-group assessment while identifying contributions in any group product.

Pupils

Like teachers, pupils have a range of opinions about working in groups; again most research refers to small groups of 4 to 8 pupils. A child's ability to work within groups will be limited by previous experiences of working with groups, liking of others within the group, and the general 'cultural' support for group work in the classroom. Small groups may be an alienating experience for a child who is teacher-dependent. The threat of working with other pupils who are not supportive may force the child into a passive role. Pupils' attitudes vary with regard to group work according to Cowie and

Rudduck (1989), including: those who value group work, practical users (for particular occasions in which they feel they may make some gains), and non-valuers. Liking of group work will be affected by pupils' perceptions of their teachers' attitudes to group work (Cullingford, 1988). Pupils who are unfamiliar with new ideas and new groupings will seek greater reliance on the teacher. And, if teacher directions are not clear or if teachers hover around groups and cause suspicions that the group is not working effectively, pupils will shift their attention from the group work to the teacher. Unease, lack of direction or suspicions of group effectiveness from the teacher causes some pupils to be 'fence-sitters' in their lack of group commitment (Galton and Williamson, 1992). Further problems may arise in groups where children are asked to expose their thoughts to a hostile group. If the child fears being 'put down' by a group, then he/she may not take the risk of explaining ideas or making contributions to effective group learning (Galton, 1990).

Groups do have their positive points for pupils. Dunne and Bennett (1990) found that pupils familiar with the ideas being discussed and the materials available will have little need of teacher attention and are very capable of looking after each other. Pupils who experience effective group work understand that they can learn from one another, and find security in doing so (Cullingford, 1988). Interestingly, one common criteria used to group pupils, that of friendship, is only critically accepted by children; they recognize the advantage of trusting and working with someone that they like, but are also aware that friends may not be the best group partners. Friends may 'muck about' and draw the child away from the work at hand.

Children's liking for group work is strongly associated with the legitimacy and structure given to classroom groupings by the teacher. Their liking is also affected by the relationship that children engender amongst themselves. For groups to be effective, pupils must feel secure, have the ability to communicate effectively amongst themselves, and understand that the teacher approves of such behaviour.

TRAINING AND GROUPS

Use of groups will depend on many factors. If teachers and pupils have positive experiences of group work, they will participate. Tension arises when groups do not 'click' or work together immediately and teachers and pupils may retreat from using small groups for learning in the future. Many studies of small groups find that they must have time to prove their effectiveness; small groups rarely work effectively the first time. These studies suggest that training of pupils for group work is necessary. Training can be undertaken in a number of ways. Minimally, the pupils must have and use skills of listening, questioning, challenging, helping and providing explanations to others (Bennett and Dunne, 1990). Webb (1989) finds that the most effective groups display high levels of elaboration and explanation of problems in their discussions, and group members can be trained to provide this type of interaction. These skills can be approached by direct training exercises or as part of a social skills programme that emphasizes security, communication and joint problem-solving (as described in Kutnick and Marshall, 1993; and Hall, Chapter 8). The need for a progressive building-up of these skills should also be coupled with the achievement of success by groups (Galton and Williamson, 1992). Teachers must be in a position to provide and support group skills by subtly intervening in group work to legitimize their effectiveness, allowing more advanced groups the freedom to explore how effectively its members may work together without having teacher intervention and allowing time in class to develop the skills. If allowed to develop effective group work skills, these groups also provide social and emotional benefits for children (Biott, 1987). Without training for effective group work, there is only limited likelihood that work in small groups will be successful. Although consideration of training has focused on small groups, the effective use of all other types of classroom groupings will require (or draw upon) similar skills if they are to be successful.

A GLOSSARY OF TERMS

Two areas of conflict concerning grouping have been identified in this chapter. The first conflict is between the ideologies of government and teachers (especially in the UK). Government has argued that traditional, whole-class teaching practices should be increased in primary schools and that 'progressive' practices fail to increase school achievement (see letter from Secretary of State for Education in Clarke, 1991). On the other hand, educational research (Bennett, 1976; HMI, 1978; Galton *et al.*, 1980; Mortimore *et al.*, 1988; Tizard *et al.*, 1988; Galton and Williamson, 1992; and Alexander *et al.*, 1992) has found that primary school practice is already overwhelmingly didactic and traditional in its orientation to knowledge and classroom working tasks. The second conflict is between teachers' ideology and their practice in the classroom. However much a teacher may favour a child-centred and active orientation in the classroom, it is difficult to bring about in practice, especially with regard to effective use of groupings for learning. In both these areas of conflict, arguments are voiced as if the situation were 'all-or-none', i.e. teachers should only use one type of practice (and avoid others). In fact, it has been found that teachers actually use a range of groupings in their classrooms (Alexander *et al.*, 1992; and OFSTED, 1993). The term 'fitness for purpose', used by Alexander *et al.*, appears as an analytic tool for the choice of effective grouping for learning in this and the succeeding chapter. Fitness for purpose applies to size of group (along the continuum from individual to whole class), the social context of instruction (theories of learning that support various groupings, teacher and pupil preference for their use), how various groups may be formed and structures (including ability, training for group interaction, friendships), empirical evidence concerning the effectiveness of various types of groups for various learning tasks, and possible problems that these groupings may cause in the classroom. At the least this chapter should dispel the idea that 'fitness for purpose' is easily identified. On the other hand, the terms defined below introduce a number of concepts and practices so that further chapters can take the discussion into greater depth.

GLOSSARY

Describing group size:

- **whole-class:** all pupil members of a class whose actual number, age, gender and ability mix will be decided by school and education authority policy.
- **small group:** usually 4 to 6 pupils together for seating and/or learning purposes. This grouping is predominantly used in co-operative learning studies.
- **triads:** three pupils working or playing together. Often used with microcomputers where one child operates the keyboard and others discuss the computer task.
- **dyads:** two pupils working or playing together. This grouping is used predominantly in cognitive studies and peer tutoring.
- **individualization:** each pupil has a unique work sheet/assignment differentiated by ability and application for the child.
- **individuation:** each pupil in a class works on the same work sheet/assignment, but only works by her/himself.

Describing pupil ability:

- **streaming:** differentiating between classes on the basis of homogeneity of ability such that classes in any year will represent high-ability, middle-ability and low-ability pupils.
- **banding:** differentiating by ability between classes but on a broader ability span than in streaming; classes may contain a mix of high- to middle-ability pupils and middle- to low-ability pupils.
- **mixed-ability:** classes in any year group composed of the full ability range of pupils (although teachers may stream small groups for curriculum and other work within each class).
- **homogeneous grouping:** small groups within a class composed of pupils of the same/similar ability.
- **heterogeneous grouping:** small groups within a class, each composed of the full range (mix) of pupil ability.

Describing grouping practices:

- **argumentation:** pairs of pupils agree key points for or against a proposition (or problem) identified by the teacher. Two pairs (one pair representing arguments for and one pair representing arguments against) then work together to discuss and present the full range of arguments about the proposition.
- **co-operation:** pupils are assigned separate sub-tasks which are brought together in a joint group outcome.
- **collaboration:** pupils are assigned the same task and share in a joint group outcome.
- **peer tutoring:** pupils work together in a teaching/learning situation in which one pupil is assigned the role of tutor (through either advanced knowledge or training) and other pupils learn from the tutor.
- **socio-cognitive conflict:** while interacting with peers, the child is confronted with alternative and conflicting perspectives, especially when approaching a problem. These additional perspectives may not be correct in themselves, but combined with the child's own perspective help to create a more adequate solution to the problem.

Describing theoretical issues:

- **contact theory:** a social psychological theory which states that co-operation can take place only if each pupil in a group makes an individual contribution, all contributions are of equal importance and the outcome is measured as an achievement of the total group effort.
- **zone of proximal development:** from Vygotsky (1978) 'the distance between the actual developmental level as determined by independent problem solving and the level of potential development as determined through problem solving under adult guidance or in collaboration with more capable peers'.
- **relational development:** if a relationship of trust and interdependence can be generated amongst pupils then they will be more likely and willing to co-operate with one another.
- **behaviourist approach:** belief and practice that classroom behaviours (such as co-operation) are likely to recur if they are rewarded. Teachers need to set up the original practice and ensure that a positive outcome is praised or provided with other tangible positive reinforcement (as merit points).

THE STRUCTURE OF THIS VOLUME

This book can be read in two distinct ways. First, read as a consecutive series of chapters, the book sets out theoretical and practical grouping methods and evidence of applications of grouping methods in classrooms. Second, individual readers may explore specific techniques of classroom grouping to incorporate into their practice. The editors provide overview chapters that lay out pedagogic and motivational issues concerning grouping pupils. The editors also introduce each chapter to provide an explanation for the inclusion of the chapter in the volume and the relationship of that chapter to the pedagogic principles of the book. Individual chapters introduce a range of grouping techniques, explain how each technique may work in class, and provide discussion as to why the technique may work. Authors were selected for their national and international status in the field of grouping children to enhance the prospects of school learning.

The first section of the volume provides theoretical and empirical overviews of pupil groupings used in the classroom. Kutnick, in Chapter 2, reviews studies of the grouping continuum (from individual to whole class) to ascertain whether particular groupings are more likely to enhance pupil achievement on particular types of classroom tasks, establishing a pedagogy of groupings.

Chapters in the second section provide specific evidence of the grouping continuum, from whole-class to individual approaches. Merrett challenges assumptions that small groups work effectively by comparing amount of 'time-on-task' by group and individual seating arrangement. He reports that seating pupils in small groups can detract from time that pupils have to consider various classroom tasks. Bennett provides arguments that small groups are very effective in supporting learning if teachers are able to structure group composition, interaction skill and appropriateness of task. Taking Bennett's ideas further is a stimulating consideration of argumentation, or the structuring of small groups for specific discussions, by David and Roger Johnson (who have a strong reputation for their work in co-operative learning).

Working with even smaller groupings, Topping provides a practical example and discussion of pairings that are used for peer tutoring in a wide variety of classroom purposes. Light, again working predominantly with pairs of pupils, brings the reader up to date with the literature on cognitive development and how it is enhanced in the social interaction of the classroom context. Light's chapter combines practical and theoretical issues. Another combination of practical/theoretical is presented by Hall, who draws upon experiential and humanistic psychology to develop social relationships amongst pupils and support their learning. Rogers sums up the second section by focusing on motivational issues that support and allow pupil groupings to work effectively.

The third section describes practical applications of the previous techniques in the classroom. The editors draw upon two concerns for classroom and teacher. Edwards explores a number of curriculum applications of classroom grouping, based on the variety of learning tasks within a classroom learning cycle (returning to an integrated pedagogy of classroom groups). Smith and colleagues have worked with school bullying for a number of years, and now draw upon their experience to discuss how co-operative group work can help to overcome a number of problems generated by and within bullying situations.

REFERENCES

Alexander, R. (1984) *Primary Teaching*. Eastbourne: Holt, Rinehart & Winston.

Alexander, R., Rose, J. and Woodhead, C. (1992) *Curriculum Organization and Classroom Practice in Primary Schools: A Discussion Paper*. London: DES.

Allport, F. (1924) *Social Psychology*. New York: Houghton Mifflin.

Bearison, D. (1982) New directions in studies of social interaction and cognitive growth. In F.C. Serafica (ed.), *Social-cognitive Development in Context*. New York: Guildford Press.

Bennett, N. (1976) *Teaching Styles and Pupil Progress*. London: Open Books.

Bennett, N. and Dunne, E. (1990) Implementing co-operative groupwork in classrooms. In V. Lee (ed.), *Children's Learning in School*. London: Hodder & Stoughton.

Bennett, N., Desforges, C., Cockburn, A. and Wilkinson, B. (1984) *The Quality of Pupils' Learning Experiences*. London: Lawrence Erlbaum Associates.

Biott, C. (1987) Co-operative group work: pupils' and teachers' membership and participation. *Curriculum*, **8**, 5-14.

Bossert, S., Barnett, B. and Filby, N. (1984) Grouping and instructional organization. In P. Peterson, L. Wilkinson and M. Hallinan (eds), *The Social Context of Instruction*. Orlando, Fla: Academic Press.

Bowles, S. and Gintes, H. (1976) *Schooling in Capitalist America*. New York: Basic Books.

Brown, W., Ragland, E. and Fox, J. (1988) Effects of group socialization on the social interactions of preschool children. *Research in Developmental Disabilities*, **9**, 359-76.

Bruner, J. (1986) *Actual Minds, Possible Worlds*. Cambridge, Mass: Harvard University Press.

Clarke, K. (1991) *Primary Education: A Statement by the Secretary of State for Education and Science*. London: DES.

Cowie, H. and Rudduck, J. (1988) *Co-operative Group Work: An Overview*. London: BP Education Service.

Crombie, R., Lowe, T. and Stigston, A. (1989) Group work and teacher skill: the role of the educational psychologist. *Educational Psychology in Practice*, **5**, 23-9.

Cullingford, C. (1988) Children's views about working together. *Education 3-13*, **16**, 29-34.

Dean, J. (1992) *Organizing Learning in the Primary School Classroom*. London: Routledge.

Dewey, J. (1916) *Democracy and Education*. New York: Macmillan.

Doise, W. and Mugny, G. (1984) *The Social Development of the Intellect*. Oxford: Pergamon.

Dreeban, R. (1984) First-grade reading groups: their formation and change. In P. Peterson, L. Wilkinson and M. Hallinan (eds), *The Social Context of Instruction*. Orlando, Fla: Academic Press.

Dunne, E. and Bennett, N. (1990) *Talking and Learning in Groups*. London: Macmillan.

Eggleston, J.F., Galton, M. and Jones, M. (1976) *Processes and Products of Science Teaching*. London: Macmillan.

Galton, M. (1990) Grouping and groupwork. In C. Rogers and P. Kutnick (eds), *The Social Psychology of the Primary School*. London: Routledge.

Galton, M. and Patrick, H. (eds) (1990) *Curriculum Provision in Small Primary Schools*. London: Routledge.

Galton, M. and Williamson, J. (1992) *Groupwork in the Primary School*. London: Routledge.

Galton, M., Simon, B. and Croll, P. (1980) *Inside the Primary Classroom*. London: Routledge & Kegan Paul.

Good, T. and Marshall, S. (1984) Do students learn more in heterogeneous or homogeneous groups? In P. Peterson, L. Wilkinson and M. Hallinan (eds), *The Social Context of Instruction*. Orlando, Fla: Academic Press.

Hadow Report (1926) *Education of the Adolescent*. London: HMSO.

Hadow Report (1931) *Report of the Consultative Committee on the Primary School*. London: HMSO.

Hadow Report (1933) *Report of the Consultative Committee on Infant and Nursery Schools*. London: HMSO.

HMI (1978) *Primary Education in England*. London: HMSO.

Kutnick, P. (1988) *Relationships in the Primary School Classroom*. London: Paul Chapman.

Kutnick, P. (1990a) A social critique of cognitively based science curricula. *Science Education*, **74**, 87-94.

Kutnick, P. (1990b) Social development of the child and the promotion of autonomy in the classroom. In C. Rogers and P. Kutnick (eds), *The Social Psychology of the Primary School*. London: Routledge.

Kutnick, P. and Marshall, D. (1993) Development of social skills and the use of the microcomputer in the primary school classroom. *British Educational Research Journal*, **19**, 517-33.

Mortimore, P., Sammons, P., Stol, L.D. and Ecob, R. (1988) *School Matters: The Junior Years*. Wells: Open Books.

Newman, D., Griffin, D. and Cole, M. (1989) *The Construction Zone: Working for Cognitive Change in School*. London: Cambridge University Press.

OFSTED (1993) *Curriculum Organization and Classroom Practice: A Follow-up Report*. London: DFE.

Pepitone, E. (1980) *Children in Co-operation and Competition*. Lexington, Mass: Lexington Books.

Perret-Clermont, A.-N. (1980) *Social Interaction and Cognitive Development in Children*. London: Academic Press.

Plowden Report (1967) *Children and Their Primary Schools*. London: HMSO.

Rogers, C. and Kutnick, P. (1990) (eds), *The Social Psychology of the Primary School*. London: Routledge.

SEAC (1990) *Teacher Assessment in the Classroom*. London: Heinemann Educational.

Tann, S. (1981) Grouping and groupwork. In B. Simon and J. Willcocks (eds), *Research and Practice in the Primary School*. London: Routledge & Kegan Paul.

Thompson, E.P. (1963) *Making of the English Working Class*. Harmondsworth: Penguin.

Tizard, B., Blatchford, P., Burke, J., Farquhar, C. and Plewis, I. (1988) *Young Children at School in the Inner City*. Hove: Lawrence Erlbaum.

Webb, N. (1989) Peer interaction and learning in small groups. *International Journal of Educational Research*, **13**, 21-39.

Vygotsky, L. (1978) *Mind and Society: The Development of Higher Mental Processes*. Cambridge, Mass: Harvard University Press.

Chapter 2

Use and Effectiveness of Groups in Classrooms: Towards a Pedagogy

Peter Kutnick

INTRODUCTION

Most reviews of groups in schools begin by comparing the types of studies and are dominated by the cultural distinction between the United States and the United Kingdom. It is an unavoidable division in approach. Group work in classrooms is represented quite distinctly in these cultures. A majority of the American studies test specific hypotheses and take an experimental approach to the study of groups; in the UK studies come from a different tradition, observing what teachers actually do in class. There are advantages and disadvantages to both of the approaches.

Grouping is a means for classroom and learning organization. Teachers obviously must make a 'best choice' of grouping (by structuring size, composition and task) for their classroom purposes. This chapter explores the various types of groups that can be used, how the choice of grouping should relate to the type of classroom learning task that is being undertaken, and why this is so. The term group or grouping is used in the widest possible sense – from the whole class being the group to the whole class providing a grouping method of individualization.

CLASSROOM GROUPS IN THE US

Reviews of research in the United States consistently find that small groups are an under-used resource in the classroom (Bennett and Dunne, 1990; Galton and Williamson, 1992). For the most part, these reviews state that the predominant grouping for classroom instruction is the whole class, although a number of teachers have extended their repertoire to include small groups during the 1980s (Peterson *et al.*, 1984). In accordance with social psychological theory (especially contact theory) small groups are arranged to enhance co-operation and allow for individual achievement through group incentives, with each member equally accountable for some part of the group's achievement. The particular 'co-operative' arrangement, while having a basis in psychological theory, is also rooted in American legislation for 'integrated' classrooms (where all pupils have an equal opportunity to succeed). These integrated classrooms are not simply idealized images, and a number of co-operative experiments show positive educational effects.

Many of the US experiments have been remarkably successful, although the studies have a limited definition of success and usually take place over a short time period only (Bennett and Dunne, 1990). For a fuller description of American studies see Chapters 4 and 5; the following is only a brief introduction. Reviewers frequently cite co-operation studies undertaken by Robert Slavin and David and Roger Johnson as evidence of effective group work. These researchers integrate co-operative learning into classrooms and show its effectiveness in comparison to individual and whole-class teaching. Slavin (1990) devised a number of approaches to co-operative learning that involve contact theory. The various approaches (student-teams achievement divisions, team-games tournament, team-assisted individualization, co-operative integrated reading and composition) follow this scheme: 1) teachers give a preliminary classroom 'quiz' to provide a baseline pre-test of individual pupil competence within the subject concerned; 2) teachers provide a task that can be divided so that each group member has an individual sub-task to learn; 3) group members learn their sub-task and then teach the sub-task to all other members of their group; 4) all group members are tested on all sub-tasks (a post-test); 5) for each pupil, a change score is calculated as the difference between the pre-test and post-test and an average of the change scores (the actual improvement) is calculated for each group; 6) teachers distribute group-based rewards either competitively between classroom groups for a top score or to any group that reaches a criterion of improvement. Extensive comparisons of Slavin's co-operative approaches to traditional classes show: comparable or (in a majority of studies) greater academic achievement in co-operative classes, with increased pro-school attitudes and mixed gender, race and ability friendships and a heavy reliance on structuring tasks and reward by the teacher.

Roger and David Johnson (1987) do not structure as elaborate a design as Slavin. The Johnsons provide common tasks for students to undertake as a group. Comparisons of their group task outcomes are made with individualized and whole-class groupings who undertook a similar learning task. Comparisons show enhanced achievement in the co-operative grouping as well as more positive development of pupils' self-esteem.

Another co-operative approach to small-group work is the 'jigsaw' of Aronson *et al.* (1978). This approach is similar to Slavin's planned task, but interaction between classroom groups is considered as well. Aronson divides each class into a number of base groups and assigns all base groups the same task. The task is divided into sub-tasks. Each group member within a base group is assigned a sub-task. Within the class, all pupils assigned the same sub-task are asked to work together and learn about their sub-task in expert groups. Pupils then return to their base group to teach their sub-task to other base group members. Group members are then tested for their knowledge on all sub-tasks. This complicated interchange is depicted in Table 2.1.

Studies of the Jigsaw approach find increased academic achievement when compared to normal classes, along with more positive attitudes to school and improved self-esteem.

Another distinct, and insightful, American approach to small-group work is presented by Noreen Webb (1985; 1989; 1991). Webb does not structure her groups to

Table 2.1 *The Jigsaw approach with three sub-tasks (1, 2, 3) and three groups (A, B, C).*

1. Base group (task assignment)	2. Expert group (sub-task learning)	3. Base group (sub-task teaching)	4. Testing of all group members on all sub-tasks
A(1), A(2), A(3)	A(1), B(1), C(1)	A(1), A(2), A(3)	
B(1), B(2), B(3)	A(2), B(2), C(2)	B(1), B(2), B(3)	
C(1), C(2), C(3)	A(3), B(3), C(3)	C(1), C(2), C(3)	

be co-operative or collaborative, but tries to ascertain what activities actually make a group more effective in learning. She assigns her groups a problem to solve, expecting that group members will help each other. Group members are not assigned specific roles but are expected to master the task on an achievement test. Group members show a range of on- and off-task interactions which either facilitate or hinder group problem solving. On-task interactions include asking questions, offering explanations, giving 'terminal' answers of right and wrong. Off-task interactions include conversations that do not relate to the work at hand and 'putting down' other group members. Groups that use a high amount of explanation are most likely to achieve. Explanations that provide a high level of elaboration concerning the problem are most effective. And, elaboration is more likely to take place in English and social studies than in mathematics.

The US studies show that co-operation and collaboration are effective approaches to promote learning and have additional social and emotional advantages for small groups. These studies do not comment on the other types of grouping (except that traditional, didactic teaching may bring positive results in the mastery orientation that often characterizes mathematics subject teaching; Forman, 1989) and mainly focus on problem-solving and application activities. Studies of co-operative and collaborative grouping show these approaches to be effective, but effectiveness is established only with clear planning of tasks to suit that type of group. Co-operative and collaborative groups must have good communication skills, especially of elaboration, to maintain and develop group discussion. Planning for the outcome of group work is important, whether one accepts Slavin's suggestion of group reward for co-operative effort or the alternative collaborative encouragement of group efforts.

CLASSROOM GROUPS IN THE UK

Many types of grouping have been in evidence in UK classrooms. Groupings include individualized approaches, small groups of 4 to 8 pupils and whole-class approaches. Research undertaken on these groupings focuses on teaching style, type of small-group learning tasks, and teacher–pupil interaction. Most studies use observational methods rather than structured experiments to gather data. In general, the results show little evidence that teachers structure small groups for reasons other than classroom organization. There is little or no evidence that particular groups are assigned particular tasks, and little comparative testing between types of grouping. Studies find that teachers use a range of organizational styles with regard to grouping and, unlike in the United States, the government has kept a watchful eye on groupings. Thus, the following studies include academic research and reports from government inspections.

A number of studies explored grouping methods and their effects in classrooms before Neville Bennett's *Teaching Styles and Pupil Progress* (1976), but few of the previous studies caused as much 'stir'. Bennett's large-scale survey in the north of England found that teaching styles varied from traditional (whole-class) to child-centred. Using traditional academic tests in the core subjects and creative writing, Bennett found that children taught as a traditional, whole-class grouping achieved the highest test scores. Readers should note that comparative results between traditional and child-centred approaches may not be as drastic as initially perceived, especially as very few teachers (approximately 17 per cent) used the latter. Bennett's study gave focus to questions which compared presence and effectiveness of classroom grouping with regard to learning. Bennett's critical starting point was the recommendations of the Plowden Committee (1967).

With regard to grouping in classrooms, Galton (1990) summarizes the Plowden recommendations as: collaborative groups should be used to overcome management problems in large classes; groups should be arranged and changed according to subject and other needs; pupils working in collaborative groups have the opportunity to explain and teach each other; small groups should allow a positive environment in which the shy and timid child may best respond; and effective groupings of pupils should allow the teacher the freedom to work with individual pupils who need extra help and support.

Perceived benefits of classroom groups expressed in the Plowden Report are similarly expressed by others, such as Kerry and Sands (1982) who state: collaboration amongst pupils will increase their ability to co-operate, pupils will be able to learn from others, and these groupings will remove the stigma of failure. While Bennett set the proverbial 'traditional cat amongst the progressive and grouping pigeons', a great opportunity was opened to ascertain the validity of Bennett's findings and question whether effective grouping practices were being undertaken within the UK.

The first large-scale, post-Bennett research in this area was an observational study that sought evidence of teaching and grouping style in the UK (Galton *et al.*, 1980). Their ORACLE survey observed teachers in junior schools in five education authorities. With regard to the use of groups in the classroom they found: 1) pupils were most likely to sit around tables in physical groups; 2) teachers, who used a wide range of teaching styles, rarely planned for group work; 3) teachers dominated 30 per cent of the classroom talk (80 per cent of teacher talk was directed towards individual pupils, 12 per cent to the whole class and 9 per cent to groups); 4) a number of small groupings were used, which included individualized seat work, joint (or collaborative) group work and co-operative group work (seat work was used most often and collaboration was found in the sharing of materials as opposed to problem solving); 5) teachers, in the main, taught to the individual pupil and generally used didactic methods rather than structuring relevant group co-operative or collaborative tasks; and 6) pupils did not show a great propensity to work together.

Preceding the ORACLE publication, Bassey (1978) questioned 900 primary school teachers about preferred teaching styles. He found a majority used whole-class methods; group work was used to a very limited extent. Bennett *et al.* (1984) observed groupings of infant pupils sitting around tables but undertaking individualized learning. The children talked amongst themselves but exchanges were usually at a low functional level, with little evidence of elaboration. Many of their individualized tasks were of a cognitive nature. Children rarely used co-operative skills and were dependent on teachers for help (if there was any misunderstanding), feedback about right and wrong answers, or direction for further tasks. Teacher dependence caused management problems. Children often queued around the teacher's desk to await her attention. Their noise and movements caused disruption within the classroom and teachers had to focus attention on maintaining 'order' in the queue rather than help with the learning task. Bennett's study shows a classic mismatch between cognitive task and individualized grouping methods.

Evidence of structuring classes into physical groups while teaching the pupils in a traditional manner was also presented in a large-scale study in Inner London schools by Tizard *et al.* (1988). She found that 65 per cent of all teacher–pupil contacts were with the whole class, 17 per cent on a one-to-one basis and 19 per cent with groups. Whole-class contact was mainly via individualized work, where each member of the class undertook the same task and each child had responsibility only for her/his own work. At the junior level, the study by Mortimore *et al.* (1988) of 400 Inner London schools again found evidence that the predominant teaching style was didactic with teacher–pupil interaction focusing on the individual. Teachers physically grouped pupils in 70 per cent of the classes while stating that they preferred teaching their classes in groups. Teacher–pupil interaction was mainly directed towards individuals (67 per cent), then the whole class (23 per cent) and groups (9 per cent). Of the teachers who grouped their classes, most based the groupings on children's ability levels. Classes taught in groups (especially using the 'rotating group' method) were less 'effective in learning outcomes if too many activities took place simultaneously'.

Results indicating a teacher preference for the whole-class approach to grouping were again found in Galton's ORACLE 2 study (see Galton and Williamson, 1992), undertaken more than 10 years after the original ORACLE study. Approximately two-thirds of the teachers stated that they used groups in their classroom; most pupils were physically grouped by mixed ability or friendships; most teacher interactions were with individuals (72 per cent), followed by whole class (19 per cent) and small groups (9 per cent). A majority of teachers stated that they favoured discussions amongst groups with individual pupils' assessments, but the relationship between this aim and actual classroom practice was weak. And, most group work did not call for within-group interaction – pupils were unlikely to maintain collaborative efforts if the teacher was not present to direct them towards collaboration. Pupils preferred not to collaborate within groups and this was explained by the lack of desire to take risks in groups. Pupils were unlikely to be supported within the group by positive and helpful feedback from other group members (Galton, 1990).

Overwhelmingly, these survey and observational studies show that teachers use a variety of groupings in class. Small groups are the most likely seating arrangement, while whole-class and individualized grouping is the predominant teaching mode. Teachers, for the most part, do not assign tasks that draw upon small-group capabilities (of co-operation and collaboration) and pupils do not show preferences for working in small groups – in fact, they can find small groups quite threatening. Teachers' use of whole-class and individualized approaches is not confined to particular regions in England or to particular age groups. There is enough survey evidence to show that these approaches probably characterize most primary and secondary schools throughout the country.

Lack of small group use does not mean that there is no evidence of this grouping. At ideological and physical levels, teachers of the post-Plowden era have taken up the call for small groups in the classroom. Influential government inspections of primary schools have continually asserted the important role of small groups in the classroom, and current recommendations call for a stronger pedagogical basis for the use of all types of classroom groups. Based upon survey and observational research, the HMI provide the following insights into classroom groups: in many schools in England the teaching style was overwhelmingly didactic (75 per cent of teachers were categorized as such, with only 5 per cent being exploratory, or child-centred) and the small groups used were structured according to subject being studied – with reading, mathematics and writing being undertaken in homogeneous ability groups and art, craft and physical education undertaken in mixed-ability groups (HMI, 1978a). From inspections of 80 infant schools HMI (1982) recommended that children as young as 5 could benefit from small-group co-operative experiences within the curriculum. The survey of mathematics teaching (HMI, 1989a) found that co-operative groups were a strong feature of the best mathematics teaching, and a majority of small groups in mathematics were homogeneous in their ability range; similarly, the survey of science teaching (HMI, 1989b) found the best work undertaken in small-group investigations. A government-sponsored investigation of the literature about practice in primary schools (Alexander *et al.*, 1992) reported advantages for all types of groupings in schools, individualized, small-group and whole-class, but recommended that teachers give pedagogic consideration to their choice of grouping rather than using groups as an organizational device or in response to ideological fashion (see Alexander, 1984). A follow-up survey to the review (OFSTED, 1993) found that most teachers observed in primary schools used small groups for classroom organizational purposes, particularly to provide ability-differentiated assignments to pupils in mathematics and English. Again, OFSTED found that group assignments did not entail collaboration and pupils worked mainly as individuals in a small group context. UK primary school teachers have been under ideological pressure (from training institutions and government) to integrate a variety of groupings into their teaching style. Surveys show they have effectively taken up this opportunity. Reliance solely on survey research in the UK, though, would omit a number of further insights.

Some UK studies adopted experimental and comparative methods, focusing on processes taking place within small groups. Boydell (1975) found that pupils placed in groups often work as individuals. Within these unoriginal results, she found most talk within the group was task-related, usually of low-order direction giving (telling what the task was about and how to proceed with it). She also found that small groups of mixed gender were often dominated by boys. Domination of talk by boys was also found in experimentally structured collaborative groups by Tann (1981). Boys asked questions and disagreed with others while girls sought more consensus. Tann found that teachers gave few instructions concerning group interaction. Groups, for their part, showed developmental phases of: orienting themselves towards the task, developing a working consensus, and bringing the task to a conclusion. The most effective outcomes were derived from groups in which the pupils challenged and reasoned with each other. These groups were able to raise meaningful questions, listen to each other, and manage disputes amongst themselves. Bennett and Dunne (1989) compared classroom groups assigned to undertake individual work with individual outcomes, individual work with a joint outcome (collaboration), and co-operative work with a joint outcome. Results showed that the co-operative groups displayed the highest levels of abstract (or elaborated) talk likely to lead to development of understanding. Bennett and Dunne further compared co-operative and individualized small groups and found more task-related talk in co-operative groups than in groups with an individual orientation (this finding contrasts with those of Wheldall *et al.* (1981) and Bennett and Blundells (1983) that pupils are more likely to spend more time-on-task when working in traditional rows than when working in a group around a table). Bennett and Dunne also found that quality of interaction varied by subject even in co-operative groups; language tasks had an abstract orientation, mathematics tasks were more directive and corrective.

These surveys and experimental/comparative studies provide a number of insights for effective small-group work. Studies show a large performance difference between structured and unstructured groups. When small groups are organized by teachers, they are usually subject-oriented, with core curriculum groups most likely to be ability-related. Boys often dominate the verbal interaction in mixed-gender groups. Teachers, for the most part, organize these small groups as a management strategy within the classroom. Teachers may also group pupils for socio-personal reasons, which again does not have a pedagogic basis.

Galton and Williamson (1992) sum up their review of small-group work in school with the following points: when children sit in groups they are likely to achieve more if they are encouraged to co-operate either by working towards a common shared outcome or by making an individual contribution towards a common goal; groups function best when they are of mixed ability and include pupils from the highest-ability group within the class; children perform in different ways according to the nature of the task – problem-solving tasks with a clear testable outcome tend to generate a greater degree of collaboration than more 'open-ended' tasks; for successful collaboration to take place pupils need to be taught how to collaborate so that they can have a clear idea of what is expected of them; and there remains considerable doubt about the value of building individual rewards into a collaborative exercise.

STYLES OF GROUP WORK: TOWARDS A TASK ORIENTATION AND AN UNDERSTANDING OF GROUP STRUCTURES

Qualifying concepts about structuring groups

Classroom groupings of various sizes and compositions have been used for a variety of purposes. Groups have been involved in activities such as discussion, problem solving, production of items, simulations, role play, transmission of information. Crombie *et al.* (1989) identified a 'continuity' of grouping including isolated individual work, work in rows, parallel work between small groups, whole-class work (that draws upon interpersonal skills of informal aiding of others), peer tutoring, federal (or co-operative work), and consensus (collaborative) work used in classrooms. Cowie and Rudduck (1989) identified a number of techniques to ensure effective group work: buzz groups where individuals in pairs exchange views about an immediate problem; snowball groups where initial small groups (of 2 or 3 pupils) meet and discuss a problem then compare their analysis with another small group with the objective of coming to a consensus; and cross-over groups which work in a jigsaw fashion. Given the range and uses of these groups, some way of organizing our knowledge becomes imperative if we are to make any pedagogic sense for the classroom.

Learning tasks

A useful analysis of the learning tasks found in classrooms has been presented by Norman (1978). This analysis reminds both researchers and teachers that learning involves more than the development of cognitive understanding within separate curriculum areas. Norman's analysis describes five types of learning tasks that characterize a continuity of classroom learning activity: incremental – introduces new ideas, procedures or skills or demands recognition and discrimination; restructuring – demanding a child invents or discovers an idea for her/himself; enrichment – demands application or synthesis of familiar skills to new problems; practice – demands the tuning of new skills on familiar problems; and revision – demands the use of skills which have not been practised for some time. As Edwards points out (Chapter 11), the learning tasks may be viewed as a developmental process, although only one task may predominate classroom activity at any point in time. Bennett *et al.*'s (1984) survey of infant classrooms found learning tasks dominated by practice (60 per cent), followed by incremental (25 per cent), restructuring and enrichment tasks (7 per cent) and revision (6 per cent). The following section investigates the pedagogic relationship between learning task and group construction. There are clear indications that particular groupings may maximize or hinder pupil learning tasks.

Group structure

Bossert *et al.* (1985) clarified that a relationship between group interaction and classroom tasks must exist if effective learning is to take place. Effectiveness is created if the type of interdependence amongst pupils within a group corresponds with task differentiation. The teacher is required to structure both group interdependence and task differentiation appropriately. Table 2.2 identifies how interdependence and differentiation may be co-ordinated to structure particular classroom activities.

Table 2.2   *Classroom activities structured through the relationship between interdependence amongst pupils and task differentiation (Bossert et al., 1985).*

Pupil interdependence	Task differentiation		
	None	Between groups	Within groups
Independent	Whole-class worksheet	Separate reading groups	Separate individualized programme
Interactive	Whole class with co-operation	Separate reading groups with co-operative tasks	Common individualized programme
Interdependent	Common group projects	Group product	Co-ordinative group task

Table 2.2 asks the teacher to co-ordinate the assigned task to the individual or group and indicates that various pupil groupings are skilled to act interdependently or independently. If task and interdependence are co-ordinated, the type of classroom assignment is easily identified (e.g. whole-class involvement does not require differentiated tasks and asks pupils to work independently from one another). If there is too much ambiguity within the activity, insecurity will enter the group interaction and pupils may feel threatened (Doyle, 1983). Insecurity limits pupils' ability to take risks and their discussion may become very restricted. If threatened, pupils are likely to provide simple, low-order and corrective responses amongst themselves or 'opt out' of discussion by adopting strategies such as 'knife edging' or 'fence sitting' (Galton and Williamson, 1992). Pupils will 'knife edge' by remaining dependent on teacher presence and direction for the group to function. 'Fence sitting' describes lack of participation by group members when they feel they may be judged harshly or inappropriately by other group members. If any classroom grouping is to work to its best ability there must be clear relational guides and task differentiation to ensure that the activity is appropriate to the desired ends and the activity must be clear and unambiguous.

Process skills within groups

Webb (1989) found that discussions within groups which lead to positive task achievements follow a developmental pattern and require particular support. Upon assignment of a well-defined task group members spend time clarifying what they have been asked to do. When discussion of the problem begins, pupils draw upon skills such as 'scaffolding' the problem for others, providing 'reciprocal teaching', 'resolving conflicts' between points of view and 'modelling' various processes of understanding. Pupils must be in a position to ask for and receive help from other group members. Task achievement is not simply a matter of receiving help, but of receiving high levels of explanation or elaboration; responses must be sensitive to the pupil's level of need, for pupils will not work effectively within the group without this sensitivity. Pupils' use of elaboration and sensitivity may not be natural in all groups, and Webb reports that training in these skills improves their use within the group. Elaboration and sensitivity allow the discussion and participation necessary for successful group work as well as greater autonomy from teacher dependence (Murrey, 1988).

GROUP SIZE AND PEDAGOGIC IMPLICATIONS

The relationship between group size and classroom pedagogy explores the size continuum (from individual to whole-class) and effectiveness in learning tasks. Only a few generalizations can be made about all groupings; these include: interaction involving all group members is more likely in small groups than in large groups (Bossert *et al.*, 1985; Nasasti and Clements, 1991); in larger groups there may be a 'diffusion of responsibility' or shirking amongst group members who believe that it is not their responsibility to initiate and carry on discussions (Webb, 1989).

Individuals as groups

Dean (1992) states that individualized classes can provide differentiated tasks for pupils across the ability range. Differentiated work, though, forces pupil reliance on teacher if tasks need explanation or approval and can cause management problems (Bennett *et al.*, 1984). Pupils are more likely to spend more 'time-on-task' when working in traditional, individuated classes (Wheldell *et al.*, 1981; Bennett and Blundell, 1983) although these studies do not account for type of task given to pupils. Cox and Berger (1985) noted that individualized work may relate best to drill and practice-learning tasks as opposed to problem-solving tasks which thrive in social situations. Individualized and individuated tasks place pressures on the teacher to match tasks to pupil level for every individual pupil. Large class-size may decrease the efficiency with which a teacher can approach all pupils. These pressures may force the teacher to hold unduly low expectations for the progress of pupils (a concern reported on by Alexander *et al.*, 1992).

Dyads

Classroom dyads are used in two types of learning approach, both having to do with incremental learning. The types represent an expert/novice approach and a mutual coming together of equals. The expert/novice approach is described in Vygotsky's dynamic zone of proximal development (1978; see glossary, p.10). Peer tutoring (see Chapter 7) is one expert/novice approach and a teacher working with an individual pupil is another. The expert/novice approach, especially in peer tutoring, is effective because of the close and sensitive nature of the relationship between teacher and learner. This dyadic type is particularly effective in cognitive problems that have a finite solution (Rogoff, 1990) although it has been used in other learning situations. Damon and Phelps (1989) characterize the expert/novice type as having an inequality of knowledge between participants while striving to maintain a mutuality of interest.

Expert/novice contrasts with a collaborative/co-operative approach in which there is an equality of knowledge and mutuality of interest. Collaborative and co-operative approaches have been found to be most effective in open-ended problem solving, especially related to spatial and creative, as opposed to formula-led procedural tasks (Damon and Phelps, 1989), and in brainstorming to generate a range of new ideas (Doise and Mugny, 1984). Collaborative dyads have been found more effective than individuals or larger groups in solving conservation problems (Bearison *et al.*, 1986; Cox and Berger, 1985; and Kutnick and Thomas, 1990). There have been few studies of the process which make collaborative dyads so effective. It is safe to speculate that there is a high level of elaboration between members with little potential of threat or dominance between pupils. Forman (1989) suggests that the interaction of equality and mutuality is really a bi-directional zone of proximal development.

Teachers use pairs of pupils for a variety of tasks. If the teacher wishes all children to generate ideas for class discussion pupil dyads are likely to ensure the involvement of all children in the class. Within the dyad each child can discuss ideas with a partner; this amount of involvement would be impossible in didactic classrooms – where the teacher can only focus on individual children (leaving the rest to fend intellectually for themselves). Communication and sensitivity to another's perspective are demanded in dyads; perhaps this is why dyads have become the focus of the traditional zone of proximal development as well as studies of problem-solving/conservation. Each of the dyadic types discussed can be used effectively in classrooms. For the dyads to be effective, though, pupils must be able to communicate effectively; allowing development of individual understanding through shared experiences (see Edwards and Mercer, 1987). Equality of knowledge may differ in each of the dyadic types, but mutuality between partners is a necessity for the dyads to be effective. Mutuality is not a simple matter of assigning two pupils a joint problem to solve; it is the development of an underlying sense of closeness or trust that allows for sensitive interaction between partners.

Triads

Placing pupils in small groups of three is a frequent occurrence in many classrooms. This practice is heavily criticized in the educational and psychological literature. In reviews of problem solving, use of triads is discouraged (Kagan, 1988; Webb, 1989; and Bennett and Dunne, 1990). Pupils' own discussions of their preferences for group work (Cullingford, 1988) stress that groups larger than two allow for possible domination and dislike to develop. According to Damon and Phelps (1989), the triad represents equal or unequal knowledge relationships but an exaggerated power relationship that may destroy the possibility of mutuality developing. The power relationship of triads is often explained as two pupils collaborating but working against the third pupil. The above should not be read as a blanket condemnation of triads in the classroom, even in problem-solving situations. When pupils have to work with apparatus, especially computers, the dynamics of a triad will allow two pupils to discuss problems while the third pupil manipulates the computer. Similarly, in Bennett and Cass's (1989) comparative study of homogeneous and heterogeneous triads, they found that the combination of one high-attaining pupil with two low-attaining pupils was effective in promoting understanding amongst the low-attaining pupils (this could be seen as a triad involving peer-tutoring). Teachers should be aware that the triad is the most likely grouping to bring out power disparities between pupils (two pupils siding against the third) unless tasks are structured to avoid this.

Mid-size or small groups

Groups of 4 to 8 pupils are more commonly referred to as a 'classroom group'. Studies which focus on this group size draw on a range of tasks and construct the groups in various ways, making it difficult to generalize any findings. Johnson and Johnson (1987) state that the small group, when pursuing a task in a co-operative manner, is more effective in the full range of learning tasks than individual or whole-class grouping except when the group undertakes a rote learning task. The previous review of UK classroom research found that very few of the small groups found in most primary school classrooms were actually assigned co-operative tasks or practised skills that would enhance a co-operative outcome. Galton and Williamson (1992) classify the range of small groups, tasks assigned and outcomes in their survey in Table 2.3.

Table 2.3   *Galton and Williamson's (1992) classification of group type, task and outcome*

Type	Task demand	Intended outcome
1. Seating groups	Each pupil has a separate task	Different outcomes: each pupil completes a different assignment
2. Working groups	Each pupil has the same task	Same outcome: each pupil completes the same assignment independently
3. Co-operative group	Each pupil has a separate but related task	Joint outcome: each pupil has a different assignment
4. Collaborative group	Each pupil has the same task	Joint outcome: all children share same assignment

The distinction between co-operation and collaboration is important as it does affect the type of task that may be assigned to a small group. Co-operative group work, as defined by Galton and Williamson, is 'where pupils work on the same task but each have individual assignments which eventually are put together to form a joint outcome' (1992, p. 10). Collaborative group work 'involves all children contributing to a single outcome and often involves problem-solving activities, particularly in cases where the group has to debate a social or moral issue and produce an agreed solution or recommendation' (p. 10).

Surveys of UK primary schools find that seating and working groups are more frequently used in classrooms. Seating and working groups do not require the quality of task preparation, sub-task assignment and social skills amongst participating pupils that is necessary for effective co-operative and collaborative groups. These seating and working groups may, in fact, be less functional in classrooms than teachers suspect. When children sit in a group but are not assigned collaborative work, they are likely to spend much of their time off-task. Wheldall *et al.* (1981; also see Chapter 3) suggest that traditional seating arrangements provide a more effective working environment for task orientation. If children are assigned co-operative tasks by their teachers, then we would expect a different outcome from that cited by Wheldall. Bennett and Dunne (1990) compared task-related talk amongst group members placed in co-operative and work groups and found a higher proportion of task-related talk in co-operative groups (88 per cent) than in work groups (66 per cent).

Many teachers are concerned that the learning taking place in co-operative and collaborative groups may not transfer to the individual (Gabbert *et al.*, 1986). In one sense, the mass of North American experimental studies have shown that appropriately structured co-operative groups are very effective in the transfer of knowledge from group to individual (in accordance with Vygotsky's (1978) description of the social nature of learning). To allow for effective co-operative and collaborative group learning the task must be structured appropriately and the group must be aware that they are working towards a collective end-product (Slavin, 1990); groups must have skills to develop and support discussion, especially the use of elaboration and sensitive support (Webb, 1991; Dean, 1992); these groups should be limited in size – usually between 4 and 6, although computer and other object-based work will require smaller numbers if everyone is to have access (Cox and Berger, 1985; Kutnick and Marshall, 1993). Learning tasks most effectively undertaken in co-operative and collaborative groups include enrichment tasks of application and synthesis work; work that draws upon multiple perspectives of group members, such as collection of information for a database, and integrates cognitive skills by identifying and challenging individual approaches to problem solving. Small groups can be used to promote cognitive development but need to be highly structured such that paired discussion can then be 'snowballed' into larger groups, composed of several pairings, and these groups can then compare perspectives (see argumentation as discussed in Chapter 5).

Not all groups, even co-operative and collaborative groups, will be totally effective in promoting learning amonst all group members. Groups will go through a phase of 'newness' in which their performance will be slowed by the need to develop meaningful learning relations amongst pupils. According to Brophy and Good (1986), a 'small group requires a well chosen assignment . . . (in which they are) willing to engage and able to complete successfully as well as rules and procedures that enable students to get help or direction without disrupting the teacher's lesson'. If there are a number of small groups in class, then the number of activities taking place should be limited (to a maximum of four) if effective learning is not to be disrupted (Mortimore *et al.*, 1988; and reinforced in Alexander *et al.*, 1992). Teachers should consider the make-up of group membership (see discussion of group make-up below).

Whole-class groups

Whole-class grouping, or the traditional/formal approach, is a relatively under-researched area. Whole-class teaching is an efficient means of transmitting information to a large number of children simultaneously, especially useful when the class is assigned an individuated worksheet. Entertainment and common stimulus for the class (in the form of storytelling) works well with the whole class. Whole-class grouping also 'provides order, control, purpose and concentration lacking in modern classes' (Alexander *et al.*, 1992).

Whole-class grouping places the teacher in didactic control of knowledge and socialization in the classroom, and with this responsibility some cautions should be noted. In working with the whole class, Alexander, Rose and Woodhead note that the teacher often 'pitches' work to the middle level of ability and this may understimulate high-ability pupils while placing low-ability pupils in a situation where they cannot succeed. Teacher–pupil interaction is likely to be dominated in the opposite way, the extremes of high and low ability will require more teacher attention while the middle-ability pupil may be neglected. Given the demands for teacher attention from the extremes of the ability range it should not be surprising that whole-class groups display extremes of very high and very low in achievement scores (Good and Marshall, 1984).

Regarding learning tasks more commonly associated with whole-class groups, revision and practice are most likely to be successful. Johnson and Johnson (1985) found that rote learning is the only learning task that a whole class can undertake more effectively than co-operative groups. The efficiency of whole class for revision, practice and rote learning is likely to be explained by the control that teachers are able to assert, leading to more time-on-task. Finally, Johnson *et al.* (1985) pose that pupil participation can be increased in a large group if initial (cognitive and problem-solving) activities are started in small groups that are instructed to 'snowball'.

To help summarize this complex overview of group sizes and their relationship to learning, Table 2.4 has been created from the relevant literature.

Table 2.4   *The relationship of group size to effective classroom learning.*

Group size	Learning task	Knowledge relationship	Social relationship	Common name
Individual	practice, revision	unequal (teacher: pupil)	hierarchical	individualized individuated
Dyad	incremental, restructuring	equal (pupil: pupil)	mutual	brainstorming, conservation, problem solving
	incremental	unequal (tutor: pupil)	mutual	peer tutoring
Triad	incremental, restructuring with computer or other apparatus	equal (pupil: pupil) with additional pupil working apparatus	mutual	conservation, problem solving
Small group	enrichment	unequal (pupil: pupil)	mutual	co-operative group
		equal (pupil: pupil)	mutual	collaborative group
Whole-class	incremental, practice, revision	unequal (teacher: pupil)	hierarchical	lecturing, individualized, individuated

OTHER ASPECTS OF GROUP MAKE-UP AND PROCESS

Ability

One major problem for any teacher working with groups is how to distribute the range of pupil ability amongst groups. This problem asks whether groups should be of homogeneous (or singular) ability or heterogeneous (mixed) ability. The choice is not simple. Influential educationalists (for example see HMI, 1989a; 1989b) find good learning practices in homogeneous-ability groups when studying the core curriculum subjects. Earlier HMI reports (1978b) found that the move from streamed to mixed-ability classrooms (albeit in secondary schools) maintained academic achievement in all pupils while substantially increasing pro-school attitudes amongst pupils. Homogeneous grouping may become the source of labelling pupils and the onset of self-fulfilling prophecies, so that top-ability and bottom-ability pupils polarize in their attitudes towards each other, resulting in friction in the classroom (Bossert *et al.*, 1984).

Webb (1989; 1991) finds advantages and disadvantages in homogeneous-ability grouping. Homogeneous high-ability groups do not display high-level elaborative interactions when asked to jointly solve a problem; most pupils want to work as individuals. Homogeneous low-ability groups have little stimulus (from more knowledgeable group members) for high-order elaborative interactions and much of their interaction is off-task. Similarly, Good and Marshall (1984) found that homogeneous low-ability groups were problematic in the classroom because they were prone to interruptions, their members often brought behavioural problems into the group, they spent less time-on-task, and were very passive in the learning process.

According to Webb, only the homogeneous middle-ability groups show high elaborative interactions that support achievement, and most of these interactions take place between the higher- and lower-ability members of middle-ability groups. Webb's evidence concerning heterogeneous/mixed ability groups finds that these groups were more likely to use high elaborative interactions leading to problem-solving achievement. She suggests that mixed-ability groups should be 'banded' such that each group does not contain the absolute extremes of high and low ability, where some polarization may occur. Better results are produced if groups are composed of high to low/middle-ability and high/middle- to low-ability members. Webb cites research by Rosenbaum (1984) and warns that pupils at the margin (or extremes) of ability cause most problems and concerns for the teacher unless they are provided an appropriate grouping that draws upon their skills without being threatened.

Gender

Few studies have explored or compared the effectiveness of single-sex and mixed-sex groups in the classroom. Pupils, themselves, often express a preference to work with same gender partners, although this is not characteristic of pupil choice until they reach the junior school (about 7 years of age), according to Bennett and Dunne (1990). Tann's (1981) experimental structuring of collaborative tasks used mixed-gender groups and found boys to be argumentative in discussion, while girls tried to reach agreement in a more consensual manner. This difference in approach to solving problems led to boys having a low tolerance for girls in their groups. Tann's work indicates that single-sex groups may be a solution to problems of imbalance in interaction and domination between boys and girls. Webb (1991) is more positive in her review of mixed-gender groups. She found that an imbalance in number of boys and girls leads to gender differences similar to those found by Tann, but recommends equal numbers of boys and girls in each group to achieve balance in discussion and successful problem solving. This recommendation coincides with Slavin's (1990) finding that mixed-gender co-operative groups were academically successful and likely to encourage cross-gender friendships.

Friendship

Teachers often allow friendship to be the basis of small groups and seating arrangements in the class. Friendship is an easy means of grouping because pupils are not likely to object to sitting with someone they like. Friendship, though, can be very stereotypical in the classroom. Social psychological processes of similarity and familiarity lead to ability, gender and racially biased friendships (usually referred to as 'cliques' in sociometric studies such as Nash, 1976; and Pollard, 1985). Teachers should be cautious in their use of friendship groups as friendship does not allow for the integration of 'loners' (those who are not liked by anyone in the classroom) and groups may object to loners assigned to the group. Friendship groups may characteristically polarize the group members – boys not wanting to work with girls, bright children not wanting to work with slow learners, etc. Friendship, thus, may limit achievement in problem-solving tasks (Webb, 1991) and general development of co-operative skills in the classroom. Friendship may work well in recreational activities.

Age

Normal development of co-operative skills (see Kutnick, 1988) takes place throughout the years of primary schooling. Webb (1983) states that children as young as 7 can benefit greatly from co-operative groups. HMI (1982) recommend that effective small-group work can be undertaken from the start of primary school, i.e. at approximately age 5. Co-operation is certainly affected by children's ability to understand and interact with other children's perspectives, but this ability is the result of experience and culture and should not be dependent on age in school. The earlier that children have the opportunity to co-operate and receive training in co-operative skills then the earlier they will demonstrate their ability to co-operate.

Personality

Very little research has been undertaken into the role of personality and group work. Webb (1989) differentiates between extrovert and introvert personality types and ability to interact in co-operative and collaborative groups. As reason would indicate, extrovert personalities are more likely to interact in small groups and introverts are less likely to interact. The role of personality, though, may be countered if both types of personality are 'trained' in process, communication and support skills.

Use of rewards

When small groups are asked to undertake co-operative and collaborative tasks for learning, there is an expectation that the motivation to work within the group will be enhanced if the product of their efforts is rewarded. Rewards may be of an intrinsic or extrinsic nature, and they may apply to individual members of the group or the group as a whole. Both Webb (1989) and Slavin (1990) found that individual rewards discouraged group work and whole-group rewards were most likely to promote help and elaboration within the group. Slavin (1983) states that co-operative group achievements should be given a tangible, extrinsic reward. Damon and Phelps (1989) actively discourage the use of extrinsic rewards, especially with regard to incremental and restructuring (cognitive) tasks; small-group learning of new knowledge and skills should provide its own intrinsic reward. There will be less pressure to use overt rewards if co-operation is the norm of the classroom (Nastasi and Clements, 1991). In all cases of group work, teachers will need to support the motivation to work within the group towards a common product. The teacher must give legitimacy to group processes of discussion, security and other actions required to enhance within group understanding. The product of the group's efforts must be suitably acknowledged by the teacher as a meaningful learning experience.

DRAWBACKS TO CLASSROOM GROUPINGS

This chapter has argued that the variety of groups found in classrooms and their effectiveness in promoting learning will depend on which learning task is assigned, group composition (especially size and ability range), the process skills of pupils and the planned outcome of group efforts. Any inappropriate mixture of task, process skills and outcome will result in ineffective learning achievements as well as classroom management/control problems.

Drawbacks of individual and whole-class groups

Inappropriate mixture of incremental and restructuring tasks assigned to individual work is likely to result in management problems for the teacher (Bennett *et al.*, 1984): teachers were hindered in providing positive feedback and matching succeeding tasks to pupil development by having to maintain control of pupils' behaviour in the queue (see p. 17). The social context that best supports incremental and restructured learning will be difficult to structure into individual and whole-class groups, in the latter individual on-task work will be hindered by the discussion amongst group members that facilitates cognitive development.

Drawbacks of small groups

Small groups work most effectively when assigned incremental, restructuring and enrichment tasks. If pupils are not allowed to be 'weaned' off their dependence on teachers, cognitive development in small groups is unlikely to be effective. Thus, classroom time must be given to the development of process skills necessary to maintain discussion and within-group support. Pupils will also need time to learn how to work co-operatively and collaboratively. Teachers need to change their focus of encouragement from the individual to the group (Alexander *et al.*, 1992). Teachers will also need to assign tasks in such a way as to involve all pupils. Without individual responsibility to the group, Bennett and Dunne (1990) point to the possibility of 'free-riders' (those who do not contribute but take credit for group effort), 'suckers' (hard workers who slacken off), and 'ganging-up' for a simple solution. If pupils within a small group display any of these behaviours the possibility of rejection, domination and argument within the group is increased. Unless groupings are carefully structured to avoid gender and ability stereotypes pupils' desire to work with friends will cause polarization between boys and girls and between the extremes of ability. Classroom isolates will be rejected from all groups (Cowie and Rudduck, 1989). Finally, small groups need the freedom to talk and move around the classroom if they are to be effective. These aspects of effective small-group work can easily go wrong if the relationship of task to process skills and outcome are not co-ordinated. Behaviours such as talking out of turn, hindering others, slowness/idleness, untidiness and movement out of seat are likely to disturb other pupils and teachers in primary and in secondary schools (Merrett and Wheldall, 1984; Houghton *et al.*, 1988); yet focused talking, movement and activity are also the behaviours that attest to groups working effectively. Effective small-group work and classroom management must coincide to provide the right environment for learning. Teachers bear a major responsibility in arranging the task, developing process skills amongst pupils, and setting standards and expectations which are distinct from the traditional didactic classroom.

CONCLUSION

This chapter brings together information from surveys and experiments, shows the range of classroom groupings currently being used and their general effectiveness. Some form of grouping will always exist in classrooms. Knowledge gained from this chapter should help to balance the relative usefulness of one form of grouping against another. The ability to make a balanced judgement also coincides with government pressure (in the UK) that teachers should use the full range of groupings available. Choice between forms of grouping is not simple: it is not enough to simply advise a teacher that not enough time has been spent in whole-class grouping. Rather, the choice of classroom group should be made to fulfil pedagogic needs of the pupils.

Planning for pedagogic needs must involve an awareness of the task assigned to any grouping, the make-up and processes that characterize a grouping, and the expected outcome of group efforts. Teachers should not simply group their classes because of the number of tables, chairs, etc. They should first consider the type of learning task being undertaken and relate this to particular groupings. Within any school day a number of learning tasks will be undertaken – for each learning task a particular group size and structure will better enable some groups to work together more effectively than others. Table 2.5 helps to qualify the task and grouping most likely to succeed.

Table 2.5   *Relationship between task and grouping make-up.*

Task	Group size	Knowledge relationship*	Social relationship[+]
incremental	dyad	unequal	hierarchical
		equal	mutual
restructuring	dyad	unequal	hierarchical
		equal	mutual
enrichment	small group	unequal	mutual
		equal	mutual
practice	whole-class	unequal	hierarchical
	individual	unequal	hierarchical
revision	whole-class	unequal	hierarchical
	individual	unequal	hierarchical

* Unequal knowledge relationship means one group member knows the answer to the task and other members must learn from the first. Equal knowledge relationship means that all group members are equally naive as to the solution of the assigned problem.
[+] As with the knowledge relationship, hierarchical social relationship means that one group member is seen to be more powerful than others. Mutual social relationship means that all group members are equally powerful.

Teachers must, if they are to use groupings successfully, be actively involved in group structuring and assessment. It is very difficult to listen to and observe every group working in a classroom and easy to misinterpret the quality of group talk. One simple recommendation is to tape-record group interaction, and listen to the quality of conversation later in the day. Quality conversation is essential if the group is to work effectively. Table 2.6 amalgamates ideas from a number of studies concerning effective communication processes, and identifies whether there is some form of explanation/elaboration going on within the group. It may be used as a checklist for each pupil in the group.

Table 2.6 *One method of recording quality participation by all group members.*

Types of conversation	Pupil 1	Pupil 2	Pupil 3
Statement or elaboration of problem			
Question			

Response:
  elaboration
  corrective			

Off-task statements			

The table will help identify who is participating and at what level that participation takes place. Teachers should remember that level and quality of participation will depend on how prepared the pupils are to interact with each other and whether group skills have been developed. This type of assessment will also identify discussion and problem-solving skills that pupils must demonstrate in National Curriculum Attainment Targets.

Consideration of the potential and actual use of groupings in the classroom is very complex but can bring many learning and social benefits to the classroom. Teachers have a number of roles to play in the choice of appropriate pupil grouping. They are ultimately responsible for control and learning in the classroom. They must plan for the quality of relationships between teachers and pupils and amongst pupils themselves. Teachers must also consider conflicts between their roles of control, tutoring, and structuring classrooms for mutual and collaborative work between pupils.

REFERENCES

Alexander, R. (1984) *Primary Teaching*. Eastbourne: Holt, Rinehart & Winston.

Alexander, R., Rose, J. and Woodhead, C. (1992) *Curriculum Organization and Classroom Practice in Primary Schools: A Discussion Paper*. London: DES.

Aronson, E., Bridgeman, D. and Gellner, R. (1978) The effects of a co-operative classroom structure on student behaviour and attitude. In D. Bar Tal and L. Saxe (eds), *Social Psychology of Education: Theory and Research*. New York: Wiley.

Bassey, M. (1978) *900 Primary School Teachers*. Slough: NFER.

Bearison, D., Magzamen, S. and Filardo, E. (1986) Socio-cognitive conflict and cognitive growth in young children. *Merrill-Palmer Quarterly*, **32**, 51-72.

Bennett, N. (1976) *Teaching Styles and Pupil Progress*. London: Open Books.

Bennett, N. and Blundell, D. (1983) Quantity and quality of work in rows and classroom groups. *Educational Psychology*, **3**, 93-105.

Bennett, N. and Cass, A. (1989) The effects of group composition on group interactive processes and pupils' understanding. *British Educational Research Journal*, **15**, 19-32.

Bennett, N. and Dunne, E. (1990) Implementing co-operative groupwork in classrooms. In V. Lee (ed.), *Children's Learning in School*. London: Hodder & Stoughton.

Bennett, N., Desforges, C., Cockburn, A. and Wilkinson, B. (1984) *The Quality of Pupils' Learning Experiences*. London: Lawrence Erlbaum Associates.

Bossert, S., Barnett, B. and Filby, N. (1984) Grouping and instructional organization. In P. Peterson, L. Wilkinson and M. Hallinan (eds), *The Social Context of Instruction*. Orlando, Fla: Academic Press.

Boydell, D. (1975) Pupils' behaviour in junior classrooms. *British Journal of Educational Psychology*, **45**, 122-9.

Brophy, J. and Good, T. (1986) Teacher behaviour and student achievement. In M. Wittrock (ed), *Handbook of Research on Teaching*, 3rd ed. New York: Macmillan.

Cowie, H. and Rudduck, J. (1988) *Co-operative Group Work: An Overview*. London: BP Education Service.

Cox, D. and Berger, C. (1985) The importance of group size in the use of problem-solving skills on a microcomputer. *Journal of Educational Computing*, **1**, 459-68.

Crombie, R., Lowe, T. and Stigston, A. (1989) Group work and teacher skill: the role of the educational psychologist. *Educational Psychology in Practice*, **5**, 23-9.

Cullingford, C. (1988) Children's views about working together. *Education 3-13*, **16**, 29-34.

Damon, W. and Phelps, E. (1989) Critical distinctions among three approaches to peer education. *International Journal of Education Research*, **13**, 9-19.

Dean, J. (1992) *Organizing Learning in the Primary School Classroom*. London: Routledge.

Doise, W. and Mugny, G. (1984) *The Social Development of the Intellect*. Oxford: Pergamon Press.

Doyle, W. (1983) Academic work. *Review of Educational Research*, **53**, 159-99.

Edwards, D. and Mercer, N. (1987) *Common Knowledge: The Development of Understanding in the Classroom*. London: Methuen.

Forman, E. (1989) The role of peer instruction in the social construction of mathematical knowledge. *International Journal of Educational Research*, **13**, 55-70.

Gabbert, B., Johnson, D. and Johnson, R. (1986) Co-operative learning, group-to-individual transfer, process gain and the acquisition of cognitive reasoning strategies. *Journal of Psychology*, **120**, 265-78.

Galton, M. (1990) Grouping and groupwork. In C. Rogers and P. Kutnick (eds), *The Social Psychology of the Primary School*. London: Routledge.

Galton, M., Simon, B. and Croll, P. (1980) *Inside the Primary Classroom*. London: Routledge & Kegan Paul.

Galton, M. and Williamson, J. (1992) *Groupwork in the Primary School*. London: Routledge.

Good, T. and Marshall, S. (1984) Do students learn more in heterogeneous or homogeneous groups? In P. Peterson, L., Wilkinson and M. Hallinan (eds), *The Social Context of Instruction*. Orlando, Fla: Academic Press.

HMI (1978a) *Primary Education in Englnd*. London: HMSO.

HMI (1978b) *Mixed-ability Teaching in the Secondary School*. London: HMSO.

HMI (1982) *Education 5-9: An Illustrative Survey of 80 First Schools in England*. London: HMSO.

HMI (1989a) *Aspects of Primary Education: The Teaching of Mathematics*. London: HMSO.

HMI (1989b) *Aspects of Primary Education: The Teaching of Science*. London: HMSO.

Houghton, S., Wheldall, K. and Merrett, F. (1988) Classroom behaviour problems which secondary school teachers say they find most troublesome. *British Educational Research Journal*, **14**, 295-310.

Johnson, D. and Johnson, R. (1985) The internal dynamics of co-operative learning groups. In R. Slavin, S. Sharan, S. Kagan, R. Lazarowitz, C. Webb and R. Schmuck (eds), *Learning to Co-operate, Co-operating to Learn*. New York: Plenum.

Johnson, D. and Johnson, R. (1987) *Learning Together and Alone*. Englewood Cliffs: Prentice-Hall.

Johnson, D., Johnson, R., Roy, P. and Zaidman, B. (1985) Oral interaction in co-operative learning groups: speaking, listening and the nature of statements made by high-, medium-, and low-achieving students. *Journal of Psychology*, **119**, 303-21.

Kagan, S. (1988) *Co-operative Learning: Resources for Teachers*. University of California, Riverside.

Kerry, T. and Sands, M. (1982) *Handling Classroom Groups*. Nottingham: University of Nottingham School of Education (mimeo).

Kutnick, P. (1988) *Relationships in the Primary School Classroom*. London: Paul Chapman.

Kutnick, P. and Marshall, D. (1993) Development of social skills and the use of the microcomputer in the primary school classroom. *British Educational Research Journal*, **19**, 517-33.

Kutnick, P. and Thomas, M. (1990) Dyadic pairings for the enhancement of cognitive development in the school curriculum: some preliminary results on science tasks. *British Educational Research Journal*, **16**, 399-406.

Merrett, F. and Wheldall, K. (1984) *Positive Teaching: The Behaviourist Approach*. London: Allen & Unwin.

Mortimore, P., Sammons, P., Stol, L.D. and Ecob, R. (1988) *School Matters: The Junior Years*, **16**, 48-52.

Murrey, M. (1988) Negotiation and collaboration in problem-solving groups. *Education 3-13*, **16**, 48-52.

Nash, R. (1976) *Classrooms Observed*. London: Routledge & Kegan Paul.

Nastasi, B. and Clements, D. (1991) Research on co-operative learning: implications for practice. *School Psychology Review*, **20**, 110-31.

Norman, D.A. (1978) Notes towards a complex theory of learning. In A.M. Lesgold (ed.), *Cognitive Psychology and Instruction*. New York: Plenum.

OFSTED (1993) *Curriculum Organization and Classroom Practice: A Follow-up Report*. London: DFE.

Peterson, P., Wilkinson, L. and Hallinan, M. (eds) (1984) *The Social Context of Instruction*. Orlando, Fla: Academic Press.

Pollard, A. (1985) *The Social World of the Primary School*. London: Holt, Rinehart & Winston.

Rogoff, B. (1990) *Apprenticeship in Thinking: Cognitive Development in Social Context*. New York: Oxford University Press.

Rosenbaum, J. (1984) The social organization of instructional grouping. In P. Peterson, L. Wilkinson and M. Hallinan (eds), *The Social Context of Instruction*. Orlando, Fla: Academic Press.

Slavin, R. (1983) *Co-operative Learning*. New York: Longman.

Slavin, R. (1990) Co-operative learning. In C. Rogers and P. Kutnick (eds), *The Social Psychology of the Primary School*. London: Routledge.

Tann, S. (1981) Grouping and groupwork. In B. Simon and J. Willcocks (eds), *Research and Practice in the Primary School*. London: Routledge & Kegan Paul.

Tizard, B., Blatchford, P., Burke, J., Farquhar, C. and Plewis, I. (1988) *Young Children at School in the Inner City*. Hove: Lawrence Erlbaum.

Vygotsky, L. (1978) *Mind and Society: The Development of Higher Mental Processes*. Cambridge, Mass: Harvard University Press.

Webb, N. (1983) Predicting and learning from student interaction: defining the interaction variables. *Educational Psychologist*, **18**, 33-41.

Webb, N. (1985) Verbal interaction and learning in peer-directed groups. *Theory into Practice*, **24**, 32-9.

Webb, N. (1989) Peer interaction and learning in small groups. *International Journal of Educational Research*, **13**, 21-39.

Webb, N. (1991) Task-related verbal instruction and mathematics learning in small groups. *Journal for Research in Mathematics Education*, **22**, 366-89.

Wheldall, K., Morris, M., Vaughan, P. and Yin Yuk No (1981) Rows *v.* tables: an example of the use of behavioural ecology in two classes of 11-year-old children. *Educational Psychology*, **1**, 171-83.

Part 2

Techniques

Chapter 3

Whole-Class and Individualized Approaches

Frank Merrett

EDITORS' INTRODUCTION

In the following chapter Merrett begins the process of considering the potential benefits that might be gained from the introduction of group work by making an assessment of the influence of seating arrangements on whole-class teaching. The essential point to emerge here is that while the physical organization of a class is not the same thing as grouping it does have a significant and potentially important influence upon the effectiveness of the work that takes place within the classroom context.

In the process of elaborating this point Merrett draws attention to the importance of considering why a teacher might impose a particular physical organization upon the classroom. One possibility is that teachers may well follow the expectations of others, concerned to present the 'correct' image to influential colleagues or superiors. Teachers may also make decisions regarding the organization of the classroom with managerial concerns uppermost in their minds.

However, it becomes apparent during the course of this chapter that if groups are to be used for pedagogical reasons then it is essential that there is careful and full consideration given to the relationship between the organization of the classroom and the nature of the activities and tasks presented to the pupils. The move from a managerial focus to a pedagogical focus should not however be taken to mean that management takes a back seat. Indeed, Merrett leads us to the conclusion that training in the management of groups is an essential pre-requisite of the development of a pedagogy of group-based teaching.

INTRODUCTION

As soon as a society accepts the idea of compulsory full-time schooling for all children it is faced with a dilemma. There are many, many children and few teachers; even fewer trained teachers. The most common solution to this problem lies in the organization of children into very large groups and the use of a system of didactic teaching involving a great deal of rote learning. The core of this type of teaching is that we have one person (the master) who instructs a large number of others. We can observe this solution in operation all over the Third World. I have seen it myself in the

Bahamas, in Jamaica, in Belize, in Nigeria, in South Africa and in India. The general pattern is that the teacher talks or instructs and then the children recite the material and learn it off by heart. Alternatively, they might be required to copy vast amounts of material from a blackboard into their notebooks. A somewhat more enlightened way of proceeding is where the teacher talks and demonstrates and then gives the pupils the chance to practise a series of examples in order to exercise and establish new skills. Both of these systems, however, call for the provision of books and pencils or pens, or some other means of writing, and pose considerable logistical problems.

The reason why so many people think that teaching is an easy option is because they remember, or think they remember, that they were taught by people telling them things. However, we know that teaching is not telling. There is a great deal more to teaching than merely telling and that is where the great debate between discovery teaching and didactic learning following an expository model really starts. Teaching, like nursing or the sacred ministry, is thought of by many people as a vocation because it provides an opportunity for serving the community, especially the younger members of it, that is very attractive. To accept some responsibility for the development and nurture of the nation's youth is a high calling and it is answered by many from the worthiest of motives. Thus, in many communities teachers are, quite properly, held in high esteem. This esteem comes from the fact that it is accepted that not only have they chosen their profession but that they have been specially prepared for it by the training they have received. Many of those who decide to take up teaching as a career do so because they find academic learning to their taste. Most of them found learning at school relatively easy and obtained satisfaction from it.

Because they were successful they probably received plaudits from their teachers and their families and friends so that the whole process of learning was pleasurable for them. Later on they would receive satisfaction from the tasks themselves; the intrinsic reinforcement that comes from knowing that one has been successful in a task or in completing an assignment. Success in academic learning may well encourage such people to suppose that others, too, will find learning a pleasurable experience and this may awaken an interest in helping other people to learn. However, their own experience of learning is not necessarily a very good preparation. They may well find the problems of less able pupils difficult to understand and to sympathize with. Expert performers will find themselves addressing the rudiments of their subject again and again with pupils who appear to be making little progress; this can be a very depressing experience.

Ideally, teaching should take place when someone who is ready to learn, that is, someone who has all the prerequisite skills and knowledge, feels a need for some new information, technique or skill. He or she goes to someone who is both expert in the particular area and with the time and ability to do the teaching. On a one-to-one basis learning takes place and the new material or skill is acquired. The learner may then go away to practise and gradually to refine and improve the skill or develop his or her understanding of the new body of knowledge.

In the last resort every person has to learn whatever they want to learn for themselves. Each of us needs to come to a personal understanding and grasp of material to be learned or to acquire the skill through practice and constructive feedback. One cannot learn by proxy. Nevertheless, a lot of the learning which is essential to human beings is social learning and has to be learned in social situations. It seems sensible, therefore, to arrange for such learning to take place in a social context within the classroom. Some skills require social intercourse and cannot be learned in isolation. You cannot learn to converse whilst living on your own like Robinson Crusoe. In some other fields we need, ultimately, to become totally independent and self-reliant. Reading is a case in point. In the end, we want children to be completely independent readers able to tackle any sort of text for their immediate purpose. On the way, however, they will need support and practical help in decoding and interpreting and this will have to come from some other agency be it parent, sibling, friend or teacher.

Some things are best learned together or actually require a social context. As Bruner and Haste (1987) suggest: 'Making sense is a social process; it is an activity that is always situated within a cultural and historical context'. For example, discussion or collaborative work towards producing a newspaper, a radio programme or a play needs group organization. Other learning, such as developing skill in calculation, composition and so on, calls for concentrated practice on the part of the individual for which calm, quietness and absence of interruption are essential. In such situations, distraction from the close presence of other people or from excessive or intrusive noise cannot be tolerated. Such conditions are almost essential for composing a letter, for calculating or for reading. Now these kinds of arrangements are governed by antecedents which include the classroom setting which, in turn, depends to a large extent upon the kind of furniture available and how it is arranged.

As Galton (1990) affirms, there is no doubt that one of the most striking changes to have taken place in primary school classrooms since World War II has been the use of more informal seating arrangements. This was dependent upon the provision of lighter furniture which could be used more flexibly. When I began teaching in 1946 pupils still sat in rows facing the teacher and the blackboard. We never thought of changing this arrangement simply because the desks provided forced children to sit side by side in pairs, with convenient storage spaces in front of them and were, in any case, far too heavy to be moved about. In some school rooms they were actually screwed to the floor. What caused the change were, of course, the recommendations of a number of official reports, beginning with the Plowden Report (DES, 1967), for individualization in teaching and for teaching small groups rather than the whole class together.

The Plowden Report made no specific recommendations about seating arrangements but the photographs comparing children sitting in rows and those working in small groups using discovery methods were there to tell their own story. The Plowden Report did, however, recommend the abandonment of streaming and the acceptance of discovery learning. Sections of the Report dealt with flexibility in the timetable and in the curriculum, with use of the environment and discovery methods. This came to be known as progressive or 'child-centred' education and was advocated up and down the country by inspectors, advisers and above all, by lecturers and tutors working in colleges of education and other institutions dealing with the professional training of teachers. The practice of progressive education has not been without its critics, however, including the writers of the *Black Papers* (Cox and Dyson, 1969a, 1969b, 1970; Cox and Boyson, 1977).

The *Black Papers* brought together a large number of contributions from those interested in the educational scene who were concerned at the wholesale adoption of discovery methods of teaching. It was suggested that this had caused academic standards to fall and social behaviour to decline. Some, such as Johnson, writing in *Black Paper 1* (pp. 4-9), suggested that the current freedom in primary schools, which was a reaction to the unnecessary regimentation of earlier years, was a very mixed blessing. Bantock, in *Black Paper 2*, examined the basic concept of discovery learning in some detail and, referring to methods of teaching and learning, concluded, 'There is, in fact, no one way'. Others including Pinn and Froome, both heads of primary schools, referred to the way in which the adoption of an idea which appears to be embraced by those with influence, is difficult for classroom teachers to sidestep. In order to get promotion they are almost forced to be in the van and when appointed to positions of authority force others to follow their way, whether they want to, and whether they have the necessary skills, or not.

In the United Kingdom it has been the custom for teachers to be allowed to teach in their own idiosyncratic ways. There has been no orthodoxy. Indeed, acceptance of this principle has been one of the reasons given by teacher educators for not providing models for beginners or guidelines for classroom management. The argument to support this view has to do with the avoidance of stereotyping. It seems strange that a movement encouraging freedom and variety in the way children learn should, in fact, be placing additional constraints on the freedom of teachers in this way. Surely, what ought to govern the practice of teachers is the suitability of a particular method, treatment or grouping arrangement for the teaching/learning task in hand, taking into account the facilities available.

Teachers have to cope not only with the actual business of teaching but also with the organizational structure of *schooling*. This structure tends to make the business of teaching very artificial. The most natural way for learning to take place, as suggested above, is for the pupil who has a real need to know something, or to learn some skill or process, to approach someone who already has that skill or knowledge with a request for help. But this hardly ever happens in schools. Because of the way in which schools are organized, teachers have to teach classroom groups which can be quite large and heterogeneous. Managing groups is quite separate from the business of teaching skills and imparting knowledge. Teachers have to be able to do both. Teaching in schools is carried on in classes where pupils have been organized into groups for instruction and where learning is pre-organized and prescribed within the limits of a syllabus and a timetable, for at least some of the lessons. Teaching has no chance of being spontaneous and personal but instead is organized into periods and made formal in nature. Quite apart from the business of teaching academic skills or bringing about the understanding of important human issues, teachers have to learn to manage groups of pupils in order to teach them. To be able to do this expertly and well is fundamental to survival for teachers at all levels. In a recent survey (Merrett and Wheldall, 1993), using a structured interview schedule, 176 secondary teachers were invited to say how important they thought classroom management was to them and their professional colleagues. Using a Likert scale specifying 'very important', 'important', 'neutral', 'not important' and 'of no importance at all', 93 per cent said that they thought it was 'very important', the rest chose 'important'. The other choices did not figure at all. They were then asked where they learned the skills of classroom management and 82 per cent believed that they had accomplished this 'on the job'.

Teachers faced with 30 or so children and half an hour of time have to decide how best to spread their resources. If they decide to use individual coaching they will have 60 seconds or less to spend with each child (assuming that they are able to give the whole of their attention to the task of teaching and do not have to spend time on matters of order and control). Deciding that this is worse than useless most teachers used to opt for class teaching for many purposes, in which case they would have the choice either to teach the whole group together as a group, or to teach individuals whilst the rest sit and wait, or to group the class and teach the groups one by one. One early solution to this problem, developed by Bell and Lancaster, was by using tutors to instruct the groups.

Andrew Bell was appointed in 1789 to be superintendent of the Military Male Asylum in Madras, which was, despite its rather forbidding name, the semi-official charity school for the orphaned sons of soldiers. Bell organized his school into classes according to achievement and boys were promoted or demoted according to their performance. In each class boys were paired so that, for example, in a class of 24 the 12 best students acted as tutors to the others. Bell maintained that both tutor and tutee gained from this system. The classes were taught by monitors who, in turn, were taught by teachers: a very economical use of manpower. Lancaster carried the germ of this idea into the school he opened in Borough Road, London, in 1798 and developed certain 'improvements' on what was called the 'Madras' system. Basically, he used the same monitorial structure in order to teach the rudiments of skill and knowledge. He suggested that under his system the teacher did not have to be directly concerned with the tiresome repetition of the rudiments of learning referred to earlier. It is interesting to note that he regarded his principal improvement to have been the introduction of the 'key' syllabus.

Class teaching was the norm in most schools until the movement for child-centred or progressive teaching, with discovery learning as the most favoured method, became the vogue and its chief physical manifestation was the almost ubiquitous use of table grouping in primary school classrooms. When the Plowden Report was published in 1967 I was abroad and when I returned in 1969 the movement towards table group seating in primary school classrooms was almost complete. The influence of what appeared to be a reasonable practice supported by a few people eminent in the educational world but backed by no empirical evidence was sufficient to bring about a fundamental change in classroom practice.

Basically, the reasoning seems to be overwhelmingly correct. Since teachers cannot deal with individuals and the class unit is too large to be meaningful it makes sense to deal with the whole by breaking it down into manageable groups. This fitted well with the philosophy of unstreaming and the idea that children learn best in a situation where knowledge and information come most easily through discussion. Added advantages appeared to be that children would learn to respond to each other amicably in small social groups and that the intellectually gifted would be able to help their less well-endowed colleagues. The ideas seemed so eminently reasonable and acceptable that few took the trouble to question the fact that no empirical evidence had ever been produced to support them.

Some research has been carried out on seating arrangements and their effects and early work included an observational study by Dawe (1934). She was chiefly interested in examining the responses to story-reading from infant children seated in different parts of the classroom and how best to stimulate discussion amongst them.

Schwebel (1969) observed children in 14 classrooms and noted that the pupils seated near the front of the class were more attentive than those at the back. Teachers were asked to rate their pupils with regard to attentiveness, disruptiveness, shyness and likeability. Pupils were then randomly assigned to seats and after three weeks teachers were again asked to rate the pupils. Teachers' perceptions of their pupils had changed markedly, indicating that variations in class seating affect both teachers and their pupils. Rubin (1973) studied 84 students in four groups with a wide range of ability. The students were seated in different places (selected randomly) each week and asked to comment (using semantic differential scales) upon their position, the person next to them and so on. Seating position was found to correlate with performance, attitudes and behaviour. Ankey (1974) also carried out studies comparing the effects of different seating arrangements and found a horseshoe arrangement to be most satisfactory.

Other studies, chiefly with children deemed to have emotional and behavioural difficulties, have been carried out comparing different seating arrangements and their effects on pupil behaviour. For example, Shores and Haubrich (1969) compared the work of four such children in programmed reading and arithmetic when seated in rows and when working in separate cubicles. Their on-task levels improved when they were more isolated from the rest of the group but not their academic performance. Saunders (1970) examined the effects of seating 'disturbed' children within groups of children with more acceptable behaviour. Despite working with a large number of pupils in 12 classes the results were inconclusive.

However, the first systematic study involving the manipulation of seating arrangements for a whole class was carried out by Axelrod *et al.* (1979), who observed two classes under rows and tables style seating arrangements. Pupils in a class of 17 below-average 7- to 8-year-old children were observed daily and their on-task behaviour sampled whilst they engaged in formal academic work. For nine sessions the children were seated in four groups of four and one of five around tables. This was followed by ten days in which they sat in rows followed by a further seven days of tables, as before, and finally seven more days seated in rows.

On-task behaviour was defined as 'orientation toward the appropriate material, attention to the teacher when she was speaking, complying with teacher requests, raising a hand for teacher assistance and being out of seat with teacher permission'. Each child was observed in turn for one minute per lesson and was rated as on- or off-task every ten seconds. Reliability was measured by having two people observing simultaneously on some occasions. These checks indicated good inter-observer agreement of between 92 and 96 per cent. The results showed a much higher level of on-task behaviour whilst children were sitting in rows than when they were sitting around tables.

In a second study a class of 32 average seventh grade (11- to 12-year-old) children were observed and disruptions were recorded. Disruptions (talk-outs) were defined as 'any audible verbal sound made by a student without the teacher's permission'. The number of talk-outs was recorded daily during 55-minute life sciences lessons in which work book assignments were completed. Once again inter-observer agreement was acceptably high. In this study the first five days of observation was with pupils sitting around tables. In a second phase observation was carried out whilst children sat in rows and this was followed by five more observation days with pupils seated around tables. Once again the results were quite clear. Disruption averaged 58 per cent under tables conditions, 30 per cent when they were seated in rows and 50 per cent when they were again seated around tables. This shows quite clearly that seating arrangements affect the behaviour of pupils.

Wheldall *et al.* (1981) replicated the Axelrod *et al.* study within a British educational context. Children's on-task behaviour was examined in two top junior classes. In one school the subjects consisted of a group of 28 mixed-ability children aged between 10 and 11 years. The school was situated in an urban residential area and the teacher was female with thirteen years of teaching experience. The second class contained a similar group of 25 academically mixed 10- to 11-year-olds. This school was situated on a large council estate. The class teacher was again female and had taught for ten years. The pupils in this second class were generally regarded within the school as being boisterous and somewhat difficult to teach. As is common with junior school classes in Britain, the pupils in both these classes were normally seated around tables. In the first class observations were carried out whilst children were engaged in formal academic work. In the second class pupils were observed engaged in a variety of subjects but not in PE, art or music.

In both classes the children were systematically observed daily for two weeks in their usual seating arrangements, i.e. in groups around tables. This was followed by a further two weeks in which they were seated in rows and finally for another two weeks when they were again seated around tables. Daily estimates of on-task behaviour for each child were averaged for each class and plotted to compare levels of on-task behaviour under the two conditions for both classes. In each class every child was observed twice by an independent observer in a different order each day for two periods of 30 seconds. This was done systematically using a procedure which would tend to underestimate the level of on-task behaviour.

'On-task' behaviour was defined very similarly in both studies as compliance with teacher's instructions, eye contact with the teacher when requested, eye contact with their textbooks and materials when asked to get on with their set work. 'Off task' behaviour included calling out, interrupting a neighbour, talking to a neighbour, being out of seat without permission, non-compliance with teacher instructions and not getting on with the set work (Wheldall *et al.*, 1981, pp. 175-6).

In order to provide some measure of reliability a second observer independently observed and recorded the behaviour in each class once in each of the three conditions. The second observer observed the children alongside and in the same order as the first observer and both kept separate, independent records.

There was evidence of good inter-observer agreement in both studies at around 90 per cent, suggesting that the data were acceptably reliable. Mean on-task behaviour for both classes was higher when the children were seated in rows than when seated around tables. Mean on-task behaviour in class A was 72 per cent under the tables condition, 88 per cent when in rows and 69 per cent when they again returned to tables. Similarly, for class B mean on-task behaviour was 67 per cent when around tables, 84 per cent when in rows and 72 per cent on return to tables. Examination of the fine-grain results suggested that these results were not entirely unequivocal. As Wheldall argued, some children will behave well whatever the seating arrangements and the effect of their behaviour will iron out some of the variations brought about by changes in the seating arrangements. He, therefore, examined the effects of changing seating arrangements on the small number of children in both classes with low initial on-task behaviour and here the results are absolutely clear. He concluded that 'children whose behaviour is low when seated around tables benefit considerably in terms of increased on-task behaviour when seated in rows'. This conclusion is related to the type of work they were being asked to do, namely, academic work such as developing skills in calculating, writing or reading which normally require quietness and concentrated application to the task.

Wheldall went on to replicate these findings (Wheldall and Lam, 1987) in three classes in a special school for behaviourally troublesome children with moderate learning difficulties whilst they were engaged in mathematics and English lessons. The effects were expected to show themselves more clearly among children who had learning and behaviour problems and who might be expected to benefit from the structure provided by more formal seating arrangements. Once again children were observed daily, but this time in four two-week phases; first seated round tables then in rows, then again around tables and, finally, once more in rows. Percentage on-task behaviour was recorded together with rates of pupil disruption and of teacher approval and disapproval. In all three classes on-task behaviour doubled from around 35 per cent to 70 per cent as conditions changed from tables to rows.

In addition, the rate of disruption was three times higher in the tables conditions than in rows conditions. There was an effect also on the teachers' behaviour. Teacher positive comments increased during the rows conditions while negative comments decreased. There is clearly a correlation between seating arrangements and teacher behaviour as well as between seating and pupil behaviour.

Wheldall, speaking as an applied behaviour analyst, argued that antecedents or setting conditions, such as manipulation of seating arrangements, are reasonably easy for teachers to carry out and that they can have important and immediate effects upon the study behaviour of pupils in the classroom. He suggested that when in certain social situations we wish to encourage interaction in a group, as for a discussion or in order to play a game like bridge, we arrange seating so as to make interaction easy. On the other hand if we want to write a letter say, or fill in an application form or income tax return it is unlikely that we would wish to find ourselves in a group where other people might easily interact with us. We are much more likely to seek a quiet place where we are not likely to be disturbed by anybody else. He concludes by suggesting 'it could be argued that it amounts to little short of cruelty to place children in manifestly social contexts and then to expect them to work independently' as was the case in the classrooms used in these experiments.

Wheldall concluded his study by emphasizing that he was not suggesting a return to rows seating formation in all classrooms for all purposes. Rather, he suggested that it is the job of teachers to decide what sort of activity they are planning for their classes and to arrange the seating according to the task. If a collaborative task is being pursued then clearly to have children seated around tables will make it much easier for them to discuss and to work with each other. On the other hand, if the task given to the pupils is one which requires each to work independently then if they sit in rows they are more likely to be able to do so without being interrupted by anybody else. This is one of the reasons why rows formation is preferred when students are engaged in formal written examinations.

It might be considered by some that the use of on-task behaviour as a measure of whether children are working as the teacher has planned or whether they are producing satisfactory results might be questioned. Evidence supporting the importance of time on-task (sometimes referred to as academic engaged time) has been provided by both behaviour analysts and non-behavioural educational researchers. A number of researchers, including Rosenshine, Berliner and Anderson, have demonstrated that academic engaged time is a critical variable in academic progress in all subjects (Rosenshine and Berliner, 1978; Anderson, 1981; Fisher and Berliner, 1985). The conclusion of Rosenshine and Berliner (1978) was that:

> A fairly clear and consistent pattern emerges from the studies cited. The primary finding is that student time spent engaged in relevant content appears to be an essential variable for which there is no substitute. (p. 12)

At the very naive level of casual observation it is apparent that a child who is wandering around the classroom and, therefore, not on-task is very unlikely to be doing the task set by the teacher. The same child will quite possibly be engaging in behaviour likely to prevent others from working also. On the other hand, there is, of course, no guarantee that pupils who are sitting in their places and apparently working are actually achieving anything. Hastings (1990) refers to the child who has developed all sorts of ploys to give the impression of being on-task when, in fact, he or she is doing very little.

The effect of different seating arrangements on the quantity and quality of work produced among two classes of 10- and 11-year-old children was examined from a different perspective by Bennett and Blundell (1983). The children of two classes were matched for size, age and sex and the work they produced in reading, language and mathematics was considered. The pupils spent the first two weeks in their normal classroom groupings around tables. The second two-week period was spent in rows and then they were moved back again into groups. The findings indicate that the quantity of work completed generally increased when children were sitting in rows whilst the quality of the work was maintained. In this study the researchers were simply concerned with the quantity and quality of work produced and did not consider the nature of on-task behaviour at all but their work combined with that of Wheldall and his associates provides convincing evidence that whether on-task is measured or the work output is measured the result is the same. Seating arrangements do affect the outcomes. At the conclusion of his researches described above, Wheldall made the point very strongly that some seating arrangements were more suitable than others for certain kinds of work and that flexibility was the essential requirement.

Thus, what children are achieving in the classroom will not depend solely upon the seating arrangements adopted by the teacher but also upon the kind of work which is set. Her Majesty's Inspectorate have over many years drawn attention to the importance of matching the task set to the ability of the pupils. What must also be considered is the match between the task and the arrangements for grouping. Galton (1990) reporting on the ORACLE study says that it was common to see examples of joint group work in most classrooms involving common tasks but generally the members of the groups had individual assignments. These joint activities, however, were seldom used for teaching basic skills of computation, for teaching English or science but were largely restricted to art and craft or general studies where there was a practical element and where equipment of various kinds was being used. In the

ORACLE study radio microphones were used to pick up the childen's talk so that a close study could be made of its nature. It is interesting to note that only about 20 per cent of pupils' conversations were related to the task in hand. This is a far cry from the expectations of the writers of the Plowden Report and the supporters of collaborative learning. It does not indicate a high level of useful and purposeful verbal interchange.

Because of the progressive nature of teacher training establishments and the idealism of new recruits to the profession one might expect child-centred education and discovery learning to be the norm in primary classrooms. Merely looking at the seating arrangements in the vast majority of primary classrooms one might easily be persuaded that this was so. However, things are not always what they appear to be, even in the curriculum areas of primary education. A paper by Barker-Lunn (1984) suggests that,

> The situation which this survey has revealed is in marked contrast with the assumed stereotype that was prevalent in the 1960s and 1970s. The Plowden Committee set up in 1963 to inquire into the state of primary education, lent its approval to what was described as progressive education. Its report conveyed the impression – without supplying supporting evidence – that progressive methods were practised by a large number of teachers and were becoming the norm in primary schools. This became the view accepted by the general public . . . This view of junior school education persisted not only in the absence of supporting evidence but even when contradictory findings were published. From 1963 to 1967 the foundation (i.e. NFER) carried out a longitudinal study which found no evidence to suggest that large numbers of teachers were practising progressive methods. A few years later, in 1973, the Bullock Committee carried out a survey of teaching practices which furnished convincing evidence that informal and progressive approaches had barely established a foothold in primary schools. (p. 186)

She concludes,

> What is clear from the 1980 survey, however, is that the most recently available evidence shows that the vast majority of junior school teachers are firmly in control of their classrooms. They prefer a didactic approach rather than a reliance on discovery methods; they are making increasing use of class teaching; and there is no need to exhort them to go back to basics. Indeed, the development of and practice in the basic skills of both English and mathematics would seem to be the predominant features of junior school classrooms. (p. 187)

It is very interesting to observe that although discovery learning is assumed to be in progress, but is not, the seating arrangements most appropriate for it are still maintained. Are primary school teachers thinking about the process or are they simply doing what they were told is the right way to arrange their rooms? Teachers in secondary schools have tended to be more traditional in their approach to styles of teaching and have not been challenged over these issues in the same way as have their colleagues in primary schools. It seems strange that a seating arrangement believed to be so essential for all class activities at the primary school level should suddenly, with the transfer to secondary schooling, be found to be inappropriate in most cases. It suggests that a useful study might be made into the metamorphosis that has taken place over the six weeks or so of the summer holiday period.

In 1992 Bennett and Dunne published a book called *Managing Classroom Groups*, in which they examined the whole business of teaching children in groups as the Plowden Report recommended. They began by considering how much of teachers' time is taken up with responding to the demands of their pupils for help, advice and assistance and how little is left for the much more important tasks of monitoring and diagnosis. They then considered the nature of co-operative grouping and how such groups can be organized to leave teachers with time for these activities. They looked in detail at group and classroom processes. They made valuable suggestions about how teachers should design tasks appropriate to group work considering separately the cognitive and social aspects. They discussed in detail the management of group work, the training of pupils in the necessary group work skills and how the outcomes of such working conditions may be assessed.

There is no doubt that their work has made a very real contribution to the whole business of teaching children in groups. This is a very important new step but it calls for a whole new set of skills for teachers to learn. Managing a class as a whole group is a difficult and demanding task. Managing a class which is divided up into groups where each may be following a different track is immensely more difficult. Still more difficult is the task of evaluating the output of each individual child, of monitoring the progress of each and especially of arranging that each one is led forward to the next stage in their learning programme. At the moment, precious little time is given in establishments concerned with the professional preparation of teachers to the matter of classroom management. This was referred to in the Elton Report (DES, 1989), which commented on the fact that the 'group management skills', which the authors themselves regarded as of prime importance, seem to be little regarded by teacher trainers. The authors affirmed that this assumption is accompanied by the belief that such skills cannot be learned. Of the teachers referred to earlier (Merrett and Wheldall, 1993) who thought that classroom management was so important to them, 82 per cent believed that they had learned their classroom management skills 'on the job'. If teachers are not being taught basic classroom management now who is to teach them the much more complex skills needed to manage groups?

Two factors that are seldom taken into consideration are the children's expectations and their perceptions of what goes on in classrooms. What research has been carried out shows that pupils have very definite views about how they expect their teachers to behave and what virtues they expect them to display and how they, in turn, ought to be responding to this. Galton (1990) in considering pupils' perceptions of collaborative group work found that, for the most part, there was a strong rejection of it. Children understand well enough that there are certain skills that they need to acquire and that some areas of knowledge and information are of interest and importance to them. They know that in order to acquire these they will need concentrated practice for which they require quiet, privacy and freedom from interruption. They are also interested to know what they can achieve on their own. At the same time they need to acquire skills which will enable them to co-operate with others, to complete joint enterprises that are impossible for the individual and to learn from their peers. Work which calls for individual work and effort and that which involves collaboration and co-operation are both necessary.

Another strong factor in the whole equation is the expectations of parents. They remember how they learned when they were at school and their expectations are partly coloured by these recollections. From consideration of the present Government's views it would seem that we are coming full circle with pressure to go back to the old, more formal ways of teaching and learning. Perhaps this change of heart is a reflection of a regime which claimed to be adopting a child-centred system but which was, in fact, operating traditionally but disguising this fact through overt organizational procedures like having the classroom furniture arranged as though for group work.

Ultimately, it is the job of teachers to be in charge. They are professionally responsible and it is their concern to arrange for children to optimize their potential. In order to do this they need to provide both individual and co-operative learning situations. Whatever organizational style they choose to adopt, one way of doing this is to follow the way of Positive Teaching (Wheldall and Merrett, 1989; Merrett and Wheldall, 1990). By using this approach teachers will seek to negotiate rules or guidelines for conduct with their pupils to the benefit of both parties. Teachers will learn to be more aware of their own responses to their pupils' work and behaviour. They will seek to change their own behaviour by learning to observe more carefully what is happening in their classrooms and to pay more attention to the good work and acceptable behaviour that is being displayed, instead of taking it for granted. Blanchard and Johnson (1983) in *The One Minute Manager* suggest that the best way of managing (and here they are talking about business management) is to creep around and find people doing the right thing and to reward them with praise, attention, extra facilities or responsibility or pay, and so on. We can adapt this to the classroom situation. Positive teachers will observe their pupils carefully and try to optimize their performance by catching those who are doing the right thing. They will try to increase their skill in observation and find those who are working well or behaving well and pay attention to them. By doing so they will optimize their pupils' efforts to the benefit of all. This they can do whether they teach their classes as wholes or whether they have, for some specific purpose and with due attention to the nature of the tasks being set, organized their pupils into groups.

REFERENCES

Anderson, L.W. (1981) Instruction and time-on-task: a review with implications. *Journal of Curriculum Studies*, **13**, 289-303.

Ankney, R.F. (1974) Effects of classroom spatial arrangement on student behaviour. *Dissertation Abstracts International*, **35**, 2799A.

Axelrod, D., Hall, R.V. and Tams, A. (1979) Comparison of two common classroom seating arrangements. *Academic Therapy*, **15**, 29-36.

Barker-Lunn, J. (1984) Junior school teachers: their methods and practices. *Educational Research*, **26**, 178-88.

Bennett, N. and Blundell, D. (1983) Quantity and quality of work in rows and classroom groups. *Educational Psychology*, **3**, 93-105.

Bennett, N. and Dunne, E. (1992) *Managing Classroom Groups*. Hemel Hempstead: Simon & Schuster.

Blanchard, K. and Johnson, S. (1983) *The One Minute Manager*. London: Fontana.

Bruner, J. and Haste, H. (1987) *Making Sense*. London: Methuen.

Cox, C.B. and Dyson, A.E. (1969a) *Black Paper 1: Fight for Education*. London: Critical Quarterly Society.

Cox, C.B. and Dyson, A.E. (1969b) *Black Paper 2: The Crisis in Education*. London: Critical Quarterly Society.

Cox, C.B. and Dyson, A.E. (1970) *Black Paper 3: Goodbye, Mr Short*. London: Critical Quarterly Society.

Cox, C.B. and Boyson, R. (1977) *Black Paper 1977*. London: Temple Smith.

Dawe, H.C. (1934) The influence of size of kindergarten group upon performance. *Child Development*, **5**, 295-303.

DES (1967) *Children and Their Primary Schools*. (The Plowden Report). London: HMSO.

DES (1989) *Discipline in Schools*. (The Elton Report). London: HMSO.

Fisher, C.W. and Berliner, D.C. (eds) (1985) *Perspectives on Instructional Time*. New York: Longman.

Galton, M. (1990) Grouping and group work. In C. Rogers and P. Kutnick (eds), *The Social Psychology of the Primary School*. London: Routledge.

Hastings, N. (1990) Questions of motivation. *Support for Learning*, **7**, 135-7.

Merrett, F. and Wheldall, K. (1990) *Positive Teaching in the Primary School*. London: Paul Chapman.

Merrett, F. and Wheldall, K. (1993) How do teachers learn to manage classroom behaviour? A study of teachers' opinions about their initial training with special reference to classroom behaviour management. *Educational Studies*, **19**, 91-106.

Rosenshine, B.V. and Berliner, D.C. (1978) Academic engaged time. *British Journal of Teacher Education*, **4**, 3-16.

Rubin, C.N. (1973) A naturalistic study in proxemics: seating arrangement and its effect on interaction, performance and behaviour. *Dissertation Abstracts International*, **33**, 3829A.

Saunders, B.T. (1970) Modification of emotionally disturbed behaviour in the elementary school child through the manipulation of classroom seating arrangements. *Dissertation Abstracts International*, **31**, 1088A.

Schwebel, A.I. (1969) Physical and social distancing in teacher–pupil relationships. *Dissertation Abstracts International*, *31*, 155IB.

Shores, R.E. and Haubrich, P.A. (1969) Effects of cubicles in educating emotionally disturbed children. *Exceptional Children*, **36**, 21-4.

Wheldall, K. and Lam, Y.Y. (1987) Rows versus tables. II: The effects of two classroom seating arrangements on classroom disruption rate, on-task behaviour and teacher behaviour in three special school classes. *Educational Psychology*, **7**, 303-12.

Wheldall, K. and Merrett, F. (1989) *Positive Teaching in the Secondary School*. London: Paul Chapman.

Wheldall, K., Morris, M., Vaughan, P. and Ng, Y.Y. (1981) Rows versus tables: an example of the use of behavioural ecology in two classes of 11-year-old children. *Educational Psychology*, **1**, 171-84.

Chapter 4

Co-operative Learning

Neville Bennett

EDITORS' INTRODUCTION

This is a chapter which establishes much of the basic case that can be made out for group work and the reader will find much here that will help in the provision of a framework for the work discussed in the chapters which follow.

Bennett makes it clear that research into co-operative group work has a number of different concerns and starting points. The work may be concerned with either process or product (more often it seems the latter) and these may in turn be based on different theoretical models.

Bennett's careful assessment of this research helps to make it clear that one needs to be careful in using the general term 'co-operation'. Different approaches, and different theoretical starting positions, will provide for the adoption of approaches which need not be considered to be interchangeable. Indeed, one conclusion which emerges quite strongly from the following chapter is that one has to be concerned with 'the problem of the match'. Teachers need to be able to make clear and appropriate decisions about the intended outcome of a particular co-operative exercise before making decisions regarding the type of task to be used and the particular group structure which would be best employed.

This suggests a need for training for teachers, but Bennett argues for the need for training for pupils. The various group processes require skill to carry out and one ought not to assume that all pupils possess such skill.

Finally, Bennett discusses the important distinction between developmental and motivational theoretical frameworks for co-operative work. These need not be regarded as being necessarily in conflict, but the reader will doubtless find it helpful to keep the distinction in mind while reading further chapters.

INTRODUCTION

It has been argued that co-operation is central to human existence (Argyle, 1991), but of all the prominent institutions of our society, schools seem least characterized by co-operative activity. Nevertheless there has, in recent years, been a developing interest in the use of co-operative groups as effective learning contexts in classrooms. This interest has largely been fuelled by the increasing realization of the link between learning and social interaction. As such there is a move to the implementation of co-operative grouping to achieve a better balance between whole-class, individual, and group teaching. This chapter sets out the rationale for co-operative grouping, and describes several types of group before considering group processes and outcomes, and what factors can aid or hinder these.

RATIONALE FOR CO-OPERATIVE GROUPING

The interest in children learning co-operatively in groups stems from various sources. These include a realization among educators of the value of interpersonal processes in both learning and social relationships, an increasing awareness of the value of co-operation and problem-solving in the development of understanding and a desire to move away from instructional models which view teachers as the only source of knowledge and skills.

This interest has been informed by two different theoretical perspectives: the *developmental* approach, drawn from cognitive psychology, and the *motivational*, derived from social psychology.

Developmental perspective

Conceptions of the learner in developmental psychology have shifted in the last decade from that of a 'lone scientist' to that of a 'social being'. Bruner and Haste (1987) describe the change as follows:

> A quiet revolution has taken place in developmental psychology in the last decade. It is not only that we have begun to think again of the child as a social being – one who plays and talks with others, learns through interactions with parents and teachers – but because we have come once more to appreciate that through social life, the child acquires a framework for integrating experience, and learning how to negotiate meaning in a manner congruent with the requirements of the culture. 'Making sense' is a social process; it is an activity that is always situated within a cultural and historical context.
> Before that, we had fallen into the habit of thinking of the child as an 'active scientist', constructing hypotheses about the world, reflecting upon experience, interacting with the physical environment and formulating increasingly complex structures of thought. But this active constructing child has been conceived as a rather isolated being, working alone at her problem-solving. Increasingly we see now that, given an appropriate, shared social context, the child seems more competent as an intelligent social operator than she is as a 'lone scientist' coping with a world of unknowns.

This view of the child as a social being rather than a lone scientist constitutes an attack on the view of learning which assumes that genuine intellectual competence is a manifestation of a child's largely unassisted activities (see Wood, 1988, for example). It stresses far more the importance of the social setting in learning, and emphasizes in particular the role of negotiating and sharing in the classroom. As Vygotsky (1978) argued, 'Learning awakens a variety of internal developmental processes that are able to operate only when the child is interacting with people in his environment and in co-operation with his peers.' Social interaction is assigned a central role in facilitating learning. Vygotsky's notion of the zone of proximal development identifies the gap between what a learner can do alone and unaided, and what can be achieved with the help of more knowledgeable others. 'What a child can do today in co-operation, tomorrow he will be able to do on his own' (Vygotsky, 1962). It is now commonly agreed that the foundation of learning and development is co-operatively achieved success, and that the basis of that success is language and communication (c.f. Wells *et al.*, 1990).

This belief that talk is central to learning is not, of course, new. The Bullock Report (1975) devoted itself entirely to language, and welcomed the growth in interest in oral language, 'for we cannot emphasize too strongly our conviction of its importance in the education of the child.' It argued that all schools ought to have, as a priority objective, a commitment to the speech needs of their pupils. And, more recently, the authors of the English 5-11 National Curriculum recommended a separate language component for speaking and listening, thus demonstrating their belief in oracy. 'Our inclusion of speaking and listening as a separate profile component in our recommendation is a reflection of our conviction that these skills are of central importance to children's development' (HMI, 1989).

Motivational perspective

Whereas the developmental approach focuses primarily on the quality of interactions during collaborative activities, the motivational perspective emphasizes the reward or goal structures under which members of the group operate. Advocates of this approach maintain that if co-operative learning increases student achievement, it is because the use of co-operative rewards, such as individual or team points, creates peer norms and sanctions supporting individual efforts. 'In other words, rewarding groups based on group performance creates an interpersonal reward structure in which group members will give or withhold social reinforcers (praise, encouragement) in response to their group mates' task-related efforts' (Slavin, 1987).

Co-operative grouping can thus be justified in terms of established theories of children's learning, and of meeting the demands of the National Curriculum. The advice of the National Curriculum Council (1989) on the English Curriculum thus emphasizes the use of language, not to communicate what is known, but as an instrument of learning: 'It is time for children to think aloud, to grapple with ideas and to clarify thoughts' through exchanges of ideas and views both with other pupils, and the teacher.

CURRENT PRACTICE IN BRITISH PRIMARY SCHOOLS

This advice, although in line with current views on children's learning, is not in line with current primary practice in Britain, which is ostensibly based on the individual-ization of learning. The Plowden Report (1967) advocated individualization of learning, but recognized a practical difficulty. If all teaching were on an individual basis only seven or eight minutes a day would be available for each child. The report therefore advised teachers to economize by 'teaching together a small group of children who are roughly at the same stage'. Further, these groups should change in accordance with children's needs, the implication being that the class would be organized flexibly, with groups forming and reforming according to children's needs and activities. Various advantages were perceived for group work: it would help children learn to get along together in a context where peers could help one another and realize their own strengths and weaknesses as well as those of others; it would make their learning clearer to individuals if they had to explain it to others; it would give pupils opportunity to teach as well as to learn. It was hoped that apathetic children would be infected by the enthusiasms of a group while able children would benefit by being caught up in the thrust and counter-thrust of conversation in a small group of children similar to themselves.

Unfortunately, research on classroom grouping practices over the last fifteen years has provided little support for this rosy picture. For example, in a survey of over 500 primary schools in the late 1970s Her Majesty's Inspectorate (1978) reported that three-quarters of classes were grouped according to ability for maths; and two-thirds of 7-year-olds and over one-half of 9-year-olds were grouped in this way for reading (c.f. Bennett *et al.*, 1986).

Research that has focused on the observation of group activities in classrooms has also reported sobering findings on contemporary practice, particularly in junior classes. Here, most children sit in groups, but for the great majority of the time they work as individuals on their own, individual, tasks. In other words, pupils work *in* groups, but not *as* groups. Further, whilst working in groups the amount of task-related talk is low, interactions tend to be short, and the opportunity to co-operate is slim. Finally there appears to be a clear sex effect in interaction. The great majority of talk is between pupils of the same sex, even in mixed-sex groups (Galton *et al.*, 1980). The small amount of research carried out at infant level indicates that there, too, children work in, not as groups, but that the sex effect is far less noticeable. Levels of task-related talk are higher, but little of it is task-enhancing, i.e. aids the children in understanding their work (Bennett *et al.*, 1984).

Although similar large-scale studies have not been carried out recently, accounts of HMI and others indicate that little change has taken place (Galton and Williamson, 1992; Pollard *et al.*, 1994). What seems to have happened is that teachers have taken note of Plowden's views in having children work in groups, but have preferred to retain individualization rather than to introduce co-operation in that context.

The unfortunate outcome is a high level of low-quality talk and a dearth of co-operative endeavour.

Typical grouping practices are shown schematically below:

Figure 4.1 represents four children as a group sitting together, but working on their own individual tasks (a, b, c, d) and aiming for an individual outcome or product.

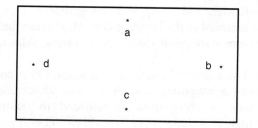

Figure 4.1 *Children working individually on individual tasks for individual products.*

This arrangement is widespread, and seen typically in maths where children often work on the same structured scheme, but at different stages within it. This occurs whether or not children are grouped by ability.

The second variant, shown in Figure 4.2, is more common when teachers set a class task, to be completed individually, e.g. the writing of a story. Here the children are engaged on the same task (a) but the aim is for an individual, not a group, outcome – each has to write their own story.

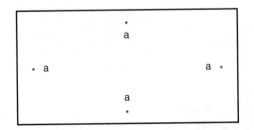

Figure 4.2 *Children working individually on identical tasks for individual products.*

The demand for co-operation is apparent in neither type of group, although it would be easier to achieve in the latter. Indeed, children often seem confused in this situation about whether they are allowed to co-operate or not. The point to bear in mind, however, is that it is these types of group that tend to generate talk of low quality, often not related to the tasks being worked on.

CO-OPERATIVE GROUPS

There is a wide variety of co-operative groups, mostly American, with a bewildering array of names: STAD, Jigsaw, COOP-COOP, etc. (see Kagan, 1985 for full descriptions).

Three are briefly described below to illustrate the range.

Student Teams – Achievement Divisions (STAD) (Slavin, 1983)

Pupils are assigned to teams of four or five which are as heterogeneous as can be arranged in terms of ability, sex and, where appropriate, race. Following a class presentation by the teacher the group works together in a *collaborative* learning process to master the material of the learning unit. Most often the team members quiz each other, working from worksheets that consist of facts, skills or information to be mastered.

Pupils are evaluated on mastery by individual quizzes. Quiz scores are transformed into team scores using a weighting system for individual scores based on prior performances. Rewards or recognition is provided to teams for high weekly performance and/or high cumulative standings. Slavin (1990) provides a number of variations and a handbook for structuring these co-operative learning groups in his review.

Jigsaw (Aronson, 1978)

As its name suggests each group member is only provided with one part of the material to be learned. Each task is divided into as many parts as there are group members and each member studies only one of those. However they do not study their parts in their group, but with members of the other group (expert groups) who are studying the same part. They then return to their own group and teach their part to the others. Finally all members of the group are quizzed on all sections of the task. Groups are composed of 5 or 6 pupils, a heterogeneous cross-section of the class.

Group Investigation (Johnson and Johnson, 1975)

This model was designed to provide pupils with broad and diverse learning experiences, in contrast to the STAD and Jigsaw approaches, which are oriented to the learning of facts and skills. It consists of six stages. Pupils identify sub-topics within an area identified by the teacher, and organize themselves into heterogeneous groups of three to six children. The group plans the learning task, usually a complex problem-solving task, and determines the goal(s) and how it is to be studied. The necessary information is collected, analysed and evaluated, before preparing the final report, event or summary. This is then presented to the class, and evaluated by their peers and teacher.

It can be seen that both STAD and Jigsaw embody interdependent tasks, i.e. the group members have to rely on each other to fulfil the demands of the task, and both incorporate rewards – quiz scores, etc., although they are awarded to the whole group in STAD, but to individuals in Jigsaw. These two models exemplify the motivational perspective, whereas Group Investigation more clearly links with developmental approaches.

In our work with primary teachers we have adopted a developmental perspective, working with adaptations of Jigsaw (see Figure 4.3) and Group Investigation to fit British classrooms. In reality they look little different from the versions described. The crucial differences are in the nature of the tasks set and the demand for co-operation that they contain.

In this kind of group, the task is divided into as many parts as there are group members – in this case, four (a1, a2, a3, a4). Each child works on one part of the task,

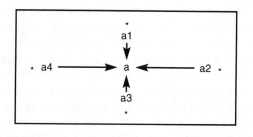

Figure 4.3 *Children working individually on Jigsaw elements for a joint outcome.*

the task being divided in such a way that the group outcome cannot be achieved until every group member has successfully completed their piece of work. At this point the 'Jigsaw' can be fitted together. Co-operation is thus built into the task structure, as indeed is individual accountability. It is difficult in this type of group task for a child to sit back and let others do all the work, especially since group members are likely to ensure that everyone pulls their weight. Examples of such tasks would be the production of a group story or newspaper, or the making of a 'set' of objects in a practical maths activity.

For the type of task in Figure 4.4, adapted from Johnson and Johnson (1975), children will need to work co-operatively since only one product will be required of the group. Activities will therefore have to be co-ordinated. Here the teacher has the choice of assigning group roles or allowing roles to emerge naturally in the group.

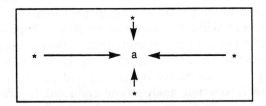

Figure 4.4   *Children working jointly on one task for a joint outcome (or discussion).*

Each individual's work will have an impact on the group product but will be worthless until it becomes part of that product. Examples can be seen in problem-solving in technology, construction activities or in discussion tasks. Although collaborative endeavour is necessary for the group to succeed, it is less easy to ascertain exactly what each pupil has contributed and individual accountability is therefore lower.

These approaches demonstrate that co-operative group work is not a single, specific form of classroom organization but encompasses different approaches, different types of task and different demands for co-operation.

STUDIES OF CO-OPERATIVE GROUPING

Changing classroom practices always present challenges irrespective of the quality of the theoretical and empirical underpinnings. Thus the implementation and acceptance of co-operative group work has been variable, mediated in part by the cultures and ideologies supporting contemporary practice in different countries. In the United States and Israel, for example, didactic teaching is the norm. Consequently the research effort has been directed toward the implementation of experimental grouping programmes, with a view to changing the social contexts of learning in the classroom. In Britain, on the other hand, the immediate social context for learning in a majority of primary classrooms is a small group of some four to six children. The research problem here has not been to change contexts, but to improve them, since typical group practice is not co-operative, and suffers from large amounts of off-task interactions, poor quality on-task interaction and marked gender effects (Bennett *et al.*, 1984).

Differences in the aims of these research studies are reflected in their design. The American and Israeli studies have tended to be input–output evaluations of grouping models, designed to ascertain their effectiveness, rather than to ascertain how groups work effectively. Group processes were largely ignored, even though these processes may have been 'planned' theoretically. The British, and some later American, studies on the other hand have tended to focus on processes.

So what evidence exists to indicate that co-operative grouping works?

Two sets of studies are relevant to the question of group effectiveness. The first set has, as indicated above, implemented a particular type of group such as STAD, and tested children at the beginning and end of the implementation to assess change. Change has sometimes been in relation to gains in achievement or in some form of social development. These studies are designed to ascertain *that* groups work, not how they work. For this reason these are labelled 'product studies'. A separate set of studies have considered *how* groups work, investigating social interaction patterns and their relationships to achievement or social outcomes. These are referred to as 'process studies'.

PRODUCT STUDIES

The claims from this set of studies about the role of co-operative grouping in improving achievement and social development are generally impressive. Johnson and Johnson (1985) for example make the following sweeping claims.

> In our studies, we have found considerable evidence that co-operative learning experiences promote higher achievement than do competitive and individualistic learning experiences. Of the 26 studies that we have done that include achievement data, in 21 studies co-operative learning promoted higher achievement, 2 studies had mixed results, and 3 found no differences . . . These studies have included college studies and students from every grade but the eighth grade. They have used curriculum in maths, English, language arts, geometry, social studies, science, physical science, and physical education. The studies have lasted from one day to nine months. They have included both males and females; upper-middle class, middle-class, working class, and lower-class students, gifted, medium-ability, and low-ability students; and students from a number of minority groups . . . It is evident, therefore, that co-operative learning procedures can provide appropriate instructional experiences for diverse students who work together.

Slavin (1987), too, is upbeat about the impact of co-operation on achievement, arguing that

> over the past 15 years there has arisen a new interest in co-operative learning methods designed for use not as a supplement to traditional instructional methods but as a coherent alternative means of organizing the classroom for instruction in fundamental curriculum areas, from mathematics to language arts to science and social studies . . . Research has established that under certain circumstances the use of co-operative learning methods increases student achievement more than traditional instructional practices.

These same authors make similar claims about improvements in the social domain. Johnson and Johnson (1985) reported that:

In our studies, we have found considerable evidence that co-operative learning experiences promote interpersonal attraction and more positive relationships among students than do competitive and individualistic learning experiences. Of the 37 studies that we have done that include interpersonal attraction data, in 35 studies co-operative learning promoted greater interpersonal attraction, and in 2 results were mixed. These findings resulted for a wide variety of age levels, subject areas, diverse students, and instructional sessions.

Slavin (1987) reports improvements in pupils' self-esteem. 'These [co-operative] methods improve student self-esteem and social relations among students, in particular, race relations and acceptance of mainstreamed students.' (See also Cowie and Rudduck, 1990.)

There is strong agreement by these American reviewers on core findings relating to gains in achievement, and in social and affective areas. Disputes abound in this, as in every, field. However, these are not disputes about whether co-operative groups are effective or not, but which type of group works best with what kind of task demand, in what kind of context, and with what age children.

Finally, although they would not claim their reports to be research, it is useful to record that HMI also appear convinced of the value of co-operative groups in improving achievement. For example, their report on mathematics in the primary school (HMI, 1989, p. 20) includes the statement: 'Co-operative work was a strong and distinctive feature of the best mathematics work seen, with pupils seeking together a solution to an intellectual or practical problem'. Issues in the implementation of effective group work are considered later.

GROUP PROCESSES

Few studies have addressed such central questions as what processes within the group relate to enhanced cognitive and social outcomes. The most frequent aspect to be studied so far has been helping behaviour. However, these studies have tended to be American, on mathematics tasks and of short duration. They have distinguished between receiving and giving help. If help is to be effective for learning there must be an explanation rather than a straight answer, it must be provided in response to the receiving pupil's needs, and be understandable. It has been suggested that the effectiveness of help received may constitute a continuum: receiving explanations is sometimes helpful, receiving information has mixed effects, and receiving the answer may actually be harmful (Webb, 1989). For example, receiving an explanation which has been requested is only useful for learning if the explanation provided was relevant, understood and applied by the receiver. Receiving information on the other hand is more likely to be helpful more often since it is easier for the helper to frame an adequate response, and for the receiver to understand it. However, receiving only the answer is unlikely to enhance the receiver's understanding.

But what does the giver gain from the helping interaction? When the first peer tutoring system was set up, some 200 years ago, it was argued that teaching was the best way of learning: *Qui docet indoctos docet se*. Most modern studies affirm this: giving explanations is positively related to achievement. In explaining to someone the giver must clarify, organize, indeed reorganize, the material conceptually. Further, if the initial explanation is not understood reformulation is necessary, utilizing perhaps different language, examples, analogies or representations. All of these, it is claimed, will consolidate or expand the giver's understanding.

The provision and receipt of information and explanations is not the only key to successful group interaction. Practice, feedback and turn-taking are other variables which can mediate achievement effects. In addition, attempts are currently being made to operationalize for classrooms the concept of cognitive conflict or controversy. This is based on Piaget's view that progress in cognitive development often occurs when cognitive conflict arises with someone who can be seen as comparable to the self but who offers a discrepant solution. Much laboratory-based research has studied and developed this argument (see Perret-Clermont, 1980; Doise and Mugny, 1984) but few studies in schools utilizing normal classroom tasks have so far been undertaken.

Finally, it is worth noting the increasing evidence of enhanced pupil involvement when working in co-operative groups. When comparisons have been made between time-on-task in groups and in whole-class activity it has been substantially less in whole classes (see Hertz-Lazorowitz, 1990). Similarly, when comparisons have been made between co-operative groups and normal classroom groups, pupil involvement in the former has been substantially higher. Table 4.1 shows the average amount of task-related talk in typical, non-co-operative classroom groups, taken from a study by Bennett *et al.* (1984) and compares these levels with those found in co-operative classroom groups (Bennett and Dunne, 1992). It is clear from these findings that children in co-operative settings demonstrate much greater involvement in their work, the average improvement being 22 per cent.

Table 4.1   *Task-related talk in co-operative and non-co-operative groups.*

	Task-related talk	
Curriculum	Non-co-operative	Co-operative
Language	70	83
Maths	63	88
Technology		93
Computer tasks		99
Average	66	88

IMPLEMENTATION

The nature and quality of group processes is mediated by several other factors which teachers will need to take note of when implementing co-operative group work in their classes. These include the composition of the group, task structures and training.

Group composition

Under this heading are considered the mix or composition of groups in terms of ability or attainment level, sex and personality.

Studies comparing groups which are homogeneous or heterogeneous in terms of children's ability or attainment level present a consistent picture. The quality of interactions is substantially different in each type of group. Of particular concern are homogeneous groups of low-ability children. When compared to high-ability groups these devote substantially less of their time to interactions concerning academic content, fewer of their requests concerning academic and procedural issues are responded to appropriately, and few explanations are offered. Not surprisingly, children in these groups show poor understanding of the task on its completion (c.f. Wilkinson and Calculator, 1982; Bennett and Cass, 1988). High-ability children, on the other hand, appear to perform well irrespective of the type of group they are played in. They tend to talk more, and more of that talk is academic in content. They are the main sources of help in groups, and provide most of the explanations.

Differential experiences for girls and boys in groups have been reported from studies of non-co-operative, as well as co-operative, groups. In the latter the sex mix of a group does appear to influence the amount and level of interaction. Studies on both sides of the Atlantic have found that girls are substantially affected in groups in which they are outnumbered by boys. They speak less, at a lower level of reasoning, and are often ignored by boys. In such groups boys are more successful than girls in obtaining help (Bennett and Dunne, 1992; Webb, 1989).

An aspect of group composition thought particularly important by teachers – pupils' personality – has attracted little systematic attention.

Task design

Although co-operative grouping has a respectable theoretical pedigree, the effectiveness of which is backed up by systematic research, very few studies have considered how best to put it into practice in classrooms. As Galton *et al*. (1980) argue:

> no serious attention appears to have been given, even in relation to the teaching of science and mathematics, to the key issue as to how the teacher, responsible for the work of a whole class (perhaps split in four, five or more groups), is to ensure that each group, engaged on co-operative tasks involving discussion and the use of materials and apparatus, is effectively and meaningfully occupied.

Consequently we have, over several years, been working co-operatively with groups of teachers in order to understand the issues involved in successful implementation in classrooms (Dunne and Bennett, 1990; Bennett and Dunne, 1992).

The most difficult area for teachers tends to be in designing tasks which are appropriate for co-operative, rather than individual, outcomes. There are two facets in planning for this: the cognitive demand of the task, and the social demand. These are shown in Figure 4.5.

How these are inter-related is best shown with a real example. Imagine that a teacher has chosen the statement of attainment from the English 'Speaking and Listening' targets: 'plan and participate in a presentation; e.g., of the outcome of a group activity, a poem, story, dramatic scene or play,' and that this statement was interpreted by the teacher in terms of children participating in a presentation of a radio news programme.

One way of fulfilling this demand in terms of a group activity is to set up a Jigsaw task; that is, children work at individual items for the news programme, but must plan

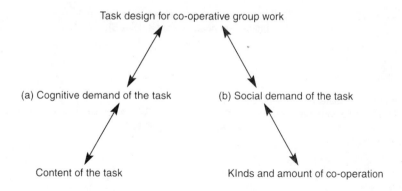

Figure 4.5 *Cognitive and social demands for co-operative tasks.*

together and must fit the individual items together to make a coherent whole.

In this case, the teacher chose a cognitive demand in terms of a statement of attainment, and then decided on a type of group embodying the social demand she desired, opting for a Jigsaw method. It would, however, be possible to decide on a method of working in groups first (say Jigsaw), and then plan the cognitive demand to fit this social demand. Either way, the two are closely linked.

The next step for the teacher is to enable the children to fulfil her plan. At the implementation stage, the pupils will have to make decisions about, for example, the new material to be used and the style of presentation, and they will have to write the items or reports. Since this is set up as a Jigsaw task, it is important that some work is undertaken as a group and some is individual. Pupils will, therefore, have to decide on who does what within the group, who writes which report, check that individual work reaches the desired standard and that they pay attention to each other's ideas, and organize the actual presentation together. Once again, the cognitive demand and the social demand are closely linked; both dictate the way in which children will be expected to operate.

Figure 4.6 represents these steps in task design and demonstrates the links between them.

Co-operative grouping is most successful when children are required to share understandings, knowledge and skills to a common end, in other words, when presented with some form of problem-solving or open task. Barnes and Todd (1977), in their detailed research study of lower secondary children, noticed that the co-operating teachers distinguished between 'loose' and 'tight' tasks for group work. Their descriptions and examples are particularly useful in terms of task design and their principles translate readily to the primary school context. Their distinction tends to reflect the difference between those activities that have 'correct' solutions and those that do not. Tight tasks are likely to need responses that are highly focused; loose tasks are unlikely to need 'right' answers and responses can be more wide-ranging.

> . . . teachers chose to set loose tasks when their pupils had much everyday knowledge that was relevant, as in *The Pearl* [the novel by Steinbeck] and in social studies topics such as 'Gang Violence'. They tended to set tighter topics in science, where the explanations they wanted were more removed from everyday ways of looking at things.

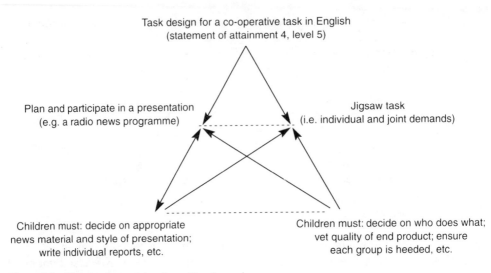

Task design for a co-operative task in English
(statement of attainment 4, level 5)

Plan and participate in a presentation
(e.g. a radio news programme)

Jigsaw task
(i.e. individual and joint demands)

Children must: decide on appropriate
news material and style of presentation;
write individual reports, etc.

Children must: decide on who does what;
vet quality of end product; ensure
each group is heeded, etc.

Figure 4.6   *Planning for social and cognitive demands.*

It became clear that the extent to which tasks were 'tight' or 'loose' had a marked impact on ways of working and many problems emerged when teachers misjudged this impact. And just as the cognitive demand of the task affects ways of working in the group, so do the social demands. The choice by the teacher of the co-operative model to be used will have a bearing on the talk, and approaches to work, that children exhibit, since different group models require different kinds of collaborative endeavour.

Training

There appears to be an assumption that pupils do not need any training in social and co-operative skills for group work to be effective. Yet research has shown that when such skills are practised the quality and effectiveness improve. Much of this research is American (Cohen, 1986; Kagan, 1988), although some British resources and techniques for training, focusing particularly at secondary school level, are provided by Cowie and Rudduck (1988) and Jenkin (1989).

Kagan (1988) has carried out most of the studies on training primary-age children. He argues that for pupils to benefit from group work 'requires a degree of tolerance and mutual understanding, the ability to articulate a point of view, to engage in discussion, reasoning, probing and questioning. Such skills are not in themselves innate, they have to be learnt, and so taught'.

Our work on training with primary school teachers has been in part based on Kagan's tasks, suitably anglicized into a 'Teambuilding' pack (Austin, 1991; Bennett and Dunne, 1992). The tasks included brainstorming rules for talk, a 'completing the circle' task which emphasized sensitivity to groups' needs through co-operation, practical tasks on helping through talk, and monitoring group processes for such skills as conciseness, listening, reflecting and allowing all members to contribute. Initial results are encouraging. In a study of four classes of children covering the age range

5 to 11 years, the amount of task-related talk increased in every class after training, and almost doubled among the youngest children (Bennett *et al.*, 1990).

Teachers should thus seriously consider the training of their pupils in social and co-operative skills. Their role in this process can be summarized diagrammatically in Figure 4.7.

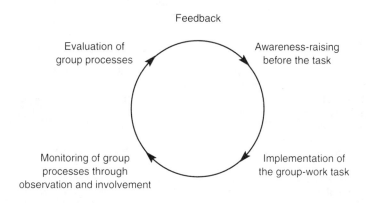

Feedback

Evaluation of group processes

Awareness-raising before the task

Monitoring of group processes through observation and involvement

Implementation of the group-work task

Figure 4.7   *A cycle of training in group work.*

Thus, children can be enabled to work more effectively in groups by making them aware of appropriate behaviours. Teachers must then observe the process of group work in order to diagnose any problems either with learning or with the social relationships of the group. These observations and general evaluation must then be fed back to the pupils to enable them to be more sensitive about the ways in which they work together. Pupils are then enabled to be more effective in monitoring their own activities in future tasks. The cycle starts again when the information gained by the teacher during this process is used to inform training activities.

CONCLUSION

Current conceptions of how children learn stress that children acquire new conceptions or understandings by making sense of new knowledge in the light of their existing knowledge. Essential to this process is language, since talk aids the organization of experience into thought. For teachers a major implication of this is for the structuring of classroom environments which offer the best opportunity for their pupils to be involved in social and cognitive activities appropriate to the building of understanding. This requires the translation of beliefs about pupils as 'social beings' into modes of classroom organization which encourage talk and co-operative endeavours. This is not to argue for the abandonment of individual or whole-class work, simply a change in balance toward more co-operative group work, particularly for problem-solving and knowledge application.

Several alternative types of co-operative grouping exist, each embodying differences in social and cognitive demands. These have been shown by research studies to be successful in their own right and be much more effective than typical classroom groups. However, work on classroom implementation demonstrates that teachers need to take careful note of how their groups are composed, how their tasks are designed, and whether, or what, training in social and co-operative skills should be considered. Careful implementation should result in enhanced social and cognitive development in the short and the long term. As Schmuck (1985) has argued, 'From the primitive hunting group to the corporate boardroom, it is those of us who can solve problems while working with others who succeed.'

REFERENCES

Argyle, M. (1991) *Co-operation: The Basis of Sociability*. London: Routledge.

Aronson, E. (1978) *The Jigsaw Classroom*. Beverly Hills: Sage.

Austin, L. (1991) The impact of training on the quality of social interaction in co-operative groups. Unpublished MEd dissertation, University of Exeter.

Barnes, D. and Todd, F. (1977) *Communication and Learning in Small Groups*. London: Routledge & Kegan Paul.

Bennett, N, Andreae, J., Hegarty, P. and Wade, B. (1980) *Open Plan Schools*. Windsor: NFER.

Bennett, N. and Cass, A. (1988) The effects of group composition on group interactive processes and pupil understanding. *British Educational Research Journal*, **15**, 19-32.

Bennett, N., Desforges, C., Cockburn, A. and Wilkinson, B. (1984) *The Quality of Pupil Learning Experiences*. London: Lawrence Erlbaum Associates.

Bennett, N., Dunne, E. and Austin, L. (1990) The impact of training on the quality of social interaction in co-operative groups. Paper presented at the European Association for Research on Learning and Instruction conference, Turku.

Bennett, N. and Dunne, E. (1992) *Managing Classroom Groups*. London: Simon & Schuster.

Bruner, J. and Haste, H. (1987) *Making Sense*. London: Methuen.

Bullock Report (1975) *A Language for Life*. London: HMSO.

Cohen, E.G. (1986) *Designing Groupwork: Strategies for the Heterogeneous Classroom*. New York: Teachers' College Press.

Cowie, H. and Ruddick, J. (1988) *Co-operative Groupwork: An Overview*. London: BP Education Service.

Cowie, H. and Rudduck, J. (1990) *Co-operative Groupwork in the Multi-ethnic Classroom*. London: BP Education Service.

Dunne, E. and Bennett, N. (1990) *Talking and Learning in Groups*. London: Macmillan.

Doise, W. and Mugny, G. (1984) *The Social Development of the Intellect*. New York: Pergamon.

Galton, M., Simon, B. and Croll, P. (1980) *Inside the Primary Classroom*. London: Routledge & Kegan Paul.

Galton, M. and Williamson, J. (1992) *Groupwork in the Primary School*. London: Routledge.

Hertz-Lazarowitz, R. (1990) An integrative model of the classroom: the enhancement of co-operation in learning. Paper presented at the American Educational Research Association conference.

HMI (1978) *Primary Education in England*. London: HMSO.

HMI (1989) *Aspects of Primary Education: The Teaching of Mathematics*. London: HMSO.

Jenkin, F. (1989) *Making Small Groups Work*. Oxford: Penguin Educational.

Johnson, D.W. and Johnson R.T. (1975) *Learning Together and Alone*. Englewood Cliffs, NJ: Prentice-Hall.

Johnson, D.W. and Johnson, R.T. (1985) The internal dynamics of co-operative learning groups. In R. Slavin (ed.), *Learning to Co-operate, Co-operating to Learn*. New York: Plenum.

Kagan, S. (1985) Dimensions of co-operative classroom structures. In R. Slavin (ed.), *Learning to Co-operate, Co-operating to Learn*. New York: Plenum.

Kagan, S. (1988) *Co-operative Learning: Resources for Teachers*. University of California, Riverside.

National Curriculum Council (1989) *English in the National Curriculum: Key Stage One.* York: NCC.

Perret-Clermont, A.N. (1980) *Social Interaction and Cognitive Development in Children.* New York: Academic Press.

Plowden Report (1967) *Children and Their Primary Schools.* London: HMSO.

Pollard, A., Broadfoot, P., Croll, P., Osborn, M. and Abbott, D. (1992) *Changing English Primary Schools.* London: Cassell.

Schmuck, R.A. (1985) Learning to co-operate, co-operating to learn, basic concepts. In R. Slavin (ed.), *Learning to Co-operate, Co-operating to Learn.* New York: Plenum.

Slavin, R. (1983) *Co-operative Learning.* New York: Longman.

Slavin, R. (1987) Developmental and motivational perspectives on co-operative learning: a reconciliation. *Child Development*, **58**, 116-17.

Vygotsky, L.S. (1962) *Thought and Language.* Cambridge, MA: IT Press.

Vygotsky, L.S. (1978) *Mind in Society: The Development of Higher Psychological Processes.* Cambridge, MA: Harvard University Press.

Webb, N.M. (1989) Peer interaction and learning in small groups. *International Journal of Educational Research*, **13**, 21-39.

Wells, G., Chang, G.L. and Maher, A. (1990) Creating classroom communities of literate thinkers. In S. Sharan (ed.), *Co-operative Learning.* New York: Praeger.

Wilkinson, L.C. and Calculator, S. (1982) Requests and responses in peer-directed reading groups. *American Educational Research Journal*, **19**, 107-20.

Wood, D. (1988) *How Children Think and Learn.* Oxford: Basil Blackwell.

Chapter 5

Collaborative Learning and Argumentation

David W. Johnson and Roger T. Johnson

EDITORS' INTRODUCTION

It would generally be assumed that co-operation and conflict were essentially incompatible. In the following chapter, David and Roger Johnson, who are two of the leading researchers into co-operative group learning methods, argue the opposite.

Argumentation, or controversy, is a method with which the Johnsons have been particularly associated. The essential aim is to encourage the processes of exploring alternative views on an issue by engaging pupils in the promotion of opposing viewpoints. However, it is most important to note the details of the procedures which the Johnsons are advocating. The controversy that is engendered is structured rather than random. Careful steps are taken to ensure that the debate is carried out within a co-operative framework, with a common concern to reach a position with which all members of the group can agree. Steps are also taken to ensure that individuals do not become 'attached' to any one particular position and thereby less willing to give open consideration to alternatives.

Again it is important to note that the authors here are arguing for a carefully structured and managed approach to be adopted by teachers within the classroom. As earlier chapters have now made clear, *placing* pupils in groups is not the same as having pupils *learn* in groups. A pedagogy of groups involves active intervention on the part of the teacher and careful consideration concerning the details of the processes involved. It is not surprising, therefore, to note that Johnson and Johnson, like Merrett and Bennett in the two preceding chapters, adopt the view that it is important to ensure that pupils are adequately equipped with the skills needed to engage fruitfully in controversy.

CO-OPERATIVE LEARNING

The purpose of this chapter is to describe two interrelated ways of using groups in school. First, teachers establish collaboration among students. Second, teachers take the naturally occurring conflict among group members and use it to enhance motivation to learn and achieve.

An essential instructional skill is knowing how and when to structure students' learning goals competitively, individualistically and co-operatively. By such structuring, teachers can influence the pattern of interaction among students and the instructional outcomes (Deutsch, 1962; Johnson and Johnson, 1989). As outlined in Johnson *et al.* (1993), teachers may structure academic lessons so that students are:

> 1. In a win–lose struggle to see who is best. When teachers structure lessons competitively students work against each other to achieve a goal that only one or a few students can attain. Students' goal achievements are negatively correlated; when one student achieves his or her goal, all others with whom he or she is competitively linked fail to achieve their goals. Teachers give students the goal of completing assignments faster and more accurately than their classmates.
> 2. Learning individually on their own without interacting with classmates. Students work by themselves to accomplish learning goals unrelated to those of their classmates. Teachers give students the goal of completing the assignments correctly to reach a pre-set criteria of excellence and evaluate students' efforts on a fixed set of standards.
> 3. Working together co-operatively to accomplish shared learning goals. Teachers assign students to small groups and give them two responsibilities: to learn the assigned material and to make sure that the other members of the group also master the assignment. Students' goal achievements are positively correlated; students perceive that they can reach their learning goals if and only if the other students in the learning group also reach their goals. Thus, students seek outcomes that are beneficial to all those with whom they are co-operatively linked.

There are four ways teachers may use co-operative learning (Johnson *et al.*, 1993): *Formal co-operative learning groups* may last from one class period to several weeks to complete any course requirement (such as decision making or problem solving), completing a curriculum unit, writing a report, conducting a survey or experiment, or reading a chapter or reference book, learning vocabulary, or answering questions at the end of the chapter). They involve setting objectives, making pre-instructional decisions, explaining the task and co-operative structure to students, monitoring students and intervening to provide task and social skill assistance, and evaluating student academic learning and having students assess how well they worked together.

Informal co-operative learning groups are temporary, *ad hoc* groups that last from a few minutes to one class period that are used during a lecture, demonstration or film to focus student attention on the material to be learned, set a mood conducive to learning, help set expectations as to what will be covered in a class section, ensure that students cognitively process the material being taught, and provide closure to an instructional session.

Co-operative base groups are long-term, heterogeneous co-operative learning groups with stable membership that give the support, help, encouragement and assistance each member needs to make academic progress (attend class, complete all assignments, learn) and develop cognitively and socially in healthy ways.

Co-operative learning scripts are standard co-operative procedures for conducting generic, repetitive lessons and managing classroom routines.

Considerable training is necessary to gain expertise in using co-operative learning. Simply placing students in groups and telling them to work together does not in and of itself result in co-operative efforts. There are many ways in which group efforts may go wrong. You can have competition at close quarters or individualistic efforts with talking. Much of our research over the past 30 years has focused on identifying what makes co-operation work, so that teachers may know how to plan lessons and activities so that the productivity of their students is maximized (Johnson and Johnson, 1989). Teachers must structure five essential elements into each lesson.

First, the heart of co-operative learning is *positive interdependence*. Students must believe that they sink or swim together. Within every co-operative lesson positive goal interdependence must be established through mutual learning goals (learn the assigned material and make sure that all members of your group learn the assigned material). In order to strengthen positive interdependence, joint rewards (if all members of your group score 90 per cent correct or better on the test, each will receive S bonus points), divided resources (giving each group member a part of the total information required to complete an assignment), and complementary roles (reader, checker, encourager, elaborator) may also be used.

The second element is *individual accountability*. The purpose of co-operative learning groups is to make each member a stronger individual in his or her right. Students learn together so that they can subsequently perform higher as individuals. To ensure that each member is strengthened, students are held individually accountable to do (and feel personally responsible for) their share of the work. The performance of each individual student is assessed and the results given back to the group and the individual. It is important that the group knows who needs more assistance, support and encouragement in completing the assignment. It is also important that group members know that they cannot 'hitch-hike' on the work of others. Common ways to structure individual accountability include (a) giving an individual test to each student and (b) randomly selecting one student's product to represent the entire group.

The third essential element is *face-to-face promotive interaction*. Once a teacher establishes positive interdependence, he or she must ensure that students interact to help each other accomplish the task and each other's success. Students are expected to discuss what they are learning, explain to each other how to solve the assigned problems or complete the assignments, and provide each other with help, assistance, support and encouragement. Silent students are uninvolved students who are not contributing to the learning of others as well as themselves. Promoting each other's success results in both higher achievement and in getting to know each other on a personal as well as a professional level.

The fourth element is *social skills*. Contributing to the success of a co-operative effort requires interpersonal and small-group skills. Placing socially unskilled individuals in a group and telling them to co-operate does not guarantee that they will be able to do so effectively. Persons must be taught the social skills for high quality collaboration and be motivated to use them. Leadership, decision-making, trust-building, communication and conflict-management skills have to be taught just as purposefully and precisely as academic skills. Procedures and strategies for teaching students social skills may be found in Johnson (1993), Johnson and F. Johnson (1994) and Johnson *et al*. (1993).

The fifth element is *group processing*. Group processing occurs when groups discuss how well they are achieving their goals and maintaining effective working relationships among members. Teachers need to provide students with the time and the procedures for discussing how well they are achieving their goals and maintaining effective working relationships. Groups need to describe what member actions are helpful and unhelpful and make decisions about what behaviours to continue or change. Such processing (a) enables learning groups to improve continuously the quality of members' learning; (b) facilitates the learning of collaborative skills; (c) ensures that members receive feedback on their participation; and (d) enables learning groups to focus on group maintenance (Johnson *et al.*, 1993).

With a thorough mastery of the essential elements of co-operation lessons cán be uniquely tailored by the teachers to their instructional needs, circumstances, subject areas and students. In addition, teachers can then diagnose the problems some students may have in working together and intervene to increase the effectiveness of the student learning groups.

Learning together to complete assignments can have profound effects. A great deal of research has been conducted comparing the relative effects of co-operative, competitive and individualistic efforts on instructional outcomes. During the past 95 years over 550 experimental and 100 correlational studies have been conducted by a wide variety of researchers in different decades with different age subjects, in different subject areas, and in different settings (Johnson and Johnson, 1989). While numerous instructional outcomes have been studied, they can be classified into three categories. First, co-operative learning promotes greater effort to achieve (includes achievement, retention, higher-level reasoning, process gain, intrinsic motivation, achievement motivation, transfer) than do competitive or individualistic learning. The more conceptual the task, the more problem solving required, and the more creative the answers need to be, the greater the superiority of co-operative over competitive and individualistic learning. Second, co-operative learning experiences promote more positive relationships among students than do competitive and individualistic learning experiences. Co-operative learning is especially needed when students are hetero-geneous in terms of ethnicity, gender, culture and achievement. In addition, co-operative experiences result in greater social support, both academically and personally. Third, co-operative learning experiences result in greater psychological adjustment, self-esteem and social competence than do competitive and individualistic learning. Each of the outcomes of co-operative efforts (efforts to achieve, quality of relationships, and psychological health) influences the others and, therefore, they are likely to be found together. Since there is considerable academic benefit to using co-operative learning, creating a co-operative context to enhance the success of conflict resolution programmes should be welcomed by most teachers.

ACADEMIC CONTROVERSY

Have you learned lessons only of those who admired you, and were tender with you, and stood aside for you?

Have you not learned great lessons from those who braced themselves against you, and disputed the passage with you?
(Walt Whitman, 1860)

Co-operation and conflict go hand-in-hand. They are fist-and-glove. The stronger the co-operation, the more conflict that will occur. When group members are committed to achieving and helping each other achieve, disagreements will occur and arguments will take place. The more committed students are to the group goal, and the more committed students are to each other, the more frequent and intense their disagreements and arguments. Within a co-operative effort, participants often disagree and argue with each other. Richard Rodgers, for example, recalling his work with lyricist Larry Hart stated, 'the noise could be heard all over the city. Our fights over words were furious, blasphemous, and frequent, but even in their hottest moments, we both knew that we were arguing academically and not personally.'

Intellectual disagreements and arguments among students do not make all teachers happy. Many teachers suppress intellectual conflict within the classroom. Students are told not to talk to each other. All communication is directed at the teacher in response to direct questions. Teachers eliminate most possibilities for intellectual disagreement and academic controversy when they use an instructional sequence of (a) lecture, (b) whole-class discussion, (c) individual worksheets, and (d) take the test on Friday. What most teachers lack is a clear procedure for structuring academic controversies among students. What most students lack is the skills to use such a procedure effectively. For these and many other reasons, academic conflicts are suppressed and avoided within most classrooms. Educators who are 'conflict-avoiders' have forgotten what John Dewey tried to make clear in his book, *Human Nature and Conduct: Morals Are Human*:

> Conflict is the gadfly of thought. It stirs us to observation and memory. It instigates invention. It shocks us out of sheep-like passivity, and set us at noting and contriving . . . Conflict is the 'sine qua non' of reflection and ingenuity.

Over the past twenty years, we have developed and tested a theory of controversy (Johnson, 1970, 1979; Johnson and Johnson, 1979, 1985, 1987, 1989). We have developed a series of curriculum units on energy and environmental issues structured for academic controversies. We have also worked with schools and colleges through the United States, Canada and Europe to field-test and implement the units in the classroom. What we have learned is summarized in this chapter. In order to create, structure and support intellectual conflict among students, educators must understand what controversy is, how students benefit, the process through which intellectual conflicts create academic benefits, the key elements that make controversy work, and the teacher's role in structuring and managing academic controversies.

NATURE OF CONTROVERSY

> The best way ever devised for seeking the truth in any given situation is advocacy: presenting the pros and cons from different, informed points of view and digging down deep into the facts.
> (Harold S. Geneen, Former CEO, ITT)

A teacher asks students to think about what problems hunting and gathering societies had to solve. Immediately, Jim jumps up and states that the major problem was how to hunt better so they could have more food. Jane disgrees. She says the major problem was how to store food so it would last longer. Jeremy stands up and tells both Jim and Jane that they are wrong; the major problem was how to domesticate the wild grains that grew in the area so that the people would be less dependent on hunting.

Jim, Jane and Jeremy begin to argue forcefully, bringing out the facts supporting why each thinks he or she is right.

Controversy exists when one student's ideas, information, conclusions, theories and opinions are incomparable with those of another, and the two seek to reach an agreement. Controversies are resolved by engaging in deliberate discourse, i.e. the discussion of the advantages and disadvantages of proposed actions as recommended by Aristotle in the *Rhetoric* aimed at synthesizing novel solutions, i.e. creative problem solving (see Follet, 1940). When controveries are structured, participants are required to research and prepare a position; rehearse orally the relevant information; advocate a position; teach their knowledge to peers; analyse, critically evaluate and rebut information; reason both deductively and inductively; take the perspectives of others; and synthesize and integrate information into factual and judgemental conclusions that are summarized into a joint position with which all sides can agree.

Structured academic controversies are more often contrasted with individualistic learning, debate and concurrence seeking. For instance, students can work independently with their own set of materials at their own pace (individualistic learning). Or students can appoint a judge and then debate the different positions with the expectation that the judge will determine who presented the better position (debate). Finally, students can inhibit discussion to avoid any disagreement and compromise quickly to reach a consensus while they discuss the issue (concurrence seeking). Concurrence seeking is close to the groupthink concept of Janis (1982) in which members of a decision-making group set aside their doubts and misgivings about whatever policy is favoured by the emerging consensus so as to be able to concur with the other members. The underlying motivation of groupthink is the strong desire to preserve the harmonious atmosphere of the group on which each member has become dependent for coping with the stresses of external crises and for maintaining self-esteem.

A key to the effectiveness of conflict procedures for promoting learning is the mixture of co-operative and competitive elements within the procedure (see Table 5.1). The greater the co-operative elements and the less the competitive elements, the more constructive the conflict (Deutsch, 1973). Co-operative elements alone, however, do not ensure maximal productivity. There has to be both co-operation and conflict. Thus, controversy is characterized by both positive goal and resource interdependence as well as by conflict. Debate has positive resource interdependence, negative goal interdependence, and conflict. Within concurrence seeking there is only positive goal interdependence, and within individualistic learning situations there is neither interdependence nor intellectual conflict.

An example of an academic controversy is as follows. In an English literature class students are considering the issue of civil disobedience. They learn that in the civil rights movement in the United States, individuals broke the law to gain equal rights for minorities. In numerous instances, such as in the civil rights and anti-war movements, individuals wrestle with the issue of breaking the law to redress a social injustice. In the past few years, however, prominent public figures from Wall Street to the White House have felt justified in breaking laws for personal or political gain. In order to study the role of civil disobedience in a democracy, students are placed in a co-operative learning group of four members. The group is then divided into two pairs. One pair is given the assignment of making the best case possible for the

Table 5.1   *Processes of controversy, debate, concurrence seeking and individualistic efforts.*

Controversy	Debate	Concurrence seeking	Individualistic
Categorizing and organizing information to derive conclusions	Categorizing and organizing information to derive conclusions	Categorizing and organizing information to derive conclusions	Categorizing and organizing information to derive conclusions
Presenting, advocating, elaborating position and rationale	Presenting, advocating, elaborating position and rationale	Active presentation of position	No oral statement of positions
Being challenged by opposing views	Being challenged by opposing views	Quick compromise to one view	Presence of only one view
Conceptual conflict and uncertainty about the correctness of own views	Conceptual conflict and uncertainty about the correctness of own views	High certainty about the correctness of own views	High certainty about the correctness of own views
Epistemic curiosity and perspective taking	Epistemic curiosity	No epistemic curiosity	No epistemic curiosity
Reconceptualization, synthesis, integration	Closed-minded adherence to own point of view	Closed-minded adherence to own point of view	Closed-minded adherence to own point of view
High achievement, positive relationships, psychological health/ social competences	Moderate achievement, relationships, psychological health	Low achievement, relationships, psychological health	Low achievement, relationships, psychological health

constructiveness of civil disobedience in a democracy. The other pair is given the assignment of making the best case possible for the destructiveness of civil disobedience in a democracy. In the resulting conflict, students draw from such sources as the Declaration of Independence by Thomas Jefferson, Civil Disobedience by Henry David Thoreau, Speech at Cooper Union, New York by Abraham Lincoln, and Letter from Birmingham Jail by Martin Luther King, Jr. to challenge each other's reasoning and analyses concerning when civil disobedience is, and is not, constructive.

This unit would typically take five class periods to conduct. During the first class period each pair develops their position and plans how to present the best case possible to the other pair. Near the end of the period pairs are encouraged to compare notes with pairs from other groups who represent the same position. During the second class period each pair makes their presentation. Each member of the pair has to participate in the presentation. Members of the opposing pair are encouraged to take notes and listen carefully. During the third class period the group members discuss the issue following a set of rules to help them criticize ideas without criticizing people, differentiate the two positions and assess the degree of evidence and logic supporting each position. During the fourth period the pairs (a) reverse perspectives

Table 5.2   *Nature of instructional methods.*

	Controversy	Debate	Concurrence seeking	Individualistic
Positive goal interdependence	Yes	No	Yes	No
Resource interdependence	Yes	Yes	No	No
Negative goal interdependence	No	Yes	No	No
Conflict	Yes	Yes	No	No

and present each other's position and (b) drop all advocacy and begin developing a group report that synthesizes the best evidence and reasoning from both sides. During the fifth period (a) the report is finalized (the teacher evaluates reports on the quality of the writing, the logical presentation of evidence, and the oral presentation of the report to the class); (b) the group's conclusions are presented to the class (all four members of the group are required to participate orally in the presentation); (c) students each take an individual test and, if every member of the group achieves up to criterion, they all receive bonus points; and (d) the group processes how well it worked together and how it could do even better next time.

Such intellectual 'disputed passages' create numerous benefits for students when they (a) occur within co-operative learning groups and (b) are carefully structured to ensure that students manage them constructively. As Thomas Jefferson noted, 'Difference of opinion leads to inquiry, and inquiry to truth.' Despite Jefferson's faith in conflict, however, many teachers are reluctant to spark disagreements in the classroom. Teachers often suppress students' academic disagreements and consequently miss out on valuable opportunities to capture students' attention and enhance learning.

HOW STUDENTS BENEFIT

> By blending the breath of the sun and the shade, true harmony comes into the world.
> (Tao Te Ching)

When students interact, conflicts between their ideas, conclusions, theories, information, perspectives, opinions and preferences are inevitable. Teachers who capitalize on these differences find that academic conflicts can yield highly constructive dividends. The outcomes of controversy may be grouped under three broad headings: achievement; positive interpersonal relationships; psychological health and social competence. It can also be fun. As Samuel Johnson once stated, 'I dogmatize and am contradicted, and in this conflict of opinions and sentiments I find delight.' Controversy can be fun, enjoyable and exciting.

ACHIEVEMENT, PROBLEM SOLVING, CREATIVITY, TASK INVOLVEMENT

Compared with concurrence seeking, debate and individualistic efforts, controversy tends to result in greater mastery and retention of the subject-matter being studied as well as greater ability to generalize the principles learned to a wider variety of situations. In a meta-analysis of the available research, Johnson and Johnson (1989) found that controversy produced higher achievement and retention than did debate (effect-size = 0.77), individualistic learning (effect-size = 0.65) and concurrence seeking (effect-size = 0.42). The dozens of studies conducted indicate that students who participate in an academic controversy recall more correct information, are better able to transfer learning to new situations, use more complex and higher-level reasoning strategies in recalling and transferring information learned, and are better able to generalize the principles they learned to a wider variety of situations.

If students are to become citizens capable of making reasoned judgements about the complex problems facing society, they must learn to use the higher-level reasoning and critical thinking processes involved in effective problem solving, especially problems for which different viewpoints can plausibly be developed. To do so, students must enter empathetically into the arguments of both sides of the issue and ensure that the strongest possible case is made for each side, and arrive at a synthesis based on rational, probabilistic thought. Participating in structured controversy teaches students of all ages how to find high-quality solutions to complex problems.

Compared with concurrence seeking, debate and individualistic efforts, controversy tends to result in higher-quality decisions and solutions to complex problems for which different viewpoints can plausibly be developed. An interesting 'real world' example is a study conducted by Dean Tjosvold (1994) with airline flight crews. Most air accidents result from 'pilot error' resulting from the failure of crew members to use their information expeditiously to cope with safety hazards. Tjosvold interviewed 27 pilots, first officers and second officers, and 8 flight attendants on how specific incidents that threatened the safety of the aeroplane were managed. Sixty incidents were provided. Respondents were asked to describe in detail a recent, significant incident in which they managed an air safety problem effectively and one that they managed ineffectively. Hierarchical regression analyses indicated that the open discussion of conflicting views and ideas within a co-operative context were powerful antecedents to using safe procedures expeditiously.

An interesting question concerning controversy and problem solving is what happens when erroneous information is presented by participants. Simply, can the advocacy of two conflicting but wrong solutions to a problem create a correct one? The value of the controversy process lies not so much in the correctness of an opposing position, but rather in the attention and thought processes it induces. More cognitive processing may take place when individuals are exposed to more than one point of view, even if the point of view is incorrect. A number of studies with both adults and children have found significant gains in performance when erroneous information is presented by one or both sides in a controversy. Ames and Murray (1982) compared the impact of controversy, modelling and non-social presentation of information on the performance of non-conserving, cognitively immature children on conservation tasks. The cognitively immature children were presented with erroneous information that conflicted with their initial position. Ames and Murray found modest but significant gains in conservation performance. Three children with scores of 0 out of 18 scored between 16 and 18 out of 18 on the post-test, and 11 children with initial scores of 0 scored between 5 and 15. They conclude that conflict qua conflict is not only cognitively motivating, but that the resolution of the conflict is likely to be in the direction of the correct performance. In this limited way, two wrongs came to make a right.

Compared with concurrence seeking, debate and individualistic efforts, controversy tends to result in (1) more frequent creative insights into the issues being discussed and (2) synthesis combining both perspectives (Johnson and Johnson, 1989). Controversy increases the number of ideas, quality of ideas, creation of original ideas, the use of a wider range of ideas, originality, the use of more varied strategies, and the number of creative, imaginative, novel solutions. Studies further demonstrated that controversy encouraged group members to dig into a problem, raise issues and settle them in ways that showed the benefits of a wide range of ideas being used, as well as resulting in a high degree of emotional involvement in and commitment to solving the problems the group was working on.

Compared with concurrence seeking, debate and individualistic efforts, controversy tends to result in greater exchange of expertise (Johnson and Johnson, 1989). Students often have different information and theories, make different assumptions, and hold different opinions. Within any co-operative learning group, students with a wide variety of expertise and perspectives are told to work together to maximize each member's learning. Many times students study different parts of an assignment and are expected to share their expertise with the other members of their group. Conflict between their ideas, information, opinions, preferences, theories, conclusions and perspectives is inevitable. Yet such controversies are typically avoided or managed destructively. Having the skills to manage the controversies constructively, and knowing the procedures for exchanging information and perspective among individuals with differing expertise, are essential for maximal learning and growth.

John Milton, in 'Doctrine and Discipline', stated, 'Where there is much desire to learn, there of necessity will be much arguing, much writing, many opinions; for opinion in good men is but knowledge in the making.' Making knowledge through disagreement does arouse emotions and increases involvement. Compared with concurrence seeking, debate and individualistic efforts, controversy tends to result in greater task involvement reflected in greater emotional commitment to solving the problem, greater enjoyment of the process, more feelings of stimulation and enjoyment (Johnson and Johnson, 1989). Task involvement refers to the quality and quantity of the physical and psychological energy that individuals invest in their efforts to achieve. Task involvement is reflected in the attitudes participants have toward the task and toward the controversy experience. We have found that individuals who engaged in controversies tended to like the task and procedure better and generally had more positive attitudes toward the experience than did individuals who engaged in concurrence-seeking discussions, individualistic efforts or debate.

POSITIVE INTERPERSONAL RELATIONSHIPS

It is often assumed that the presence of controversy within a group will lead to difficulties in establishing good interpersonal relations and will promote negative attitudes toward fellow group members, and it is also often assumed that arguing leads to rejection, divisiveness and hostility among peers. Within controversy and debate there are elements of disagreement, argumentation and rebuttal that could result in individuals disliking each other and could create difficulties in establishing good relationships. On the other hand, conflicts have been hypothesized potentially to create positive relationships among participants (Deutsch, 1962; Johnson, 1970). The evidence indicates that controversy promotes greater liking and social support among participants than does debate, concurrence seeking, no controversy or individualistic efforts (Johnson and Johnson, 1989).

PSYCHOLOGICAL HEALTH AND SOCIAL COMPETENCE

There are a number of components of psychological health that are strengthened by participating in academic controversies (Johnson and Johnson, 1989). Compared with concurrence seeking, debate and individualistic efforts, controversy tends to result in higher academic self-esteem and greater perspective-taking accuracy. Being able to manage disagreements and conflicts constructively enables individuals to cope with the stresses involved in interacting with a variety of other people.

PROCESS OF CONTROVERSY

> Since the general or prevailing opinion on any subject is rarely or never the whole truth, it is only by the collision of adverse opinion that the remainder of the truth has any chance of being supplied.
> (John Stuart Mill)

The hypothesis that intellectual challenge promotes higher-level reasoning, critical thinking and metacognitive thought is derived from a number of premises:

1. When individuals are presented with a problem or decision, they have an initial conclusion based on categorizing and organizing incomplete information, their limited experiences, and their specific perspective.
2. When individuals present their conclusion and its rationale to others, they engage in cognitive rehearsal, deepen their understanding of their position, and discover higher-level reasoning strategies.
3. Individuals are confronted by other people with different conclusions based on other people's information, experiences and perspectives.
4. Individuals become uncertain as to the correctness of their views. A state of conceptual conflict or disequilibrium is aroused.
5. Uncertainty, conceptual conflict and disequilibrium motivate an active search for more information, new experiences and a more adequate cognitive perspective and reasoning process in hopes of resolving the uncertainty. Berlyne (1965) calls this active search epistemic curiosity. Divergent attention and thought are stimulated.
6. By adapting their cognitive perspective and reasoning through understanding and accommodating the perspective and reasoning of others, a new, reconceptualized and reorganized conclusion is derived. Novel solutions and decisions are detected that are, on balance, qualitatively better.

Each of these premises is discussed below.

Step 1: Organizing information and deriving conclusions

In order to make high-quality decisions, individuals have to think of the proper alternatives, make a good job of evaluating them and choosing the most promising one. When individuals are presented with a problem or decision, they have an initial conclusion based on categorizing and organizing incomplete information, their limited experiences, and their specific perspective. Individuals organize their current

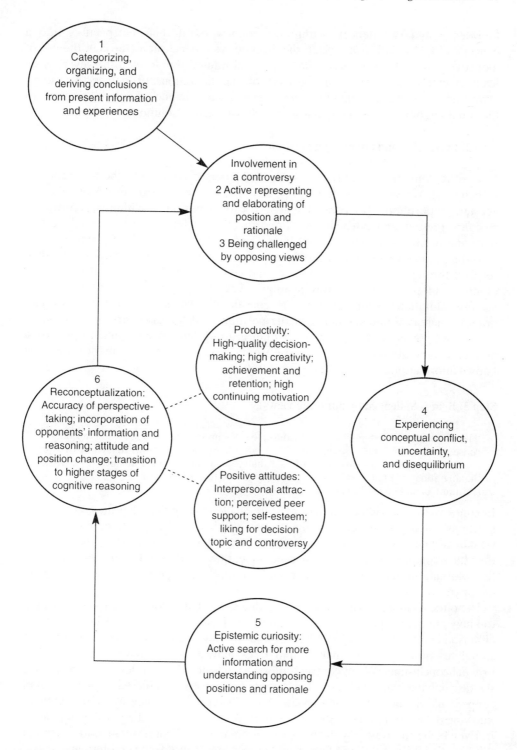

Figure 5.1 *Process of controversy* (Johnson and Johnson, 1987).

knowledge and experiences, within the framework of their perspective, into a conceptual framework from which they can derive a conclusion (through the use of inductive and deductive logic). The conceptual frameworks formed, however, often lead to inaccurate conclusions because of the limitations of perspective, one's expectations and mental set at the time, a tendency to give one's dominant response to the situation, or fixation on the first seemingly satisfactory solution generated.

Step 2: Presenting and advocating positions

Edward R. Murrow, the journalist, said, 'To be persuasive we must be believable; to be believable we must be credible; to be credible, we must be truthful.' Most students get few opportunities to present and advocate a position. Within a controversy students present and advocate positions to others who, in turn, are advocating opposing positions. Advocacy may be defined as the presenting of a position and providing reasons why others should adopt it. Decisions and conclusions are then reached through a process of argument and counter-argument aimed at persuading others to adopt, modify or drop positions. Advocating a position and defending it against refutation require engaging in considerable cognitive rehearsal and elaboration, increased understanding of the position, and the discovery of higher-level reasoning processes. Disagreements within a group have been found to provide a greater amount of information and variety of facts as well as changes in the salience of known information.

Step 3: Being challenged by opposing views

'Has anything escaped me?' I asked with some self-importance. 'I trust there is nothing of consequence that I have overlooked?' 'I'm afraid, my dear Watson, that most of your conclusions were erroneous. When I said that you stimulated me I meant, to be frank, that in noting your fallacies I was occasionally guided towards the truth.'
(Arthur Conan Doyle, *The Hound of the Baskervilles*)

In controversy, individuals' conclusions are challenged by the advocates of opposing positions. Members critically analyse each other's positions in attempts to discern weaknesses and strengths. They attempt to refute opposing positions while rebutting the attacks on their position. At the same time, they are aware that they need to learn the information being presented and understand the perspective of the other group members.

The direct evidence indicates that individuals engaged in controversy are motivated to know the others' positions and to develop understanding and appreciation of them (Johnson and Johnson, 1989). Hearing opposing views being advocated, furthermore, stimulates new cognitive analysis and frees individuals to create alternative and original conclusions. When contrary information is not clearly relevant to completing the task in hand it may be ignored, discounted or perceived in biased ways in favour of supporting evidence. When indivduals realize, however, that they are accountable for knowing the contrary information some time in the near future, they will tend to learn it. Even being confronted with an erroneous point of view can result in more divergent thinking and the generation of novel and more cognitively advanced solutions.

Step 4: Conceptual conflict and uncertainty

Hearing alternatives being advocated, having one's position criticized and refuted, and being challenged by information that is incompatible with and does not fit with one's conclusions, leads to conceptual conflict and uncertainty. The greater the disagreement among group members, the more frequently disagreement occurs, the greater the number of people disagreeing with a person's position, the more competitive the context of the controversy, and the more affronted the person feels, the greater the conceptual conflict and uncertainty the person experiences (Johnson and Johnson, 1989).

Step 5: Epistemic curiosity and perspective taking

Macbeth said, 'Stay, you imperfect speakers, tell me more.' When faced with intellectual opposition in a co-operative context, students will ask each other for more information. Conceptual conflict motivates an active search for more information (called epistemic curiosity) in hopes of resolving the uncertainty. Indices of epistemic curiosity include individuals actively (a) searching for more information, (b) seeking to understand opposing positions and rationales, and (c) attempting to view the situation from opposing perspectives.

Step 6: Reconceptualization, synthesis, integration

André Gide said, 'One completely overcomes only what one assimilates.' Nothing could be more true of controversy. When overt controversy is structured within a problem-solving, decision-making or learning group by identifying alternatives and assigning members to advocate the best case for each alternative, the purpose is not to choose the best alternative. The purpose is to create a synthesis of the best reasoning and conclusions from all the various alternatives. Synthesizing occurs when individuals integrate a number of different ideas and facts into a single position. It is the intellectual bringing together of ideas and facts and engaging in inductive reasoning by restating a large amount of information into a conclusion or summary. Synthesizing is a creative process involving seeing new patterns within a body of evidence, viewing the issue from a variety of perspectives, and generating a number of optional ways of integrating the evidence. This required probabilistic (i.e. knowledge is available only in degrees of certainty) rather than dualistic (i.e. there is only right and wrong and authority should not be questioned) or relativistic thinking (i.e. authorities are seen as sometimes right but that right and wrong depend on your perspective). The dual purposes of synthesis are to arrive at the best possible decision or solution and to find a position that all group members can agree on and commit themselves to. There is evidence that controversy leads to accuracy of perspective taking, incorporation of others' information and reasoning into their own position, attitude and position change, and transition to higher stages of cognitive reasoning, all of which contribute to the quality of individuals' reconceptualization, synthesis and integration.

KEY ELEMENTS FOR MAKING CONTROVERSY WORK

> He that wrestles with us strengthens our nerves, and sharpens our skill. Our antagonist is our helper.
> (Edmund Burke, *Reflections on the Revolution in France*)

Although controversies can operate in a beneficial way, they will not do so under all conditions. As with all types of conflicts, the potential for either constructive or destructive outcomes is present in a controversy. Whether there are positive or negative consequences depends on the conditions under which controversy occurs and the way in which it is managed. These key elements are as follows (Johnson and Johnson, 1979, 1989, 1992):

1. *A co-operative context.* Communication of information is far more complex, accurate, encouraged and utilized in a co-operative context than in a competitive context. Controversy in a co-operative context promotes open-minded listening to the opposing position, while in a competitive context controversy promotes a close-minded orientation in which individuals were unwilling to make concessions to the opponent's viewpoint and refused to incorporate any of the opponent's viewpoint into their own position.
2. *Heterogeneous participants.* Heterogeneity among individuals leads to potential controversy, and to more diverse interaction patterns and resources for achievement and problem solving.
3. *Relevant information distributed among participants.* The more information individuals have about an issue, the more successful their problem solving.
4. *Social skills.* In order for controversies to be managed constructively, individuals need a number of conflict management skills, such as disagreeing with each other's ideas while confirming each other's personal competence and seeing the issue from a number of perspectives.
5. *Rational argument.* Rational argumentation includes generating ideas, collecting and organizing relevant information, using inductive and deductive logic and making tentative conclusions based on current understanding.

STRUCTURING ACADEMIC CONTROVERSIES

> Conflict is the gadfly of thought. It stirs us to observation and memory. It instigates invention. It shocks us out of sheep-like passivity, and sets us at noting and contriving . . . Conflict is a 'sine qua non' of reflection and ingenuity.
> (John Dewey, *Human Nature and Conduct: Morals Are Human*)

Jack London is teaching a unit on the Romantic poets in a course on English literature. He assigns students to groups of four and explains to his classes, 'You are to consider two Romantic poets and choose which one is better and explain why (using the criteria we have developed as to what makes a poet great). You are to work co-operatively. You are to write a group report detailing the criteria as to what makes a poet great, the group decision (made by consensus) as to which poet is better, and a detailed rationale.' Jack divides the groups into two-person advocacy teams. 'Advocacy Team A,' he states, 'is to take the position that George Gordon (Lord Byron) is the better poet and Advocacy Team B is to take the position that William

Wordsworth is the better poet. The procedure you will follow has five steps.' First, students research the issue by reading a number of poems by their assigned author, using the criteria for great poets to analyse the poet's work, and then prepare a persuasive case as to why their poet is the better of the two. They are to learn all about their poet and prepare to teach what they know to the other pair. Second, the two advocacy teams meet and each makes a persuasive presentation advocating the best case possible for their poet. Each pair member has to do half the presentation. Third, the four group members engage in a general discussion in which they advocate their position, critically evaluate and attack the opposing position and its rationale (giving it a trial-by-fire), rebut the attacks on and defend their position, learn both positions, and compare their strengths and weaknesses. Fourth, the two pairs reverse perspectives and present the opposing position as if it were their own. Each advocacy pair presents the best case possible for the opposing position. Fifth, the group of four integrate the best reasoning from both sides, seek a synthesis, reach a consensus as to which poet is better, and prepare a group report explaining their reasoning and its rationale. The group's report should reflect their best reasoned judgement. Each group member then individually takes an examination on a comparison of the two poets. The lesson ends with groups discussing how effectively members engaged in the controversy process.

For the past several years we have been training teachers and professors throughout North America and Europe in the use of structured academic controversies. Structured academic controversies are now being used at the University of Minnesota in engineering, psychology and education courses. They are being used in elementary and secondary schools as well as universities in North America, Europe and elsewhere. The basic format for doing so follows. A more detailed description of conducting academic controversies may be found in Johnson and Johnson (1992).

Structure the academic task

The task must be structured (1) co-operatively and (2) so that there are at least two well documented positions (e.g. pro and con). The choice of topic depends on the interests of the instructor and the purposes of the course.

Prepare instructional materials

Prepare the instructional materials so that group members know what position they have been assigned and where they can find supporting information. Each position needs (a) a clear description of the group's task; (b) a description of the phases of the controversy procedure and the interpersonal and small-group skills to be used during each phase; (c) a definition of the position to be advocated with a summary of the key arguments supporting the position; and (d) resource materials (including a bibliography) to provide evidence for the elaboration of the arguments supporting the position to be advocated.

Structure the controversy

The principal requirements for a successful structured controversy are a co-operative context, skilful group members, and heterogeneity of group membership. Teachers may structure these requirements by:

1. Assigning students to heterogeneous groups of four. Divide each group into two pairs. A high-ability reader and a low-ability reader may be assigned to each pair. The responsibility of the pair is to get to know the information supporting their assigned position and prepare a presentation and a series of persuasive arguments to use in the discussion with the opposing pair.
2. Assigning pro and con positions to the pairs and giving students supporting materials to read and study. A bibliography of further sources of information may also be given. A section of resource materials may be set up in the library.
3. Structuring positive interdependence by highlighting (a) the co-operative goals (ensuring that all group members reach a consensus on the issue, master all the information relevant to both sides of the issue [measured by a test], and participate in writing a quality group report and making a presentation to the class); (b) resource interdependence (materials are jigsawed within the group) and reward interdependence (bonus points are given to members if all of them learn the basic information contained in the two positions and score well on the test).
4. Structuring individual accountability by ensuring each student participates in preparing the assigned position, presenting the position, discussing the issue, reversing perspectives, preparing the report, presenting the report, and taking an individual test on the material.

Conduct the controversy

First, teachers assign each pair the tasks of (a) learning their position and its supporting arguments and information; (b) researching all information relevant to their position; (c) giving the opposing pair any information found supporting the opposing position; (d) preparing a persuasive presentation to be given to the other pair; and (e) preparing a series of persuasive arguments to be used in the discussion with the opposing pair. Students are given the following instructions:

> Plan with your partner how to advocate your position effectively. Read the materials supporting your position. Find more information in the library reference books to support your position. Plan a persuasive presentation. Make sure you and your partner master the information supporting your assigned position and present it in a persuasive and complete way so that the other group members will comprehend and learn the information.

Second, teachers have each pair present its position to the other. Presentations should involve more than one media and persuasively advocate the 'best case' for the position. There is no arguing during this time. Students should listen carefully to the opposing position. Students are told:

As a pair, present your position forcefully and persuasively. Listen carefully and learn the opposing position. Take notes, and clarify anything you do not understand.

Third, teachers have students openly discuss the issue by freely exchanging their information and ideas. For higher-level reasoning and critical thinking to occur, it is necessary to probe and push each other's conclusions. Students ask for data to support each other's statements, clarify rationales and show why their position is a rational one. Students evaluate critically the opposing position and its rationale, defend their own positions, and compare the strengths and weaknesses of the two positions. Students refute the claims being made by the opposing pair and rebut the attacks on their own position. Students are to follow the specific rules for constructive controversy. Students should also take careful notes on and thoroughly learn the opposing position. Sometimes a 'time-out' period needs to be provided so that pairs can caucus and prepare new arguments. Teachers encourage more spirited arguing, take sides when a pair is in trouble, play devil's advocate, ask one group to observe another group engaging in a spirited argument, and generally stir up the discussions. Students are instructed to:

Argue forcefully and persuasively for your position, presenting as many facts as you can to support your point of view. Listen critically to the opposing pair's position, asking them for the facts that support their viewpoint, and then present counter-arguments. Remember this is a complex issue, and you need to know both sides to write a good report.

Fourth, teachers have the pairs reverse perspectives and positions by presenting the opposing position as sincerely and forcefully as they can. It helps to have the pairs change chairs. They can use their own notes but may not see the materials developed by the opposing pair. Students' instructions are:

Working as a pair, present the opposing pair's position as if you were they. Be as sincere and forceful as you can. Add any new facts you know. Elaborate their position by relating it to other information you have previously learned.

Fifth, teachers have the group members drop their advocacy and reach a decision by consensus. The students then (a) write a group report that includes their joint position and the supporting evidence and rationale (all group members sign the report indicating that they agree with it, can explain its content, and consider it ready to be evaluated); (b) take a test on both positions (if all members score above the pre-set criteria of excellence, each receives five bonus points); and (c) process how well the group functioned and how their performance may be improved during the next controversy. (Teachers may wish to structure the group processing to highlight the specific conflict management skills students need to master.) Students are instructed to:

Summarize and synthesize the best arguments for both points of view. Reach consensus on a position that is supported by the facts. Change your mind only when the facts and the rationale clearly indicate that you should do so. Write your report with the supporting evidence and rationale for your synthesis that your group has agreed on. When you are certain the report is as good as you can make it, sign it. Organize your report to present it to your entire class.

Teach students conflict skills

No matter how carefully teachers structure controversies, if students do not have the interpersonal and small-group skills to manage conflicts constructively, the controversy will not produce its potential effects. The social skills emphasized are those involved in systematically advocating an intellectual position and evaluating and criticizing the position advocated by others, as well as the skills involved in synthesis and consensual decision making. Students should be taught the skills of (a) focusing on the mutual goal of coming to the best decision possible, not on winning; (b) confirming others' competence while disagreeing with their positions and challenging their reasoning (be critical of ideas, not people); (c) separating your personal worth from criticism of your ideas; (d) listening to everyone's ideas, even if you do not agree with them; (e) first bring out all the ideas and facts supporting both sides (differentiate the differences between positions) and then try to put them together in a way that makes sense (integration of ideas); (f) taking the opposing perspective in order to understand both sides of the issue; (g) changing your mind when the evidence clearly indicates that you should; (h) paraphrasing what someone has said if it is not clear; (i) emphasizing rationality in seeking the best possible answer, given the available data; and (j) following the golden rule of conflict (act towards your opponents as you would have them act towards you).

SUMMARY

Walter Savage Landor once said, 'There is no more certain sign of a narrow mind, of stupidity, and of arrogance, than to stand aloof from those who think differently from us.' When teachers lecture about events and people and structure competition among students they create the conditions under which students will avoid listening to different points of view and defensively reject ideas and people that might prove them wrong. In order to avoid close-minded attempts to 'win', teachers must structure the learning situation in ways that promote interest, curiosity, inquiry and open-minded problem solving. To do so teachers must use two interrelated instructional procedures: co-operative learning and academic controversy.

Working together co-operatively to accomplish shared learning goals. Teachers assign students to small groups and give them two responsibilities: to learn the assigned material and to make sure that the other members of the group also master it. Students' goal achievements are positively correlated; students perceive that they can reaching their learning goals if and only if the other students in the learning group also reach their goals. Thus, students seek outcomes that are beneficial to all those with whom they are co-operatively linked. Co-operative learning groups may be used to teach specific content (formal co-operative learning groups); ensure active cognitive processing of information during a lecture or presentation (informal co-operative learning groups); provide long-term support and assistance for academic progress (co-operative base groups); and structure repetitive classroom routines (co-operative learning scripts). To be effective, teachers have to structure co-operative learning situations so that students perceive that they sink or swim together, are accountable for doing their fair share of the work, interact face-to-face to provide each other help and support, utilize interpersonal and small-group skills, and process how to improve the effectiveness of the group. It is these essential components that differentiate co-operative learning from traditional classroom grouping.

Teachers using co-operative learning are on very safe grounds empirically. Co-operative learning can be used with some confidence at every grade level, in every subject area, and with any task. It simultaneously effects many different instructional outcomes – outcomes related to effort to achieve, positive interpersonal relationships, and psychological health. Since each outcome can induce the others, they are likely to be found together.

Controversy exists when one student's ideas, information, conclusions, theories and opinions are incompatible with those of another, and the two seek to reach an agreement. Controversies are (a) an inherent aspect of higher-quality learning, higher-level reasoning, critical thinking, sciencing, problem solving and decision making, (b) inevitable. If students get intellectually and emotionally involved in co-operative efforts, controversies will occur no matter what teachers do. In well structured controversies, students make an initial judgement, present their conclusions to other group members, are challenged with opposing views, become uncertain about the correctness of their views, actively search for new information and understanding, incorporate others' perspectives and reasoning into their thinking, and reach a new set of conclusions.

While this process sometimes occurs naturally within co-operative learning groups, it may be considerably enhanced when teachers structure academic controversies. This involves dividing a co-operative group into two pairs and assigning them opposing positions. The pairs then develop their position, present it to the other pair, listen to the opposing position, engage in a discussion in which they attempt to refute the other side and rebut attacks on their position, reverse perspectives and present the other position, and then drop all advocacy and seek a synthesis that takes both perspectives and positions into account. Controversies tend to be constructive when the situational context is co-operative, group members are heterogeneous, information and expertise is distributed within the group, members have the necessary conflict skills, and the canons of rational argumentation are followed.

REFERENCES

Ames, G. and Murray, F. (1982) When two wrongs make a right: Promoting cognitive change by social conflict. *Developmental Psychology*, **18**, 894-7.

Berlyne, D.E. (1965) *Structure and Direction in Thinking*. New York: Wiley.

Deutsch, M. (1962) Co-operation and trust: some theoretical notes. In M. Jones (ed.), *Nebraska Symposium on Motivation*. Lincoln, NE: University of Nebraska Press.

Deutsch, M. (1973) *The Resolution of Conflict*. New Haven, CT: Yale University Press.

Follet, M. (1940) Constructive conflict. In H. Metcalf and L. Urwick (eds), *Dynamic Administration: The Collected Papers of Mary Parker Follet*. New York: Harper.

Janis, I. (1982) *Groupthink: Psychological Studies of Policy Decisions and Fiascos*. Boston, MA: Houghton-Mifflin.

Johnson, D.W. (1970) *Social Psychology of Education*. Edina, MN: Interaction Book Company.

Johnson, D.W. (1979) *Educational Psychology*. Englewood Cliffs, NJ: Prentice-Hall.

Johnson, D.W. (1980) Group processes: influences of student–student interaction on school outcomes. In J. McMillan (ed.), *The Social Psychology of School Learning*. New York: Academic Press.

Johnson, D.W. (1993) *Reaching Out: Interpersonal Effectiveness and Self-Actualization* (4th ed.). Englewood Cliffs, NJ: Prentice-Hall.

Johnson, D.W. and Johnson, F. (1994) *Joining Together: Group Theory and Group Skills* (4th ed.). Englewood Cliffs, NJ: Prentice-Hall.

Johnson, D.W. and Johnson, R. (1979) Conflict in the classroom: controversy and learning. *Review of Educational Research*, **49**, 51-61.

Johnson, D.W. and Johnson, R. (1985) Classroom conflict: controversy v. debate in learning groups. *American Educational Research Journal*, **22**, 237-56.

Johnson, D.W. and Johnson, R. (1987) *Creative Conflict*. Edina, MN: Interaction Book Company.

Johnson, D.W. and Johnson, R. (1989) *Co-operation and Competition: Theory and Research*. Edina, MN: Interaction Book Company.

Johnson, D.W. and Johnson, R. (1992) *Creative Controversy: Intellectual Challenge in the Classroom*. Edina, MN: Interaction Book Company.

Johnson, D.W., Johnson, R. and Holubec, E. (1993) *Circles of Learning: Co-operation in the Classroom* (3rd ed.). Edina, MN: Interaction Book Company.

Tjosvold, D. (1994) Flight crew collaboration to manage safety risks. Unpublished manuscript, Simon Fraser University, Burnaby, BC, Canada.

Chapter 6

Cognitive Approaches to Group Work

Paul Light and Karen Littleton

EDITORS' INTRODUCTION

Over the last ten years, some substantial strides have been made towards understanding how cognitive development takes place in a social context. Real implications have been drawn from this understanding that should help to promote cognitive development within the classroom. No longer are teachers given Piaget's logico-mathematical stages as their sole insight to children's thinking, nor can this developmental experience be pictured as a lone child interacting with physical objects. The chapter by Light and Littleton provides historical and practical accounts of children interacting with others, sharing and challenging perspectives between themselves, and conceptualizing this social experience as the basis for their cognitive development. The chapter confirms the evidence and discussion in previous chapters that learning is not an individualist enterprise.

The literature and studies reviewed by Light and Littleton are derived from theories characteristic of developmental psychology. Evidence presented reminds the reader that these theories do not exist in a vacuum; theory generation and testing must take place in the real world. While the studies discussed are predominantly experimental, many of them have taken place with primary school children within their school context. The writers are very much aware that the role of the teacher is essential in: identifying appropriate cognitive tasks; grouping pupils of various abilities into various sized groups; presenting tasks that can/should be undertaken in a collaborative fashion; and allowing for joint discussions and problem-solving experiences.

All of the studies reviewed by Light and Littleton draw upon cognitive, problem-solving tasks. The authors identify that different pupil pairings may be more or less appropriate for type of task undertaken, and draw conclusions with regard to knowledge and power relationships similar to those discussed in Chapter 2. The evidence presented correlates well with knowledge inequalities as in peer tutoring (Chapter 7), consideration of co-operative skills (Chapters 4 and 5) and the curriculum implications taken up in Chapter 11. While Light and Littleton do not discuss the social and emotional bases for effective peer interaction in cognitive development, they are aware that pupil characteristics and training are essential in structuring the social context that best supports cognitive development in pupils.

INTRODUCTION

The study of children's cognitive development (the development of their thinking, reasoning, knowledge and understanding) has long been a central concern of psychologists as well as of educationalists. Psychologists have tended to adopt experimental methods, and it is mostly this tradition of research which we will draw upon in this chapter. Conducting experiments often involves creating rather artificial situations in which to observe children's learning, and the results will not always be directly applicable to the classroom. Nonetheless, experiments can allow us to test our hypotheses objectively, something which is often extremely difficult under more naturalistic conditions.

In this chapter we shall give an account of research on cognitive development, conducted over the last fifteen years or so, which has addressed whether, when and how peer interaction facilitates children's learning and problem-solving and cognitive development. Other possible benefits of collaboration, such as its impact on children's social development or communication skills, will not be considered here, although we fully recognize their importance. Likewise we recognize that in classroom situations the continuing role of the teacher in structuring and managing group work may be of prime importance, but the studies to be discussed here focus only on the constructive processes of interaction within small groups of children working autonomously. Classroom management of these groups raises issues which go beyond the present chapter (see Eraut and Petch, forthcoming; and also Mercer and Fisher, 1992).

As with much of developmental psychology, our story starts with Piaget and his successors in the Genevan school. The first substantive section of the chapter will deal with the Piagetian legacy, and the idea of 'socio-cognitive conflict' as an explanation for the facilitation of cognitive development through peer interaction. As we shall see, the concept of 'constructive conflict' has played a key role in research in this field. The following section will cover the subsequent enrichment of this idea to encompass the role of social norms and expectations, under the label 'social marking'. We shall then broaden our range a little, moving away from Piagetian tasks to consider evidence relating to peer facilitation across a wide range of ages and types of cognitive task. Here we shall draw increasingly on the psychological perspective associated with the Russian psychologist Vygotsky, which emphasizes processes of mutual construction of knowledge and understanding.

As its title suggests, we shall concentrate in this chapter upon 'cognitive approaches', namely approaches which address the question of how group work impacts upon the intellectual skills and processes involved in children's learning. Nevertheless in our conclusion we shall draw on some recent findings to suggest that the analyses of cognitive processes in peer interaction cannot be pursued very far in isolation from the social, motivational and emotional dimensions of such interaction.

The research which we will be presenting in this chapter has not been directed primarily at influencing classroom practice. Nonetheless there may be some implicit messages for how such practice might best be managed. We hope that familiarity with this research may inform (though it cannot prescribe) the way that teachers utilize group work in support of children's education.

EGOCENTRISM AND SOCIO-COGNITIVE CONFLICT

Piaget began his research on the development of human understanding in the 1920s, and continued his work in the field for almost sixty years. Not surprisingly, then, 'Piaget's theory' is not a single, coherent position, and there are significant shifts of emphasis at different periods. The work for which Piaget is best known in the English-speaking world dates mostly from the 1940s to the 1960s. In this period he was intent on an exercise he called 'genetic epistemology', namely the production of an account of human reasoning in terms of its genesis or course of development. The detailed stage-by-stage account which resulted gave little attention to the question of what particular types of experience were necessary to induce progress. Where particular experiences were referred to, these tended to be encounters between the child and the physical world – for example, counting objects and then counting them again in a different order and then discovering that the number remained the same. Very little attention was paid to the social dimensions of experience, so that the Piagetian child could be seen almost as a solo child-scientist, single-handedly (re)discovering physics and mathematics by grappling with the puzzles and paradoxes of the natural world.

This is something of a parody of Piaget's position, of course, but it serves to contrast this later Piagetian work with his earliest researches conducted in the 1920s and 1930s. In these early studies, based for the most part on observations of his own children, Piaget developed the key concept of egocentrism. Both in his work on *The Language and Thought of the Child* (1926) and on *The Moral Development of the Child* (1932), Piaget saw the principal barrier to the pre-school child's progress as being an inability to 'decentre'; to take account of other people's points of view. The egocentric child, he suggested, does not understand the relativity of points of view, and takes his or her own view for reality. This egocentrism limits moral thinking and communication in fairly obvious ways, but also limits cognitive development in other more subtle ways. Since children cannot appreciate that the first thing that strikes them about a problem might not be the only way the problem can be thought about, they cannot reflect on alternatives or understand how different factors might interact with one another. Importantly, Piaget saw this egocentrism of children's thinking as being overcome through social experience of a particular kind.

The child's relations with adults (whether parents or others) were seen by Piaget as inherently asymmetrical, and the difference in power and status was such that children could not balance their own views against those of adults. But in more symmetrical relationships between the child and his or her peers, differences of viewpoint could provide both a divergence of views (different 'centrations' which would conflict with one another) and the social pressure to reach a resolution of this difference of view. By integrating the partial centrations in a higher-level perspective embracing both, the children could resolve their differences. Thus peer interaction was seen to hold a very special potential for helping egocentric ('pre-operational') children to overcome their egocentrism and make progress towards higher-level ('operational') thinking.

This idea lay dormant for many years, little explored in subsequent work either by Piaget or by his co-workers. But in the 1970s, at a time when social psychology was establishing itself in Geneva, these social dimensions of Piaget's theory began to be explored systematically. In these studies some of the 'hallmark' tests of operational thinking devised by Piaget in his later work were used to explore the argument that he had himself advanced many years earlier regarding the facilitatory role of peer interaction.

The principal architect of these experiments in peer interaction with Piagetian tasks was Willem Doise, together with his research associates Gabrial Mugny and Anne-Nelly Perret-Clermont. They worked extensively with a task which very obviously involved 'points of view', since it involved spatial rearrangements. The child's ability to co-ordinate different points of view was for Piaget a key index of the overcoming of egocentrism (Piaget and Inhelder, 1956). The 'three mountains' task (in which children had to reconstruct different views of an array of three papier-mâché mountains) became one of the best known 'indicators' of the achievement of decentred operational thinking.

In the version of the task used by Doise and colleagues (see Figure 6.1), a child was presented with an arrangement of model buildings on a cardboard base, making up a little village. The buildings were oriented in relation to a fixed mark on the base, such as a village pond. Another table stood to the side of the child, with another base, but this had no buildings on it, only the fixed mark. This might be in the same position vis à vis the child (Figure 6.1a) or, for example, rotated 180 degrees (Figure 6.1b). The child's task was to reconstruct the village using a second set of pieces on the second base in such a way that the buildings all stood in the same relation to the pond as they did in the original village. The task is fairly easy if the fixed mark is in the 'same' position on the second base as on the first, but much more difficult if it has been rotated relative to the child. Children's difficulties with this type of task can be used as an index of their egocentrism, since correct solution depends on the children decentring from their own point of view, allowing the fixed mark to provide the point of reference for placements.

Doise and colleagues (e.g. Doise and Mugny, 1984) used a three-step experimental design to investigate the effects of peer interaction on children's responses to this task. The first (pre-test) step involved all children being tested individually to establish their level of development in relation to the task. On the second step some children (the control group) were assigned to working alone again, while others (the experimental group) worked in pairs. Finally the third step of the procedure (post-test) involved all the children working alone again. This design allowed the researchers to ask two experimental questions. Firstly, will the children who work together on step two produce better performances than those who work alone? Secondly, will those who worked together on step two show better individual performance at post-test than those who worked alone at step two?

These two questions are both of interest, of course. In terms of the first question, there may be many situations in which the performance of the group as a group is the important thing for a teacher to foster. But the concerns of researchers in this area, and of teachers in many cases, have focused mainly on the second question, namely whether the experience of working in a pair will be of value in terms of subsequent individual performance. Here, perhaps, we see the influence of our profoundly individualistic culture!

Doise and colleagues experimented with a number of arrangements in these studies. They pre-tested children and retained only those who could solve simple versions of the task, where although the child had to turn through 90 degrees to look from one table to the other, the fixed mark was in the same position vis à vis the child on each of

Figure 6.1   *Village representations (adapted from Doise and Mugny, 1984).*

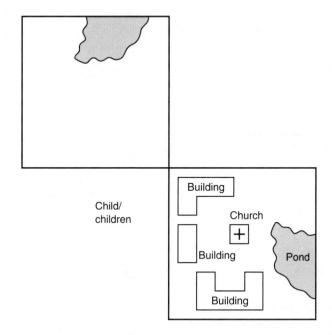

a)   *Pond in same position for child viewing two tables.*

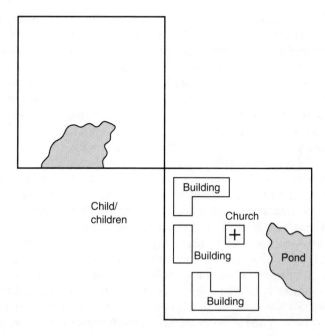

b)   *Pond rotated 180 degrees.*

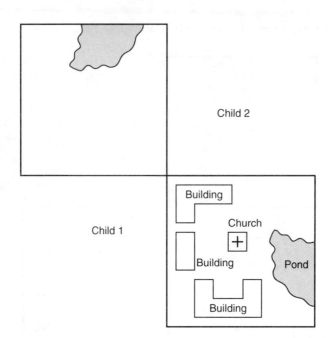

c) Pond in same position, children in different positions.

the tables. Their performances on the more complex items involving further rotations of the fixed mark were classified in three levels, from failure to take any account of such rotations (Level 1), through partial adjustment to such rotations (Level 2) to fully correct performance (Level 3).

Doise and Mugny (1984) report two studies which will serve to exemplify their work with this type of task. In the first, they pre- and post-tested 100 children aged 5-7 years individually, and in between allowed some of them (randomly chosen) to work on the task alone while others worked in pairs. The pairs included Level 1–Level 1 pairs, Level 1–Level 2 pairs and Level 1–Level 3 pairs. The partners were always from the same school class and were of the same gender. The pre- and post-tests took place about ten days before and after the experimental phase. Results showed that Level 1 subjects made rather little progress when paired with other Level 1 subjects, but also rather little when paired with Level 3 subjects. They made considerable gains when paired with a Level 2 partner. It seemed that the Level 3 subjects were rather sure of themselves and imposed their solution without much discussion, whereas the Level 1–Level 2 pairs were characterized by much more conflict and negotiation.

A second experimental design entailed creating conflicting points of view not by taking children at different levels but by placing children of the same cognitive level in different positions with respect to the array. With the tables corner to corner (see Figure 6.1c), it is possible to arrange the children's positions so that a child in one of the 'bays' has a 'simple' transposition to deal with while the child in the opposite bay has a complex rotation. If Level 1 subjects are paired together, each of them will try to impose a simple translation of positions, and these will conflict with one another, one being a correct solution and the other an incorrect solution.

Doise and Mugny (1984) report a study in which they compared pre- to post-test progress of Level 1 children, some of whom worked in pairs trying to tackle the problem together from different positions, while others worked alone but were able to move from one position to the other as they worked. The paired children made significantly more progress, lending further support to the idea that it is socio-cognitive conflict (the holding of different points of view by different partners in a social interchange) that holds the key to progress.

The other task which Doise and colleagues (but most especially Perret-Clermont, 1980) used for these experiments was the conservation task. In its best-known form this involves establishing the equality of amounts of liquid in two identical beakers and then pouring the contents of one of them into a differently shaped beaker, so that the liquid level is noticeably higher or lower. Then the child is asked if the amounts of liquid in the two containers are still the same. Pre-operational children judge them not to be, basing their response on liquid level or some other salient cue (e.g. 'this jar's fatter'). In a similar way, Piaget's research indicated that young children do not appreciate that the length of a stick remains the same despite displacements of position, or that the weight (mass) of, say, a ball of clay remains the same despite changes in shape.

Perret-Clermont used the same three-step design as was used for the 'village' studies. For children assigned to the interactive condition at the second stage, she explored various arrangements. One which proved effective was to have three children work together. Two were selected as having shown a grasp of conservation at pre-test, the third was a non-conserver. The third child was then given a jug of juice and the task of sharing the juice equally between the three of them in variously shaped beakers, so that they would all agree that they had the same. Non-conserving children exposed to this experience not only succeeded with their partners in achieving 'fair shares', but typically went on to perform well on the individual post-test.

This arrangement involves a conflict between pre-operational and operational responses to the task, but progress was also demonstrated in situations where two different pre-operational centrations were brought into conflict. Thus with two rulers initially aligned with one another, children will agree that they are the same length. If one is then displaced relative to the other, children in different seating positions may both suppose the lengths to be different, but disagree as to which is now longest. Doise and Mugny (1984) report that such contradictions of equally wrong answers (whether offered by a child or an adult) can be effective in producing progress towards higher-level 'conserving' responses which resolve the lower-level conflicts.

These studies thus lent considerable weight to the idea that peer facilitation could have rather dramatic effects on children's cognitive development, and to the idea that such benefits could be explained in terms of socio-cognitive conflict. They also helped to stimulate a much wider interest in research on the facilitatory effects of peer interaction, including much of the research discussed in the remainder of this chapter. However, as is so often the case, the initially rather simple story these studies seem to tell has become a good deal more complicated as further research has accumulated.

PEER INTERACTION AND SOCIAL MARKING

In part the need for some reappraisal of the interpretation of peer facilitation effects in terms of socio-cognitive conflict was suggested by the very effectiveness of peer interaction. For example, with conservation, it appeared that a session of only ten or twenty minutes of peer interaction around a conservation problem was often enough to shift a child from non-conserving to conserving responses. This shift is, in Piagetian terms, one of the major hurdles on the path to operational thinking, so it seems remarkable that it can be achieved so readily, with children even showing generalization to types of conservation not addressed in the group session (Perret-Clermont, 1980). Moreover, social class differences in children's responses were rather marked at pre-test with middle-class children showing a significantly greater frequency of conserving responses, but this difference disappeared by post-test. Can we really suppose that the effects of years of differential socialization can be eclipsed by ten or twenty minutes of peer interaction?

An alternative explanation is that in some way or another the experience of working together with other children on the task changes the way the children understand the questions. The work of Margaret Donaldson (1978) and others suggests strongly that children often fail Piagetian tests not because they cannot work out the answer but because they misunderstand the question that they are being asked. With the conservation task, for example, the way in which the experimenter deliberately draws the child's attention to an irrelevant cue (e.g. by pointedly pouring the juice into different shaped containers for no apparent reason) may lead the child to interpret the task in terms of appearances (which looks more now?) rather than in terms of actual amounts. In the peer interaction situation, where the children are sharing juice amongst themselves, this misleading cue is not available, and the need to establish fairness of distribution keeps the children's attention firmly focused upon the actual amounts. So it may be, as Light and Perret-Clermont (1989) have argued, that the standard individual pre-test actually gives a misleadingly poor impression of the abilities of the children, while the peer interaction condition allows them to be clearer about what is expected of them and thus to show themselves to better advantage.

One way of paraphrasing this argument is to say that it is the social norms or conventions associated with 'fair shares' that help the children to sort out what the task is about. In fact one of the main ways in which the work of Doise and his colleagues has developed since 1980 has involved recognition of the pervasive role of such norms and conventions. Doise uses the phrase 'social marking' to refer to the way that the ease or difficulty of a cognitive task can be affected by the extent to which it can be mapped on to social norms or rules with which the child is familiar.

In the case of the spatial rearrangement (village) task, social marking has been explored by, for example, replacing the houses, pond etc. with a model classroom with pupils' desks facing the teacher's desk (the fixed mark). With these materials, if the children rearrange the materials incorrectly, the children will no longer be facing the teacher. Thus the usual cognitive strategy of the Level 1 or Level 2 child will lead to a conflict with certain social conventions which these Swiss children all shared. How this would work with British primary school children, accustomed to very different classroom organizations, is an open question!

Doise (1990) describes studies in which, for example, children are pre- and post-tested on the village tasks, while in-between some of them have experience (alone or in pairs) with either the village materials or the classroom materials. Because the children were at the same level and shared the same physical relationship to the materials, not much progress was expected for those who worked with the village materials, and indeed not much was found. But the children who worked with the classroom materials did better, especially those who worked as pairs, and they carried over this advantage to the standard individual post-test a week or so later.

Another direction of work explored by Mugny *et al.* (1984) involved having an adult oppose a child's judgements in the interaction phase of the study. With the village materials, children usually gave way to adults, even when the adult was wrong. With the classroom materials, on the other hand, children tended to hold on to their own ideas more strongly, and argued for them even when the adult disagreed. In this condition, the children made significantly greater pre- to post-test progress than with the village materials.

In this more recent Genevan account, therefore, the effects of immediate face to face interaction between children working together on a task cannot be considered in isolation from the framework of social benefits and expectations that the participants bring to the situation. Peer interactions, in other words, are themselves seen to be conditioned by their social context.

Meanwhile, as we shall show in the next section, the initial studies of Doise *et al.* had begun to spawn a much wider interest in experimental research on peer interaction. This new research took from the Genevan work a general experimental approach (the three-step design with individual pre- and post-tests) and a concern with the possible role of conflict. On the other hand, the non-Genevan research has typically shown much less interest in the Piagetian repertoire of tasks, and a much less exclusive concern with children at the boundary between pre-operational and operational thinking.

PEER INTERACTION AND PROBLEM SOLVING

One of the tasks long beloved of cognitive psychologists interested in problem solving is the 'Tower of Hanoi'. This is usually presented in the form of board with three vertical pegs in it; over one peg is slipped a number of different sized tiles, with the largest at the bottom and the smallest at the top so that they form a pagoda-shaped

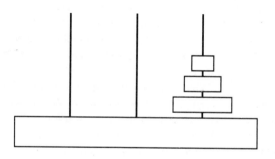

Figure 6.2 *Original set-up of 'Tower of Hanoi'.*

stack (see Figure 6.2). The task is to dismantle the 'pagoda' and reform it on one of the other pegs, but with the constraints that only one tile can be moved at a time and that a larger tile may never be placed on a smaller one. With three tiles, the problem is soluble in a minimum of seven moves.

Our own first exploration of peer interaction effects on problem solving began with this task (Glachan and Light, 1982; Light and Glachan, 1985). We pre-tested individual children, aged about 8, and then assigned them at random to either a control condition where they worked alone or an experimental condition where they worked in pairs, sitting opposite one another with the board between them. We then post-tested them all individually with a slightly different version of the task. In the first study, we obtained no evidence that the children who worked together gained any advantage from doing so. However, when we looked at what they were doing this offered no surprise. They were simply taking turns, having one move or a whole trial each, but taking little interest when it was 'not their go'. So we attached little handles to each side of the tiles and tried again with a rule which stipulated that they must co-operate on all moves and that no move could be made unless the two children moved the tile together. Under these conditions we did get evidence that children who worked together did better, and carried over some of this advantage to individual post-test.

We followed this up with a study in which the same task was presented on a computer. The children had to key in numbers to signal which tile they wanted to move where. Again, it was only when we modified the software so that both children had to key in each move that we saw any benefit for the children who worked together (Light *et al.*, 1988). What counts, seemingly, is for the children to be engaged with one another as well as with the task. Blaye (1988) came to the same conclusion on the basis of a series of studies involving 5- and 6-year-olds in a matrix-filling task presented to them on computer. Whilst the experience of working in a pair often led to greater individual progress than working alone, this was particularly noticeable when one of the children was required to indicate their choice with a lightpen while the other had to affirm their consent by using the keyboard. Once again it is co-ordinating the roles of the children that seems to be important.

In our own work we have experimented with a number of other computer-presented 'puzzles', one being a computer version of the pegboard code-breaking game 'Mastermind'. The computer generated a digitial code sequence which the children had to 'break' by trying out different sequences and getting feedback (Light and Glachan, 1985). In this study the children who worked together again enjoyed some advantage over those who worked alone. In an attempt to understand the basis of this facilitation we tape-recorded the interaction between the children. We looked in particular for 'arguments', i.e. sequences where the children were offering differing suggestions as to what move to make next, and where at least one of them was offering some kind of justification. As it happened, such arguments were fairly common in about half of the pairs and rather scarce in the other half. The improvement of children's scores from pre-test to post-test was significantly greater in those pairs who engaged in frequent argument than it was for the remainder.

This study then offered some support for the view that 'socio-cognitive conflict', or at least disagreement, may be a necessary condition for progress in peer interaction situations. More evidence comes from a more recent series of studies by Christine

Howe and colleagues at Strathclyde. These were conducted with secondary school-aged pupils using computer-based tasks related to the physics curriculum. The design of these studies has followed the familiar pattern of individual pre-tests and post-tests, and in-between a session in which children work together in pairs or small groups.

Howe *et al.* (1991), in a study concerning trajectories of objects dropped from planes, formed pairs on the basis of pre-test responses such that students (12- and 14-year-olds) in a pair were either similar or different in terms of their initial predictions and conceptions. The pairs which showed the greatest pre- to post-test gains were those where the students differed both in terms of their predicted trajectories and the conceptions on which these predictions were based. In a subsequent study (Howe *et al.*, 1992) the researchers differentiated between the actual judgements the children made and the strategies they used in approaching the problem. In this case the problem concerned comparison of the speed of two trains under various conditions. One train (on the computer screen) ran at a constant speed, while the other accelerated or decelerated, with variations of direction, starting position and so on. Subjects were undergraduates. Pre-tests were used to establish the judgements made and strategies used by each subject, and then the pairs were made up so that the partners were either similar or different in judgements or strategies. The most productive group combination in terms of conceptual change was where partners differed in both strategy and judgement. However, in this instance, the next most productive arrangement was where the partners were similar in both judgements and strategies, this being apparently more effective than where children differ on only one of these dimensions. Although Howe and colleagues offer some speculations about how this comes about, it seems on the face of it a rather puzzling outcome.

While the work of Howe and colleagues lends support to the idea that socio-cognitive conflict may be the key ingredient in peer facilitation of learning, other researchers have raised more doubts about this and have criticized the concept of conflict as vague and ill-defined (Blaye, 1988). Some researchers have found that interaction between children at the same level is actually sometimes the most effective situation. Thus, for example, Light *et al.* (1994) found with a detour problem-solving task couched as a computer adventure game that working with a partner of the same pre-test score level was more effective than working with a lower-level or a higher-level partner. So, there appear to be at least some circumstances under which learners need to be evenly matched to maximize the productivity of the interaction. It may be that the fact that the task was wholly novel for both partners was important here: they were not coming to the situation with well formed views of how the problem should be tackled, as they were in the case of Howe *et al.*'s study. In these circumstances, collaborative gains may have more to do with joint construction of understanding than with decentring through conflict in Doise's sense. In the next section we shall consider other research which bears on this issue.

CO-CONSTRUCTION AND THE ROLE OF TALK

Before turning to the main theme of this section we ought to give brief consideration to an issue which may well have struck the reader by this stage, namely why computers seem to figure such a lot in this literature. In some ways this seems paradoxical, since computers were introduced into educational thinking back in the 1960s and 1970s largely in terms of a vision of individualized education. But the reality in schools, especially primary schools, is that most use of computers is by pairs or small groups often working collaboratively at the keyboard, largely independently of the teacher. Indeed, it seems that this may prove to be their greatest strength. Teachers have long seen advantages in group work, but the logistics of the classroom often militate against these advantages being realized. Research by Galton *et al.* (1980) and Bennett (1987) has revealed that whilst children in classrooms may commonly be seen sitting together in groups, closer observation reveals that their mode of working is rarely collaborative – the children are typically found working 'in parallel' rather than in co-operation. There are indications, both in the classroom observation literature and in the experimental literature (see review by Light and Blaye, 1990), that computers may offer at least part of the answer, by providing sufficient structure and responsiveness to maintain the effective functioning of the group with the minimum of teacher intervention. This consideration, together with the practical advantages for the researcher of running experiments on the computer, has led to a heavy concentration in the peer interaction literature on facilitation of computer-based learning and problem solving.

We began this chapter with Piaget, whose theory of cognitive development had such massive influence upon contemporary thinking. But there is, today, a countervailing influence represented by the Russian psychologist L.S. Vygotsky. Vygotsky's own research and writing were done in the 1920s and 1930s, but his influence and that of Luria, one of his students, led to the development of a robust tradition of Soviet developmental psychology which has only made itself felt in the West in the last decade or so. Vygotsky saw the 'higher mental functions' (reflection, thinking, reasoning etc.) not as products of individual development but as resulting from the internalization of initially social processes. The child's understanding of the world is seen as being built up through interaction with others and most especially through language. Rather than being direct, based on experience with the physical world, the child's experience is largely mediated by others. Meanings are negotiated and established through interaction in a wide range of social contexts.

Vygotsky's work directs attention most obviously to asymmetrical interactions, between more and less expert individuals. His theory offers an account of tutoring, and draws attention to the fact that most of what children have to learn, the adults around them already know. But the concepts of negotiation of meaning and co-construction of shared understanding can be applied to peer interaction as well as to adult–child interaction. They lead us to consider collaborative rather than conflictual processes, and in particular to focus on the constructive role of discussion.

Much of the research on peer interaction conducted within this tradition has been classroom-based, and has involved larger groups than the twos and threes typically used in the more experimental neo-Piagetian tradition. Greater 'ecological validity' gained by working in more naturalistic conditions is won at the cost of some control over the conditions of working, and such studies rarely include individual pre- and post-testing or individual control conditions.

Some studies have eschewed measuring 'cognitive outcomes' altogether and have focused instead on developing criteria for discussing the variety and 'educational quality' of talk arising during children's collaborative work. Dawes *et al.* (1992), for example, investigated the nature of primary school children's talk when they are working together at the computer and identified three qualitatively different types of talk in their data: disputational, cumulative and exploratory talk. Disputational talk is effectively unproductive disagreement. Such talk is characterized by an initiation (e.g. proposition, hypothesis, instruction) followed by a challenge (be this a direct rejection or a counter-proposition/hypothesis). Such challenges typically lack clear resolution or else result in resolution which is not supported by agreement. Cumulative talk simply adds uncritically to what has gone before. Initiations are typically accepted either without discussion or with only superficial amendments. In contrast, however, exploratory talk demonstrates the active joint engagement of the children with one another's ideas. Whilst initiations may be challenged and counter-challenged, appropriate justifications are articulated and alternative hypotheses offered. Where alternative accounts are offered they are developments of the initiation. Progress thus emerges from the joint acceptance of suggestions. Whilst Dawes *et al.* acknowledge that all three types of talk are appropriate in certain circumstances, they maintain that exploratory talk offers a potential for learning over and above that offered by the other categories. According to this analysis, then, collaborative activities should be designed to foster children's use of exploratory talk.

Other researchers have also put considerable resources into analysing the verbal exchanges and patterns of interactions in medium-sized groups (six or so). Thus, for example, Celia Hoyles and colleagues (Hoyles and Sutherland, 1989; Hoyles *et al.*, 1990) have made very detailed observational studies of groups of children working on an extended LOGO project in the context of their mathematics work. LOGO is a computer programming language, being used in this case to support 'Turtle graphics' – with children controlling the movements of a screen 'Turtle' to produce geometric figures of various kinds. According to these researchers the critical role for discussion comes when there is some kind of mismatch between what a student is attempting to achieve and what their partner will allow or comprehends. The pivotal role for discussion between learners is said to occur when such 'conflict' arises, for it is here that the different perceptions of the problem and its solution have to be negotiated, articulated and made compatible within the demands and constraints of the task. Note that here the term conflict is used in a wider sense than that intended by Doise and colleagues, being rather closely related to that of negotiation.

Negotiation and verbally explicit pre-planning are central to the analysis of interaction in problem solving offered by Barbieri and Light (1992). In this study we were able to show that pairs who negotiated most explicitly and made most extensive use of verbal pre-planning while working collaboratively on a detour task tended to be the most successful at individual post-test. However, such correlations do not provide unambiguous evidence that the quality of discussion which children engage in directly affects the quality of learning outcomes. It remains possible, for example, that it was the fact that particular children had 'cracked the task' that shaped the discussion, rather than vice versa. Sorting out cause and effect in this area is not easy. In our own work we are trying to replicate these findings in a study with pre- as well as post-test data, to see how far the verbal interaction measures predict gains as opposed to absolute levels of task performance. There have been some attempts to partial out prior abilities in this way. Webb *et al.* (1986), for instance, investigated the way in which 'explanations' were associated with learning outcomes amongst pupils learning programming. They found that the frequency of both giving and receiving explanations was associated with learning achievements.

In fact getting children to talk their way through a problem without a partner present can itself be helpful to problem solving (Fletcher, 1985), while on the other hand some advantage can accrue to groups of students who work together on a problem even when they are not allowed to talk at all (e.g. Jackson *et al.*, 1992). So while language is part of the story, and probably a large part, it is certainly not all of it. A good deal more work will need to be done before we fully appreciate the ways language functions in facilitating understanding.

LIMITATIONS OF A PURELY COGNITIVE APPROACH

As Hoyles *et al.* (1992) have noted, the majority of studies investigating effective group work have neglected interpersonal variables within the pairs or groups of children, such as the children's individual characteristics and self-perceptions, and their perceptions of one another, and of the task itself. Others have also remarked on the neglect of issues such as the relative status of pupils (Laborde, 1988) and other social psychological considerations which might affect performance (e.g. Saloman and Globerson, 1989) as well as the role of training for interaction (see other chapters in this volume).

Moreover, as indicated previously, some studies (e.g. Jackson *et al.*, 1992) have come up with findings which challenge any supposition that interaction and discussion alone underpin the beneficial effects of group work. Indeed, our own work investigating children's computer-based problem solving has revealed that working in presence of other children who are similarly engaged can be facilitative even if the childen are working on different machines without any overt interaction (Light *et al.*, 1994).

A striking paper by Robinson-Stavely and Cooper (1990), involving computer-based learning in adults with little computer experience, highlights the effects of mere presence of a peer and draws attention to the power of expectancy of success in influencing both performance and the response to others in the learning situation. In their first study Robinson-Stavely and Cooper asked male and female students to complete a difficult computer task and a series of questionnaires in either the presence or the absence of another person. Those women who worked in the presence of someone else typically performed less well, reporting higher anxiety and expressing more negative attitudes towards computers than those women who were required to work alone. With the men, however, the presence of another person had the opposite effect. In a second study, Robinson-Stavely and Cooper manipulated expectations for success. Some students were given 'feedback' that they were likely to do well and others that they were unlikely to succeed. There was evidence of facilitation for 'positive expectancy' subjects and impairment for 'negative expectancy' subjects, as compared with those subjects who were required to work alone.

What emerges from Robinson-Stavely and Cooper's study is the significance of social comparison rather than simply social facilitation in the learning situation. Social comparison (and more generally the role of social representations in learning) is central to some recent French research (Monteil, 1991, 1992). This has focused on social comparison variables affecting learning in secondary school pupils. In a series of studies generating clear and replicable results, Monteil and colleagues have manipulated actual academic ability levels, inducing expectancies of success in pupils relative to their peers on particular tasks, and varying the public *vs* private nature of the subsequent learning situation. Students for whom there is a mismatch (whether positive or negative) between their general academic standing and their induced perception of their own ability relative to their peers show good learning outcomes in private or 'anonymous' learning situations, whereas those who receive 'feedback' matching their expectations learn more effectively in situations where their performance is visible to their peers (Monteil, 1992). Whether the same results would be obtained in a British or North American context, where academic success and failure are typically less strongly 'marked' in schools remains to be seen.

Monteil and colleagues interpret their results in terms of social comparisons within the peer-based learning situation, and interpret the effects of such comparisons as mediated by emotional responses to the situation, influencing the focusing of attention on task-relevant information. Their studies attest to the powerful influence of social representations (of self and of other) on school children's learning and highlight the need to pay closer attention to the ways in which children working in the various conditions we create construe the task and their own situation and ability in relation to it.

There are limitations, then, on how far we can expect to get with purely cognitive accounts of the benefits of group work. We have seen in this chapter that studies based on the cognitive–developmental theories of Piaget and Vygotsky have taken us a considerable distance in understanding how and when peer interaction facilitates children's understanding. To get much further, we shall need to integrate a fuller understanding of children's social perceptions and emotional reponses with our cognitive accounts of 'how group work works'.

Even when we have this fuller picture we should not expect to establish group work as any kind of educational panacea. To the question of whether group work leads to better cognitive outcomes, the answer will always be 'it depends'. The studies we have reviewed in this chapter at least begin to illuminate some of the conditions for productive outcomes. For example, they illustrate the importance of ensuring joint engagement with the task. They also indicate that there will be no overall recipe for pairing or grouping children. For tasks which require children to arrive at correct judgements, interactions may only be productive where group members differ in their initial viewpoints. However, for novel tasks requiring constructive elaboration of solutions not heavily dependent on prior knowledge, balanced pairings are likely to prove more effective. As we foresaw at the outset, we are a long way from being able to prescribe the ways in which group work should be used to maximize cognitive gains. But the emerging research literature will hopefully provide a valuable resource for teachers reflecting on the role of group work within their own classroom practice.

REFERENCES

Barbieri, M.S. and Light, P. (1992) Interaction, gender and performance on a computer-based problem solving task. *Learning and Instruction*, **2**, 199-214.

Bennett, N. (1987) Co-operative learning: children do it in groups – or do they? *Educational and Child Psychology*, **4**, 7-18.

Blaye, A. (1968) Confrontation sociocognitive et résolution de problème. Unpublished doctoral thesis, University of Provence, Aix-en-Provence.

Dawes, L., Fisher, E. and Mercer, N. (1992) The quality of talk at the computer. *Language and Learning*.

Doise, W. (1990) The development of individual competencies through social interaction. In H. Foot, M. Morgan and R. Shute (eds), *Children Helping Children*. Chichester: Wiley.

Doise, W. and Mugny, G. (1984) *The Social Development of the Intellect*. Oxford: Pergamon.

Donaldson, M. (1978) *Children's Minds*. London: Fontana.

Eraut, M. and Petch, R. (forthcoming) *Groupwork with Computers*.

Fletcher, B. (1985) Group and individual learning of junior school children on a micro-computer-based task. *Educational Review*, **37**, 251-61.

Galton, M., Simon, B. and Croll, P. (1980) *Inside the Primary School*. London: Routledge.

Glachan, M. and Light, P. (1982) Peer interaction and learning. In G. Butterworth and P. Light (eds), *Social Cognition*. Brighton: Harvester Press.

Howe, C., Tolmie, A. and Anderson, A. (1991) Information technology and groupwork in physics. *Journal of Computer Assisted Learning*, **7**, 133-43.

Howe, C., Tolmie, A., Anderson, A. and MacKenzie, M. (1992) Conceptual knowledge in physics: the role of group interaction in computer-supported teaching. *Learning and Instruction*, **2**, 161-83.

Hoyles, C. and Sutherland, R. (1989) *Logo Mathematics in the Classroom*. London: Routledge.

Hoyles, C., Sutherland, R. and Healy, L. (1990) Children talking in computer environments. In K. Durkin and B. Shire (eds), *Language and Mathematical Education*. Milton Keynes: Open University Press.

Hoyles, C., Healy, L. and Pozzi, S. (1992) Interdependence and autonomy: aspects of groupwork with computers. *Learning and Instruction*, **2**, 239-57.

Jackson, A., Fletcher, B. and Messer, D. (1992) When talking doesn't help: an investigation of microcomputer-based group problem solving. *Learning and Instruction*, **2**, 185-97.

Laborde, C. (1988) Divers aspects de la dimension sociale dans les recherches en didactique des mathematiques. In C. Laborde (ed.), *Actes du premier colloque franco-allemand de didactique des mathematiques et de l'informatique*. Grenoble: La Pensée Sauvage.

Light, P. and Blaye, A. (1990) Computer-based learning: the social dimensions. In H. Foot, M. Morgan and R. Shute (eds), *Children Helping Children*. Chichester: Wiley.

Light, P. and Glachan, M. (1985) Facilitation of problem solving through peer interaction. *Educational Psychology*, **5**, 217-25.

Light, P. and Perret-Clermont, A.-N. (1989) Social context effects in learning and testing. In A. Gellatly, D. Rogers and J. Sloboda (eds), *Cognition and Social Worlds*. Oxford: Clarendon Press.

Light, P., Foot, T., Colbourn, C. and McClelland, I. (1988) Collaborative interactions at the microcomputer keyboard. *Educational Psychology*, **7**, 13-21.

Light, P., Littleton, K., Messer, D. and Joiner, R. (1994) Social and communicative processes in computer-based problem solving. *European Journal of Psychology of Education*, **9**, 93-109.

Mercer, N. and Fisher, E. (1992) How do teachers help children to learn? An analysis of teachers' interventions in computer-based activities. *Learning and Instruction*, **2**, 339-55.

Monteil, J.-M. (1991) Social regulation and individual cognitive function: the effects of individuation on cognitive performance. *European Journal of Social Psychology*, **21**, 225-37.

Monteil, J.-M. (1992) Towards a social psychology of cognitive functioning. In M. von Granach, W. Doise and G. Mugny (eds), *Social Representation and the Social Bases of Knowledge*. Berne: Hubert.

Mugny, G., DePaolis, P. and Carugati, F. (1984) Social regulation in cognitive development. In W. Doise and A. Palmonari (eds), *Social Interaction in Individual Development.* Cambridge: Cambridge University Press.

Perret-Clermont, A.-N. (1980) *Social Interaction and Cognitive Development in Children.* London: Academic Press.

Piaget, J. (1926) *The Language and Thought of the Child.* London: Routledge.

Piaget, J. (1932) *The Moral Development of the Child.* London: Routledge.

Piaget, J. and Inhelder, B. (1956) *The Child's Conception of Space.* London: Routledge.

Robinson-Stavely, K. and Cooper, J. (1990) Mere presence, gender and reactions to computers. *Journal of Experimental Social Psychology*, **26**, 168-83.

Saloman, G. and Globerson, T. (1989) When teams do not function the way they ought to. *International Journal of Educational Research*, **13**, 88-99.

Webb, N., Ender, P. and Lewis, S. (1986) Problem-solving strategies and group processes in small groups learning computer programming. *American Educational Research Journal*, **23**, 247-61.

Chapter 7

Peer Tutoring

Keith Topping

EDITORS' INTRODUCTION

Peer tutoring is a well-established technique to promote learning between a tutor and tutee. As its name implies, peer tutoring is a relationship between individuals with unequal knowledge (between expert and novice) and generally taking place between social equals (mutual power relationship). This pedagogic relationship between grouping and learning tasks (see Chapter 2, Table 2.4) should be particularly effective in incremental learning, especially where there is a single correct answer (which the tutor is able to support and guide the tutee toward). Keith Topping, an educational psychologist by training and who has worked in the field of peer tutoring for many years, shows this technique to be effective for learning incrementally as well as with revision and practice tasks (see further discussion of these tasks in Chapter 11). Peer tutoring can be used across the curriculum, in primary and secondary schools, and within higher education; although most studies focus on the core curriculum subjects, especially English (reading and spelling) and mathematics in the primary school.

Topping presents practical and comparative issues. Practically, the reader should gain a firm grasp of the procedures to set up, run and evaluate peer tutoring tasks. Teachers will quickly learn that this is not a simple technique, but one which requires much planning, training, supportive material and supportive relationships. Comparatively, the value of peer tutoring has been shown for tutors and tutees – in their intellectual and social development.

While peer tutoring is a highly structured technique, Topping reminds us that it can be used flexibly. Classroom innovations and variations show that peer tutoring can allow low-ability pupils to tutor high-ability peers in areas of particular expertise. Tutoring can also take place between parallel classes and across year groups. Pupils of low ability as well as all others should share in this process which can enhance learning and self-concept.

INTRODUCTION

Picture an average primary classroom. Five groups of six children are clustered round their tables, each busy with their own activities. At one table the six children sit quietly, carrying out a traditional written exercise: they are seated as a group but do not function as a group. At another table the teacher has set a co-operative task: the creation of an optimum wheeled vehicle from limited materials. Two children want to be boss and are squabbling about design, while the rest watch passively. At a third table the children have spontaneously paired up, assigned each other the roles of tutor and tutee and are proceeding with spelling tasks selected as interesting by the tutee. They are following a procedure in which they have been trained and of which they have a graphic reminder in front of them. After 15 minutes they change roles.

This chapter explores in detail the last of these scenarios. It includes a review of definitions and typologies of peer tutoring, essential elements of successful classroom organization, research evidence on effectiveness, a specific example of a practical approach to the peer tutoring of spelling skills and a summary of points to consider when designing or modifying peer tutoring procedures or techniques.

DEFINITIONS AND TYPOLOGY

A traditional definition of peer tutoring might have been: 'more able pupils helping less able pupils in co-operative working pairs carefully organized by a teacher.' The difference in ability between the more competent tutor and the less competent tutee implied by this definition was sometimes taken automatically to imply a differential in age also. In fact, in recent times 'cross-age' tutoring has been widely supplemented with 'same-age' peer tutoring. Furthermore, new organizational structures have been developed which dispense with the need for an ability differential in the pair.

Given this development of the definition and the expansion in the use of peer tutoring to new curricular areas and other age groups (including university students and working adults) a new definition is needed which is wider but perhaps inevitably carries less information: 'people from similar social groupings who are not professional teachers helping each other to learn and learning by teaching.'

Initial objections to peer tutoring often embody resistance to more able pupils being 'used' to help less able pupils. Peer tutoring is indeed difficult to justify if it is reliant solely on the altruism of the tutor, but properly organized peer tutoring programmes target achievement gains by both tutors and tutees, as is clear from the reference in the second definition to 'learning by teaching'.

How is 'helping each other to learn' via peer tutoring different from doing just that through co-operative learning? In the many methods for co-operative learning described in the literature, a teaching or tutoring role or 'job' is rarely allocated to a participant, the more usual expectation being that 'co-operative learners' have interlocking and complementary short-term tasks which effectively 'structure positive interdependence'.

In peer tutoring, the roles of tutor and tutee are clearly allocated and the associated 'job description' carefully specified. This implies that care must be taken with matching of tutor and tutee. In addition to definite and relatively long-term role-making, often involving the specification of frequent and regular contact times, peer tutoring is usually characterized by specific procedures for the process of interaction. In peer tutoring, each member of the pair has parallel, albeit interdependent, objectives. Furthermore, tutoring usually has a high level of focus on the detail of curriculum content – although social and affective gains do occur, they are not directly targeted to the same extent as in co-operative learning.

Training for peer tutoring tends to be longer and more detailed, often including precise guidance on correction procedures, although it may be generic to a range of tutoring activities or highly specific or both. Tutoring training often is intended to have impact over a whole tutoring programme, while instructions for a co-operative learning activity are more likely to be very brief and for immediate application only.

While co-operative learning most often operates in small groups of 3 to 6 individuals, often on a same-age basis within existing class mixed-ability groups, peer tutoring typically functions in pairs and can be in a variety of constellations. Close monitoring and supervision, together with some form of evaluation, should be a characteristic of all peer tutoring projects, but in practice this depends on local pragmatics and may be no more likely in peer tutoring than in co-operative learning.

A typology of peer tutoring would categorize projects on at least six major variables, namely: age, ability, role continuity, institutional origins, group size and content nature. Peer tutoring projects may be cross-age or same-age. They may operate with same-ability or cross-ability pairs. Roles may be permanently fixed or there may be reciprocal tutoring, with roles switching at pre-defined points. The tutor and tutee may originate from within the same educational institution, or different ones – in some projects tutees are in primary school and tutors in secondary school or tutees in secondary school and tutors in college or university. Although peer tutoring usually is in pairs, some projects involve tutoring in small groups, although this latter tends to be more complex, not least in role specification, and thus more difficult to monitor.

THE SCOPE OF PEER TUTORING

The variety of peer tutoring programmes which have operated successfully is prodigious. They range from the highly structured to the relatively unstructured, from those which emphasize personal and social growth to those which lay great stress on academic achievement, from small supplementary programmes co-ordinated by one teacher to extensive schemes which involve all pupils in a school, from those which provide help for handicapped pupils of low attainment to those which were designed as enrichment for the relatively able, and from those which focus on the very young to those which concern themselves with the distinctly elderly.

In this latter respect, some successful projects have included 5-year-old tutees, and some tutors of the same age or younger, although the latter is rarer. At the other end of the age spectrum, open learning centres for low-income adults have operated on a peer tutor basis, and many other programmes in this field have utilized adult peer volunteers.

Peer tutoring is extending to increasingly esoteric subject areas and participant populations. A pack of materials for cross-age peer tutoring in science with 5- to 10-year-olds has been developed (Croft and Topping, 1992). Fitz-Gibbon and Reay (1982) have used the peer tutoring method in foreign language teaching, while Karegianes *et al.* (1980) report on the effects of 'peer editing' on writing proficiency of low-achieving high school students. Cicirelli (1976) extensively explored the use of siblings as tutors of younger children in their own family. Projects have operated with young male offenders in youth custody facilities (Posen, 1983). Peer tutoring programmes targeted on 'at-risk' adolescents and dealing with issues such as sex, HIV/AIDS and drugs are increasingly to be found.

ORGANIZATION

All children are different, and schools are even more different from each other. All successful peer tutoring projects have certain common elements, but each must be designed to fit comfortably within the ecology of a particular school at a particular time in its development. It is very important that peer tutor projects are not used to compensate for, and thereby disguise, fundamental weaknesses in professional teaching or organizational infrastructure within a school. Schools that have failed to organize other things are unlikely to have any greater success in successfully organizing peer tutoring.

Different teachers will run peer tutoring projects for very different purposes, and a success for one teacher could be construed as a failure by another teacher with different objectives and expectations. Objectives do need to be realistic. It is reasonable to expect both tutors and tutees to show increased competence in the curriculum area of the tutoring, and perhaps increased confidence and interest in that area. However, it is not reasonable to expect a brief project to make a major impact on a long-standing and widespread problem in school. A degree of reasonable caution when setting objectives creates the possibility of being pleasantly surprised subsequently.

Selection and monitoring of participants

In a project involving same-age tutoring within a single class recruitment will be no problem. The project organizer must decide whether all the class are to be involved, or whether to start with a small group of well-motivated volunteers and use them as a model of enjoyment which will persuade the rest of the class of the desirability of joining in a little later. In cross-age and cross-institution projects, recruitment is more complex.

Age differential between tutors and tutees is probably of less significance than an ability differential. Any cross-age tutoring arrangement will almost inevitably create difficulties of matching timetables and movement of pupils. While same-age and cross-age tutoring can be equally effective, there is some evidence that where ability (and therefore often age) of the tutor is substantially greater than that of the tutee, the tutee may be expected to benefit more, although this may be at the cost of the tutor benefiting somewhat less.

Most peer tutoring in schools is done in a one-to-one situation, but it can occur in small groups of three, four or five children. If this latter arrangement is to be established, it is important to make rules for the group and role of tutor or 'leader' very clear, or children may spend more time bickering about organization than actually getting on with the task in hand. Particularly for a first venture, it is important to be able to monitor closely a small number of children. Most of the research work on peer tutoring has been done with pairs rather than small tutor groups and the former arrangement is likely to prove organizationally more simple, more satisfying for 'pairs' and promote a maximum of time on task. The issue of whether research studies have shown pairs to be more effective is more complex; only Devin-Sheehan *et al.* (1976) have addressed this question and they reported that results were mixed.

The range of ability in the children is a critical factor in selection and matching of tutors and tutees. A widely used rule of thumb is to keep a differential of about two years in attainment between tutors and tutees (unless operating some form of same-ability tutoring). When drafting an initial matching on the basis of ability, it is possible to rank available children in terms of their attainment in the curriculum area of tutoring, draw a line through the middle of the list separating tutors on the top and tutees at the bottom, and then pair the most able tutor with the most able tutee, and so on.

In some projects, the alternative approach has been taken of pairing the most able tutor with the least able tutee, but this sometimes creates a situation where the gap in ability is so wide that little stimulation is available from the tutoring materials for the tutor. On the other hand, if a minimal differential in ability is not maintained, and the tutor's abilities approximate to those of the tutee, then little gain in attainment can be expected from tutees, except those resulting from increased time on task, unless the interactive structure is specifically designed for same-ability tutoring.

Pre-existing social relationships in the peer group must also be considered. To pair children with their 'best friends' of the moment may not be a good idea in all cases, particularly as the friendship may be of short duration. Obviously it would be undesirable to pair a child up with another child with whom there is a pre-existing poor relationship. Special care is necessary with pairings in cases where tutees are known to be of particularly timorous or over-dependent personality, or tutors are known to be rather dominant or authoritarian by nature.

To allow children free selection of tutor is likely to create a degree of chaos. Some tutors will be over-chosen while others may not be chosen at all, quite apart from the question of maintaining any requisite differential in ability. The gender balance in the class can present a problem, particularly if there are more girls than boys; initially many boys may express reluctance at the prospect of being tutored by a girl. Needless to say, the reluctance often disappears fairly quickly where the teacher allocates a female tutor to a male tutee and instructs them to get on with it. One effect of this kind of cross-sex tutoring may be to improve relationships and dispel stereotypes. Many of these social considerations apply equally to the establishment of pairings of mixed race. Peer tutoring can offer a focus for social contact between children who might otherwise be inclined to avoid each other owing to completely unfounded assumptions or anxieties.

It is always worthwhile to nominate a 'supply tutor' or two to ensure that absence from school of the usual tutor can be covered. Children acting as spare tutors need to be particularly stable, sociable and competent in the curriculum area of project, since they will have to work with a wide range of tutees. However, do not worry about imposing a burden on spare tutors, as they may be expected to benefit most in terms of increased ability. In cross-age or cross-institution projects, in which it may be more difficult to ascertain regular and frequent tutoring contact, more stand-by tutors may need to be appointed. If there is a danger of any volunteer tutors dropping out before the end of the project, there are again implications for nominating stand-bys to fill this sort of gap.

The question of parental agreement often arises in connection with peer tutor projects. Involvement in such a project is usually sufficiently interesting for the children as to result in many of them mentioning it at home. It is usually desirable for a brief note from school to be taken home by both tutors and tutees, explaining the project very simply, underlining that participation is purely voluntary, and reassuring parents that the project will have both academic and social benefits for tutors as well as tutees.

Materials

There is some evidence that peer tutoring is generally more effective in raising attainment when structured materials are used than in other circumstances. Certainly, carefully sequenced materials which take tutees step-by-step, ensuring success along the way, may be easier for tutors to follow reliably and may reduce the need for lengthy and complex training. On the other hand, teachers may feel that such materials can easily become stultifying, create over-dependence and inhibit generalization of skills. Also, considerable financial or time costs may be involved in purchase or preparation of structured materials.

Materials that are too highly structured may inhibit initiative and reduce opportunities for tutors to participate creatively. The restricted availability of complex and expensive structured materials may prevent additional spontaneous tutoring from occurring in project participants' own free time. In recent years, there has been more emphasis on the utilization of structured techniques which are of broad-spectrum applicability to a wide range of materials which themselves need not be structured and are readily available.

A related question concerns control of the difficulty level of the materials. In a very highly structured sequence, some form of placement test may be necessary to determine at what point the tutee should commence. Subsequently, in this situation, mastery of each task determines progression to the next, so the sequence is predetermined. Other approaches which are less dependent on highly structured materials have allowed some choice by the tutee and/or tutor from a variety of materials which are nevertheless within a compressed band of difficulty. More recently still, techniques have been developed which allow tutors and tutees free access to materials of uncontrolled difficulty. In these cases, tutors and tutees have often been taught skills to enable them to choose mutually interesting materials at an appropriate level of difficulty for both. Choice by negotiation between tutorial pair is a general rule in these circumstances. Some projects have gone further down the road towards independent control of learning by vesting responsibility for choice entirely with tutee. (Of course, in all circumstances the difficulty of the material must be controlled to be within level of the tutor's competence.) Unless the teaching of choosing skills is particularly effective, this can result in episodes of ineffective tutoring, and runs the risk of the tutor becoming bored.

Peer tutoring works partly by promoting increased time spent on task, and speed of progress through materials can often be much more rapid than is normal in ordinary classroom teaching. This can create an embarrassment for the project co-ordinator, who can find existing stocks of relevant and available materials rapidly exhausted.

A school may pride itself on the volume of relevant materials which it possesses, and forget to pay close attention to how easily tutorial pairs can actually have access to material. In reading projects, for instance, it is not enough for the school to contain a large number of books; it is also necessary for the children to have very regular and frequent access to them. It is important to be clear about which member of the tutorial pair takes the initiative on access to materials. Is this the job of tutor or tutee or both?

Highly structured materials may have the advantage of inbuilt mastery criteria which make it very clear when the tutorial pair are to move on to the next section of prescribed materials. At the other end of the spectrum, where the tutorial pair are allowed a free choice of materials irrespective of difficulty level, the issue of progression criterion does not arise, since a variability in difficulty level from week to week or day to day is usual, and accommodated by tutorial technique. The specification of progression criteria will usually be seen by teachers as requiring their professional expertise.

Contact

A basic decision is whether tutoring is to occur wholly in class time, wholly in children's break time, or in a combination of both. If tutoring is to occur entirely in class time, it can be kept under teacher supervision. If tutoring is to occur in children's break time, some very mature pairs can be left to make their own arrangements, but this is a much greater imposition on tutors and tutees alike, and the momentum of the project may begin to peter out as the novelty begins to wear off.

The best arrangement may be to schedule a basic minimum of contact during class time, but make available the possibility for tutoring pairs to negotiate further sessions in their own break time according to their own levels of enthusiasm. Some projects have arranged for contact after school, or indeed before school starts in the morning. Such arrangements are of course highly constrained by transport arrangements for homeward-bound children and should only be attempted if the enthusiasm of participants is high.

Finding physical space to accommodate pairs can be a problem. In a cross-age tutor project within one school, particularly where two full classes are involved, it is possible for half of the pairs to work in the tutee's classrom and the other half in the tutor's classroom. Finding physical space for tutoring to occur during break times may be considerably more difficult if there are problems of break time supervision and/or children are not allowed access to classrooms. Clearly, a positive social atmosphere is more likely to be fostered if children have adequate personal space and are comfortable during their tutoring. An ambience with a degree of informality is therefore preferable, but the situation should not be so informal as to incorporate many distractions from the tutoring process.

Noise too may be a problem. In same-age tutoring within one classroom, the noise generated by fifteen or more pairs of enthusiastic children reading together is quite considerable. This is exacerbated in an open-plan school, and may generate complaints from classes which are pursuing a more formal curriculum. Availability of an adequate quantity of comfortable seating can also be problematic. Even in a simple reading project, to find enough chairs which may be situated side by side and are reasonably comfortable for both participants might not be easy. Where the peer tutoring curriculum is more formal and incorporates some paper and pencil work, availability of tables also has to be considered.

In cross-age tutor projects, noise and inconvenience generated by the movement of pupils from one location to another is also relevant. In cross-institution peer tutoring, 'imported' students will need to be briefed about the layout of the building, and shown round – this is, of course, ideally done by host students.

Each individual tutoring period should last for a minimum of 15 minutes. Little worthwhile can occur in less time than this, after allowing for lack of punctuality and general settling down. If it is possible for those who so desire to continue for 20 to 30 minutes, this is advantageous. Tutoring sessions of 30 minutes certainly seem to be the most common period found in the literature. It might be possible for the minimum of 15 minutes to occur just before a natural break time, and there could be provision for tutoring pairs continuing into their own break time if they so desire. It is always better to leave a tutoring pair less than exhausted at the end of their joint experience, in order that they will come to their next session with positive attitudes and high energy levels.

To ensure that a project has a measurable impact, frequency of tutorial contact needs to be at least three times per week. Contact frequency of this order is very commonly found in the literature. Children involved in peer tutoring projects rarely objecting to daily tutoring, as most of them find it interesting and rewarding. Some pairs may organize their own impromptu sessions in their own break time whether teachers like it or not! Although the literature suggests that the greater the frequency of tutoring sessions, the more impact a project is likely to have, nevertheless a point of diminishing marginal returns may be found.

The project should be launched with reference to an initial fixed period of commitment. It is useful for both tutors and tutees to be clear about what they are letting themselves in for, and how long a course they need to be able to sustain. Additionally, the literature suggests that short-term projects tend to generate bigger effect sizes. So a minimum project period of six weeks is suggested, since it would barely be possible to discern significant impact in less time than this. Popular project periods are eight weeks and ten weeks, which fit comfortably within an average term or semester, and it is not usually desirable to fix a period of longer than twelve weeks for an initial commitment. It will be much better to review the project at the end of a short initial period, and to obtain feedback from participants and evaluate outcomes, and at that stage make conscious joint decisions about improvements or future directions. One thing to definitely avoid is letting the whole thing dribble on interminably until it runs out of steam.

Technique

There are a number of techniques for peer tutoring which have been carefully and coherently organized into easily deliverable packages. Examples of these in the reading area include 'Paired Reading' and 'Pause Prompt and Praise', designed to be relatively simple albeit structured and applicable to a wide range of materials.

In the United States, packaged techniques have sometimes tended to be even more highly structured, incorporating not only structured tutoring techniques but also highly structured teaching materials. There are obviously considerable attractions in using a pre-defined and packaged tutoring technique, since one may build on the experience of previous workers and avoid unnecessary anxiety about the appropriateness of what one is attempting. Additionally, there will usually be a background of research evidence from other workers with which one may compare one's own results. Use of a pre-existing package is thus strongly recommended for those embarking on their first peer tutoring project.

However, the highly structured packages in the United States sometimes seem mechanistic and unappealing. Certainly such techniques would appear to place a greater imposition on the altruism of tutors than do more natural techniques. Given a clear enough structure, there is no need for tutors to be particularly able or mature, but these latter characteristics may be highly desirable if tutors are to use the techniques with any subtlety and sensitivity.

TRAINING – GENERAL

Some workers have tried to avoid the rigidity at times inherent in very highly structured materials and techniques by attempting to train tutors in much more general teaching skills. These could include: how to present a task, how to give clear explanations, how to demonstrate certain tasks and skills, how to prompt or lead pupils into imitating those skills, how to check on tutee performance, how to give feedback on performance, how to identify consistent patterns of error or problem in tutee responses, and how to develop more intensive remedial procedures for those patterns of error.

It is obvious that this range of skills is quite sophisticated. Requisite skills have been categorized in a number of ways. An obvious separation is between tutoring skills needed to establish good interpersonal relationships, tutoring skills which are specific to the teaching materials in hand, and the skills requisite to systematic checking and record keeping.

Workers have dwelt on creating a positive orientation or 'set' to tutoring in tutors from the outset. In some programmes, tutors have been carefully given a complete overview of the structure of the various components and aims of the project. The importance of positive attitudes in encouraging regular attendance has been emphasized, and considerable attention given to means of establishing good rapport with tutees and stimulating positive tutee motivation. Sometimes information about problems of the tutees has been given to the tutors in order to develop empathy. Equally, tutors have sometimes been advised about the dangers of feeling too 'sympathetic' towards tutees, and falling too readily into the trap of providing unconscious prompts and excessive help which might foster over-dependence.

Ways of giving clear instructions without unnecessary elaboration or the use of difficult vocabulary have been included in some projects. The appropriate point at which to resort to demonstration of the requisite skill may be covered, as may precise details of how and when prompts or guides in practice should be used. Tutors have been trained in how to give systematic instruction, how to closely observe tutee response, and how to respond differentially to different kinds of response.

Other relevant tutor skills have included identification of areas where the tutee needs extra help, systematic mastery checking, record keeping, the issue of token reinforcement, the ability to deal with 'take-homes' and home back-up reinforcers, the ability to manage and refer to any contracts which have been made in respect of the project, and the ability to discuss the progress of the tutee with the project organizer or other supervisor and the tutee themselves.

Errors will be made by tutees. Errors imply failure, and failure creates stress. Stress can produce a negative reaction in the tutee and, possibly, in a tutor who feels that errors are an indication of incompetence on their part. To avoid irritation, frustration and disharmony in the tutoring relationship, all techniques must include some form of pre-specified error correction procedure. Whatever this is, it needs to be quick, simple and consistently applicable, easy and non-stressful for both children.

A standard simple model stipulates that whenever the tutee makes an error, the tutor signals (usually non-verbally) the error, demonstrates or models the correct response, checks that the tutee can produce the correct response unaided, and at some later point rechecks that the tutee can still emit the correct response on request. This kind of framework can be applied to almost any curriculum area and any kind of mistake, and has the advantage of not leaving the tutee to struggle for any significant length of time before help and support is forthcoming.

Specification is needed of the nature, frequency and circumstances for usage of praise in the tutoring relationship. It is useful to specify some sort of minimum frequency with which praise should be deployed, but even more important to give a clear indication of those circumstances where it should always be used. Many tutors find that the giving of verbal praise does not come naturally to them, and they may need considerable practice and feedback in this specific aspect before an adequate level of performance is achieved. In training, verbal and non-verbal aspects of praise should be emphasized, since use of routine praise words in a boring monotone will not have the desired effect. In addition, in some tutoring relationships a pat on the back or head or some other gesture may serve to add variety to social reinforcement.

Some tutors have a very restricted vocabulary of praise words, and part of tutor training could include a listing of appropriate vocabulary. Ideas for such lists can be brainstormed by groups of tutors and tutees together. In cases of doubt, tutors can be encouraged to discuss this with their tutees, since the latter may be able to generate more culturally appropriate praise vocabulary. In addition to verbal and non-verbal praise, record keeping inherent in project organization may include an element of written praise from both tutors and supervising professionals.

TRAINING – SPECIFIC

Before teachers set out to train children in particular procedures, it is clearly important that the teachers themselves are well versed in methods to be used, the technique in use and materials, especially where special or structured materials are to be an essential feature of the project. There is no substitute for being taught how to do it yourself by somebody with previous experience, and you will need to have practised the technique yourself on a child or colleague before trying to disseminate the method further.

Training children individually or in pairs may be highly effective, but would be extremely time-consuming and therefore not efficient, and most teachers opt to train children in groups. Sometimes there are initial training meetings for tutors only or training meetings for tutors and tutees as two separate groups, but in other circumstances tutors and tutees are trained together from the outset. Specify well in advance date, time and place of your training sessions. The number of training sessions, their length and frequency will also need to be made clear to all concerned. The physical space in which training is going to occur will probably need a facility for all participants to sit in a large group and listen to a talk and watch a demonstration, but there will also be a need for chairs (and possibly tables) to be available for subsequent practice, if this is to be incorporated in the same session.

Materials to be used for the training session will also need to be readily and reliably available. You may choose to have available for scrutiny a whole range of possible materials, but for actual practice it will be much better if specific items and tasks for use by each pair during the practice session have been pre-selected, thus avoiding much meandering while hunting for an appropriate item. Even in projects where tutors or tutees are to be given a fairly free choice of materials and tasks, paradoxically the training meeting might be one occasion where you need to control difficulty level of materials more rigidly.

Direct verbal instruction and written instruction cannot be assumed to be effective training methods on their own, although they form essential components of any training procedure. Certainly a verbal explanation of the overall structure and purposes of the project will be given by way of introduction, followed by further detailed explanation of materials and techniques to be used. Take care that the vocabulary in your verbal instruction is simple, and that any unusual words you use are carefully defined for the children. This issue commonly arises in relation to the use of the words 'tutor' and 'tutee', which some project co-ordinators working with young children prefer to replace with a word like 'helper'. In fact, providing care is taken to define meaning of words in advance, their use with even young children can help give the exercise an air of novelty and heighten its status.

Written instruction may take the form of continuous prose in a pamphlet and obviously the readability of the pamphlet is of paramount importance, since it is desirable that both tutor and tutee are able to refer to it. However, it may be much more useful to use various forms of check-list, flowchart, diagram, picture or cartoon, and so on. For essential reminders about most important 'rules', posters or individual 'cue cards' may be helpful.

It is possible for the teacher to demonstrate how to use the technique and materials, either with a willing and confident (intending or previous) tutee, or with another teacher playing the role of tutee, or show a video-tape of a successful practice. Once a first successful project has been run, experienced tutors and tutees can be brought back to demonstrate for subsequent groups of children, and this kind of demonstration tends to have the most impact of all. Immediate practice of tutoring technique is then essential, and feedback should be given from professionals as soon as possible. In some projects, tutors practise tutoring technique by role play on each other before being exposed to tutees, and this may be a useful form of organization if the tutoring technique is particularly complex. In many cases, however, it should be possible to proceed directly to practice in intended tutor/tutee pairs.

Behaviour of tutorial pairs needs close monitoring during the practice session, and this can put a considerable strain on staffing resources. In a practice session of 20 to 30 minutes, a professional cannot expect to observe in detail the tutoring technique of more than five or six pairs. Thus if large groups are being trained, a substantial number of 'mastery checkers' who are conversant with techniques and materials will need to be available. This is undoubtedly the most labour-intensive part of the training procedure. Those pairs who demonstrate that they have learned procedures rapidly can be praised and left to continue, but those pairs who are struggling or using deviant technique will need immediate extra individual tuition until they have fully mastered the procedures.

Once children have been brought to mastery on techniques and materials, they will need briefing about organizational 'nuts and bolts' of day-to-day running of the project. This will include details about access to materials, means of record keeping, arranging times and places for tutorial contact, and procedures for further help and follow-up. A brief written reminder of these organizational details may be helpful. Some teachers choose to establish verbal or written contracts between tutors and tutees, or between project co-ordinators and tutors and tutees.

Recording

Some form of records should be kept of the tutoring process, whether by the project organizer, tutors, tutees or some combination of these. There may be official forms constituting record sheets or cards, progress reports to complete, or probes and tests to be assessed at the appropriate moment. Clear specification is necessary of what recording materials are needed, who is responsible for keeping records safe when available, who completes them, who obtains them from stock when required, and who replenishes stock as it is depleted.

Recording provides a tangible demonstration of achievement and progress for children, and is of considerable interest for the supervising teacher. It is entirely logical that these records should be kept by the children themselves. With more wide-ranging tutorial materials, simple diaries can be kept by each pair, while projects using much more specific materials will generate more precise records. If record keeping can be shared by tutor and tutee, then so much the better.

In some projects the tutee records basic details such as date, materials completed and so on, while the tutor records some words of praise or other comment. Even quite young children prove to be surprisingly good at writing positive comments about their tutees, and learning to give and receive praise without embarrassment is a valuable component of peer tutoring. By and large, tutor comments should be as positive as possible, with any problems discussed directly with the project co-ordinator via self-referral.

Records themselves should be checked each week by the supervising teacher, who can also record some favourable comment and add an official signature, perhaps together with other signs of approval such as house points or merit marks for a particularly meritorious week's work. Participants will, however, need to be clear about who is going to check self-recording, when this is to occur, where records are to be delivered, and how frequently this is to be done.

Monitoring

During the course of the project, it is important that the co-ordinating teacher keeps a close eye on how things are going, in order to be able to nip any incipient problems in the bud, to dispense plentiful praise and enthusiasm to keep motivation high, to ensure that technique does not show signs of 'drift', to check that tutorial pairs or groups are maintaining positive social relationships, to be sure that materials are being used in an appropriate sequence or with reference to relevant levels of difficulty, and generally to keep themselves fully informed about the complexity and richness of learning which should be taking place. Especially in a first project, close monitoring will be essential to ensure that maximum benefit is gained by all participants.

The children themselves may be first to report difficulty or seek help. If a participant who is known to be of high status in the peer group can be prompted to be first to refer a fairly minor problem, other children will soon follow suit.

Many projects feature review meetings between co-ordinating teachers and tutors and tutees. These can occur with tutors and tutees separately or together, in a group or as individuals. The aim is to discuss how the project is going in general, and any specific problems occurring in particular pairs. Group sessions can be valuable for tutors and/or tutees to discover that other pairs are having the same problems. On the other hand, individual meetings will elicit more feedback from quiet and shy individuals, but will be more time-consuming.

Of all monitoring procedures, direct observation is by far the most revealing. Where a supervising teacher is present during tutoring, particularly with same-age projects in class time, much can be gleaned by observing individual pairs. The peer tutoring session is not an opportunity for the teacher to 'get on with some marking'. The least the teacher should do is set a good example by working with project materials or a surplus tutee, but it is much more useful to circulate round the group observing and guiding children as necessary.

In addition, it is possible to ask a particularly expert child tutor who is not otherwise engaged to act as an observer in a similar way and report back to the teacher. A simple check-list of elements of technique or procedure may be useful to help to structure observations of 'monitors'. This could be very similar to, although a little more elaborate than, the check-list of 'rules' which could have been given to tutorial pairs as part of the initial training procedure.

Some form of check on basic organizational parameters of the project will also be necessary. Attendance of tutors and tutees at scheduled contact time will particularly require monitoring. You may find, for instance, that tutoring sessions scheduled for the very beginning of the school day or after school may be rendered problematic at certain times of year by inclement weather and dark nights. If review meetings are to be held between tutorial participants and project co-ordinators, attendance at these and response in them needs to be checked. Availability of appropriate materials will require constant monitoring.

Evaluation

To evaluate in a way which gives results of any consistency, reliability or validity will require planning at the outset. To wait until the end of the project before attempting to evaluate its success is a recipe for confusion and self-deception. To evaluate thoroughly can be very time-consuming, and there is no point in devoting scarce time to this part of the exercise unless you have particular objectives in mind. For further details of evaluation methods, see Topping (1988).

Monitoring and evaluation information will need collating and summarizing in some way, or (to be more precise) in two ways. A very simple way of presenting favourable results and information to the children themselves is necessary to encourage them and promote further growth of confidence. A more 'scientific' collation will be necessary to present to interested colleagues, particularly those who will try to pick holes in your write-up. Feedback to children can be group or individual, with tutors and tutees separate or together. This feedback should be specific to the work and work process undertaken. Do not assume that children will be easily fobbed off by some vague generalizations.

You must make a decision about whether individual pairs are to be given information about their own progress, bearing in mind that even if they are not given comparative information they will soon be asking their friends for this in the playground, or whether the group as a whole should merely be given information about improvement based on group averages. It is useful to make the feedback process reciprocal, and encourage them to give you their views (verbally or in writing or both) on how the project went, and how it could be improved for another generation or a subsequent occasion. Very often children will make suggestions which are contradictory, and therefore rather difficult to implement, but some of their suggestions will undoubtedly be insightful and extremely helpful when organizing further projects.

EFFECTIVENESS

A number of substantial reviews of research on peer tutoring have been published, far too many to mention here. *Children Teach Children* (1971) by S. Gartner *et al.* was the first of significance, but V.L. Allen's (1976) *Children as Teachers* reached a much wider audience and remains a classic. Allen (1976) noted that more studies reported positive effects for tutors than for tutees. Peer tutoring had proved effective across barriers of gender, race and social class.

Subsequently, Sharpley and Sharpley (1981) reviewed 82 peer tutor studies, concluding that same-age tutors were as effective as cross-age tutors in inducing cognitive advances in tutees, and also that same-age tutors were themselves more likely to derive cognitive benefits as a result of their tutoring experiences. Most peer tutoring studies focused on reading skills, but 16 dealt with mathematics and a further four with spelling and language skills, while other curriculum areas included social science, French, German and Spanish languages, written expression, creative thinking, problem solving, drugs, sexuality and birth control.

Results on the effects of extrinsic reinforcement were equivocal, three studies claiming that tangible reinforcement improved functioning at least on rote learning tasks in the short term, while another three found no such effect. Studies of the relative effectiveness of trained versus untrained tutors on all types of tasks indicated that although unstructured programmes using untrained tutors could succeed, they were likely to have a lower success rate. However, of the 82 studies, in terms of academic outcomes for tutors, 21 studies reported positive effects, none reported negative effects, but 29 reported non-significant effects. For academic outcomes for tutees, 35 studies reported positive effects, no studies reported negative effects, but 27 reported non-significant effects.

Moving on from the traditional literature review, Cohen *et al.* (1982) conducted a meta-analysis of 65 studies of peer tutoring, all of which featured true control groups rather than the 'comparison' groups. Tutoring had taken place in a wide range of curricular areas. In 45 of 52 studies, tutored students out-performed control students, while in six studies control students did better and in one study there was no significant difference. Studies involving tutor training and structured tutoring tended to produce larger effect sizes. Eight studies reported improvements in student attitudes and seven studies reported improvements in tutee self-concept, although this latter effect was small. Cohen *et al.* concluded 'these programmes have definite and positive effects on the academic performance and attitudes of children who serve as tutors'.

More recently, Topping (1988) produced a 'review of reviews', commenting on the increasing involvement of students who have special needs as tutors and tutees and the extension of peer tutoring methodology to tutors as young as three years, and to increasingly exotic curriculum areas. The literature was also reviewed by Goodlad and Hirst (1989) and this volume contains considerable reportage of peer tutoring in higher education, particularly Goodlad's own work in involving undergraduates to help tutor science, mathematics and engineering in high schools.

Increasingly, specific structured 'packages' for peer tutoring of basic skills have been developed, researched and disseminated. Wheldall and Colmar (1990) have reviewed evidence on the effectiveness of the 'Pause, Prompt, Praise' technique for reading, while Topping (1990) and Topping and Lindsay (1992) have done the same for 'Paired Reading' technique. Topping and Whiteley (1990) reported that using the Paired Reading technique children tutored by parents did no better in the short term than children tutored by peers, with effect sizes of the order of 0.87 for reading accuracy and 0.77 for comprehension. Peer tutor gains were greater than peer tutee gains in reading accuracy, but this difference did not reach statistical significance. Subjective feedback from same-age peer tutees was more positive than that from cross-age peer tutees, although tutors tended to be equally positive irrespective of the differential.

Workers have increasingly experimented with reciprocation of tutor–tutee roles within dyadic pairings. Thus Pigott *et al.* (1986) reported on reciprocal peer tutoring in teams of four elementary school children working on routine arithmetic drill. Under-achieving pupils improved their performance to a level indistinguishable from that of their class mates and these gains were maintained at follow-up. Palincsar and Brown (1986) similarly described a procedure for developing reading and comprehension skills in which specific task roles rotated round a small group: predicting, question generating, summarizing and clarifying. Evaluation results were impressive. Dyadic reciprocal peer tutoring involving peer-managed group contingencies was reported by Fantuzzo *et al.* (1990), who found consistent increases in the rate of accurate arithmetic performance to a level significantly above the rates of untreated controls, which was maintained at follow-up.

The effectiveness of reciprocal peer tutoring highlights the importance of task-focused structured interaction. This is very different from a traditional conception of peer tutoring, with its associated preoccupation with the 'qualities' of a 'good' tutor. Many studies deployed under-achieving pupils as tutors in order to improve these pupils' attainment and self-esteem. An extreme example is reported by Custer and Osguthorpe (1983), who arranged for mentally handicapped pupils to tutor their non-handicapped peers in sign language, with the result that the sign language competence of both tutors and tutees improved and social interaction between the two groups improved even more.

The deployment as tutors of students with emotional and behavioural difficulties has also been widely explored. Maher (1984) deployed high school students with behavioural difficulties as cross-age tutors for elementary school pupils with learning difficulties in reading, language and mathematics. Gains in attainment for both tutors and tutees are detailed, and disciplinary referrals of tutors fell from an average of six during the baseline period to two during the intervention period, stabilizing at one during follow-up.

Cook *et al.* (1986) carried out a meta-analysis of studies of special needs students as tutors of others. In over 19 studies involvement in tutoring raised the performance of the tutors and tutees as compared with that of controls, with tutees usually achieving greater gains than tutors. Behaviour ratings of tutors showed some improvement, more than those of tutees, and both tutors and tutees showed improvement in attitude towards the school and/or the curriculum area of tutoring. However, changes in measures of self-image and sociometric integration were not to be statistically significant.

Osguthorpe and Scruggs (1990) reviewed 26 studies deploying special education students as tutors, and noted that 23 found the tutors and/or tutees performed better on outcome measures. Attempts to demonstrate the effectiveness of tutoring on 'self-esteem' had generally been unsuccessful, possibly owing to problems of measurement. These authors also emphasized the importance of adequate training and supervision.

A SPECIFIC EXAMPLE

Method

The *Cued Spelling* technique was designed specifically for use by non-professional tutors, whether peers, parents or other volunteers. The basic structure of the technique comprises 10 Steps, 4 Points to remember and 2 Reviews, as illustrated in Figure 7.1 (p.121). The 10 Steps and 4 Points apply to every individual target word worked upon by the pair, while the Speed Review covers all target words for a particular session and the Mastery Review covers all the target words for one week, or a longer period if desired.

10 Steps

The child (tutee) chooses high-interest target words irrespective of complexity (Step 1). The pair check the spelling of the word, put a master version in their Cued Spelling Diary and usually also add it to the top of a piece of paper on which subsequent attempts will be made (Step 2). The pair then read the word out loud synchronously, then the child reads the word aloud alone, ensuring tutee capability of accurate reading and articulation of the word (Step 3).

The child then chooses Cues (prompts or reminders) to enable him or her to remember the written structure of the word (Step 4). These Cues may be phonic sounds, letter names, syllables or other fragments or 'chunks' of words, or wholly idiosyncratic mnemonic devices. Tutees are enouraged to consider and choose Cues which fit well with their own cognitive structures, i.e. make sense and are memorable to them. Thus, although a parent (tutor) might make suggestions or stimulate imagination, the decision on Cueing rests wholly with the child.

Once Cues are decided upon, the pair say the Cues out loud simultaneously (Step 5). The tutee then says the Cues out loud (Step 6) while the tutor writes the word down on scrap paper to this 'dictation'; thus the tutee is provided with a demonstration or model of the required behaviour. At Step 7, the tutor says the Cues out loud while the tutee writes the word down. At Step 8, the tutee says the Cues and writes the word simultaneously.

At Step 9, the tutee is required by the tutor to write the word as fast as possible (the tutee may or may not decide to recite the Cues out loud at this Step, but may well recite them sub-vocally). At Step 10, the tutee again reads the word out loud as a reminder of the meaningful context in which the target word hopefully has remained embedded.

4 Points to remember

The 4 Points cover aspects of the technical application:

1) At every attempt at writing a target word, the tutor is required to cover up previous attempts on the work paper, to avoid the possibility of direct copying, although in fact some tutees prefer to do this themselves.

2) Every time there is a written attempt on a target word, the tutee checks the attempt and the tutor only intervenes if the tutee proves unable to check his or her own attempt accurately. If tutees have written a word incorrectly, they are encouraged to cross it out very vigorously to assist its deletion from their memory.

3) At an incorrect attempt, the correction procedure is merely that the pair return to the Step preceding the one at which the error was made.

4) Tutors are required to praise at various junctures which are specified quite clearly. Precise details of the nature of praise and the criteria for its application are intended to promote higher frequency and regularity of praise, as well as more effective use of it.

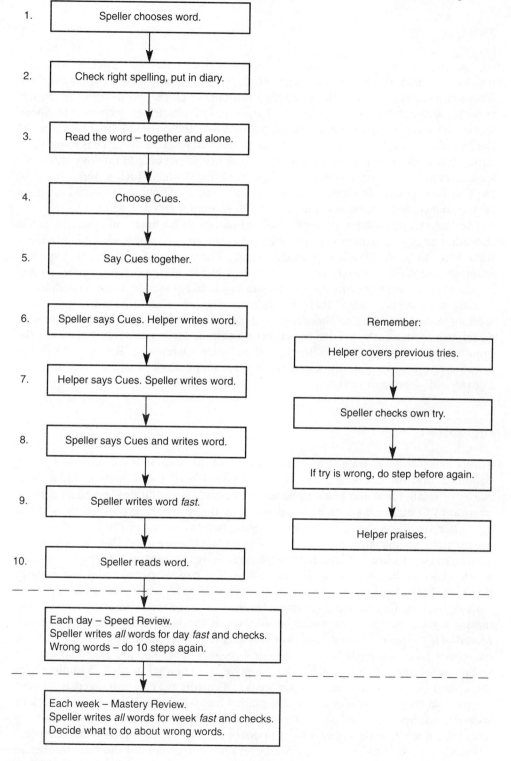

Figure 7.1 *Cued Spelling: the 10 steps.*

2 Reviews

At the end of each tutoring session, there is a Speed Review, wherein the tutor requires the tutee to write all the target words for that session as fast as possible from dictation in random order. The tutee then self-checks all the words with the 'master version' in the Cued Spelling Diary. Target words which are incorrect at Speed Review have the 10 Steps applied again, perhaps with the choice of different Cues. At the end of each week, a Mastery Review is conducted, wherein the tutee is required to write all the target words for the whole week as fast as possible in random order. No specific error correction procedure is prescribed for Mastery Review and it is left to the pair to negotiate for themselves what they wish to do about errors. Many pairs choose to include failed words in the next week's target words.

The technique has been designed and structured to be highly interactive, but in operation presents as democratic rather than didactic. It is intended to provide a framework to 'scaffold' self-managed learning. There is good evidence that spellers naturally use a great variety of strategies in a highly idiosyncratic manner, so any requirement to use a specific mnemonic strategy is likely merely to further inhibit an already poor speller. Also, there is evidence that when children select their own spelling words, they tend to choose more difficult words but are as successful as with easier words chosen by adults. Work on mnemonic strategies has emphasized the importance of meaningfulness to the subject (see Oxley and Topping, 1990, for relevant references). Thus the Cued Spelling technique fits in well with recent trends towards individualized and self-governed learning of spelling skills.

Organization

Tutors and tutees are trained together. A talk on the method is accompanied with a demonstration on video, since a live demonstration of Cued Spelling often lacks clarity of small detail and tends to be less successful. An additional practical demonstration of Cueing using a chalkboard and soliciting from the group different words and different cueing strategies for each word is helpful in making the point that there are no 'right' cueing strategies, only effective and ineffective ones. Pairs are given a 10 Step chart (see Figure 7.1) to refer to while practising the method with the tutee's own words (chosen before the meeting), using the paper, pencils and dictionaries provided. Individualized feedback and further coaching is provided as necessary.

Cued Spelling Diaries are given to each pair, each page including space to write the master version of up to ten words on all days of the week, together with boxes to record daily Speed Review and weekly Mastery Review scores and spaces for comments from tutor (daily) and teacher (weekly). The pair are asked to use the technique on about five words per day (implying a minimum time of 15 minutes) for three days per week for the next six weeks. The tutees are encouraged to choose words from their school spelling books, graded free writing, relevant project work or special Cued Spelling displays of common problem words, and collect these (in a CS 'collecting book'), so they always have a pool of suitable words from which to choose.

Tutees are asked to bring their CS Diaries once each week for the class teacher to view and keep watch on the words chosen, since some children choose words they already know while others choose extremely difficult words of very doubtful utility – in this case a formula of '3 for everyday use and 2 just for fun' might need to be prescribed. Participating children might receive a badge and parents a higher readability information sheet with further ideas on Cueing.

Cued Spelling has been much used in a reciprocal peer tutoring format, it being relatively easy to refer to a master version of correctness in a dictionary, i.e. correct and successful learning is not dependent on the omniscience of the tutor. In reciprocal tutoring, the fact that everyone gets to be a tutor is good for the self-esteem of both members of the pair, who of course end up learning their partner's words as well as their own.

Effectiveness

Oxley and Topping (1990) reported on a project in which eight 7- and 8-year-old pupils were tutored by eight 9-year-old pupils in the same vertically grouped class in a small rural school. This cross-age, cross-ability peer tutoring project was found to yield striking social benefits and the children spontaneously generalized peer tutoring to other curricular areas. Subjective feedback from both tutors and tutees was very positive. The self-concept as a speller of both tutees and tutors showed a marked positive shift compared to that of non-participant children, especially so for the tutees. After six weeks, a total Mastery Review of all target words yielded average scores of 66 per cent correct. Results on two norm-referenced tests of spelling were equivocal, since although the scores of both tutees and tutors were strikingly improved at post-test, so were those of non-participant children in the same class.

Peer tutored Cued Spelling in a class-wide, same-age, same-ability reciprocal tutoring format was reported by Brierley *et al.* (1989). All pupils in the three first-year mixed-ability classes (aged 9 to 10 years) in a middle school participated. Tutor and tutee roles changed each week. All the children were trained in a single group meeting. After six weeks, a total Mastery Review of all words covered yielded average scores of 80 per cent. On a norm-referenced test of spelling, the average gain for all children was 0.65 years of spelling age during the six-week project, certainly many times more than normal expectations. Subjective feedback from the children was very positive, 84 per cent of the children reporting feeling they were better spellers after the project.

A study of parent tutored Cued Spelling with children of 8 years of age and of the normal range of spelling ability (France *et al.*, 1993) indicated that the intervention appeared to be effective in differentially raising the spelling attainments of participants as compared to non-participants.

It can be argued that any method involving extra time on task at spelling and extra valuable parental attention and approval related to spelling might be likely to yield differential gains. A study by Watt and Topping (1993) compared Cued Spelling with traditional spelling homework (an alternative intervention involving equal tutor attention and equal time on spelling tasks), compared the relative effectiveness of parent and peer tutored Cued Spelling and assessed the generalization of the effect of Cued Spelling into subsequent continuous free writing. On a norm-referenced spelling test, Cued Spellers gained over two months of spelling age for each chronological month elapsed, while the traditional spelling homework comparison group of more able spellers gained only half a month of spelling age per month. The average score at final Mastery Review of words used in the programme was 93 per cent correct. Parent and peer tutoring were equally effective. Pre-post analysis of written work was based on samples of writing from Cued Spellers and comparison children. The average number of spelling errors per page reduced from 8.5 to 4.62 for the Cued Spellers and from 3.7 to 2.1 for the comparison children, who clearly had a lower error rate to start with and thus had less room for improvement.

PARAMETERS OF SUCCESSFUL SYSTEMS

There is now an ever-expanding wealth of knowledge and experience about systems for tutoring by non-professionals and from this it is possible to distil a checklist of engineering criteria likely to maximize success. Those educators inventing their own local procedures may find this helpful.

Objectives. Whatever benefits the programme is expected to have should be clearly articulated, not least for marketing/recruitment and subsequent evaluation purposes. The programme must not interfere with the regular school curriculum, but should dovetail into it. Keep the objectives modest for your first attempt.

Ability differential. Be clear with potential volunteers (and yourself) about the degree of ceiling competence needed in the tutor and the feasible range of ability differential (if any) in the pair. If tutor competence is in doubt there must be reference to some acceptable master source to verify correctness, since over-learning of errors would leave the tutee worse off than when they started.

Flexibility. Procedures should be applicable without major modification to participants of different ages and abilities with different needs, different learning styles and different ambitions, and in different physical environments. Clearly, the more specific the chosen materials, the less possible it is to be flexible. Likewise, the procedure should enable and facilitate the tutee to deploy a range of strategies, rather than strait-jacketing them into a single professionally preferred one. Activity should preferably be varied and multi-sensory, with alternation between different styles of reading, listening, writing, speaking and so on.

Interaction. Procedures should involve response (inter-) activity from both members of the pair, since if one declines into being merely a checker or passive audience, motivation will soon evaporate. The procedure should promote a high rate of time on task, with an emphasis on keeping going: maintaining the flow of activity increases the number of learning opportunities and helps stave off anxiety.

Satisfaction. Both members of the pair must gain some intrinsic satisfaction from the activity. Basically, it's got to be fun.

Self-management. The tutee should have a substantial degree of control over the process of tutoring and preferably over the curriculum content and materials as well. Tutee control of the amount of support offered by the tutor is especially valuable. Tutees should be able to exercise choice and initiative; deprived of the opportunity, they will never develop the skills.

Instructions. These should be simple, clear and above all specific. Instructions are probably best given as a series of finely task-analysed steps. Both tutor and tutee should be given very clear (interactive) job descriptions, since without this the process of tutoring can rapidly degenerate into a muddle. The provision of a simple visual map, chart or other cue to remind the pair of how it is all supposed to work may well be helpful.

Materials. Especially for children with learning difficulties, the curriculum materials in use should be individualized to match the tutee's needs and interests.

Error control. The tutee should not feel as if they are making many errors, since this is bad for morale. Control of errors should be through teacher-, tutor- or tutee-selected materials, careful accommodation by the tutor to the tutee's natural pacing and the provision of swift non-intrusive support. Errors are potentially the major stress point in the tutoring relationship – but be alert to other possible causes of stress and fatigue in the system.

Error signalling. When an error is made, feedback should be swift, but not so immediate that the tutee has no opportunity to detect the error. Error signalling should be positive and minimally interruptive.

Error correction. A swift, simple and specific error correction procedure must be clearly laid down, which is seen by the tutee as supportive and draws minimum attention to the error. There should be a strong emphasis on self-checking and self-correction, both higher order skills which need to be fostered.

Eliminate negatives. 'Don't say don't.' Prescribe positive error signalling and correction procedures which are incompatible with the negative and intrusive behaviours, rather than giving tutors a list of prohibited behaviours.

Accentuate positives. Be specific about requirements for praise, including what to praise (especially self-correction and initiative-taking), frequency, verbal and non-verbal aspects, and the need for variety and relevance to the task. Deploy individual token or tangible rewards only if all else fails. Some group acknowledgement of participation via badges, certificates, etc. might be valuable and acceptable, and is useful advertising.

Discussion. Emphasize that discussion by the pair promotes and confirms full understanding by the tutee in order to avoid mechanical conformity to the surface requirements of the task by either member of the pair.

Modelling. Ensure the tutoring procedure can include a demonstration of competence by the tutor which may be imitated (or improved upon) by the tutee, rather than over-reliance on verbal prompting. Tutors should also be encouraged to model more general desirable behaviours, such as enthusiasm for the topic in hand. Participant pairs will also serve as models for other pairs, and the project group should deliberately be kept in contact so that the social dynamic adds a further dimension to motivation. Remember the co-ordinating professional must model continuing enthusiasm for the programme!

Training. This is essential, and should be done with both members of the pair present via verbal, visual and written information-giving (bilingual if necessary), coupled with a demonstration, immediate practice, feedback, further coaching and subsequent monitoring. Training individual pairs is very costly, and well-organized group training is as effective while also serving to develop group support and solidarity.

Contracting. Specify an initial trial period and be very clear about the time costs for the pair should they participate. Remember little and often will be most effective, especially with tutees with learning difficulties. Expect pairs to clearly contract into participation. Ensure there is mutual feedback about effectiveness and proposed improvements by the end of the trial period. Discuss continuation options and seek contract renewal, possibly in a range of formats, by participants.

Monitoring. Emphasize self-checking. Some simple form of self-recording is desirable, and both members of the pair should participate in this. Periodic checking of these records by the co-ordinating professional is a minimal form of accountability of high cost-effectiveness. This may need to be supplemented in some cases by verbal enquiry of one or both members of the pair and/or direct observation of the pair.

Evaluating. Be clear as to the objectives of evaluation. Feeding back to the participants data on their success might increase their motivation. Publicizing the data might expand subsequent recruitment or attract additional funding. How should you review the extent to which the curriculum content of the tutoring has actually been mastered and retained in the longer term? Criterion-referenced tests closely allied to the tutoring process are likely to give the most valid (and most impressive) results, but a norm-referenced test in the same general area is a more stringent test of generalization of skills acquired through tutoring and might be construed as more 'objective' by outsiders.

Generalization and maintenance. You will need to build in means for continuing review, feedback and injection of further novelty and enthusiasm if pairs are to keep going and maintain the use of their skills. Again, the social dynamic of the group is important. You will need to consciously foster the use of these skills to different materials and contexts for new purposdes. When pairs have developed sufficient awareness of effective tutoring to begin to design their own systems, you know you have done a good job. As tutees themselves recruit a wider range of tutors, the tutee becomes even more central as quality controller of the tutoring process.

CONCLUSION

It seems clear that peer tutoring can be a very valuable and cost-effective tool in any teacher's repertoire of pedagogic methods. Although it is of broad-spectrum applicability, there is no suggestion here that it should be used constantly or routinely, since it is certainly no universal panacea. Selective and well-organized application of the method, coupled with subsequent reflection upon the processes and products of each session, will preserve its potency.

Creative individuals have continued to widen the range of operation of peer tutoring in recent years, yielding an ever-expanding typology of tutoring but resulting in looser definitions and greater difficulty in differentiating peer tutoring from other related approaches. Peer tutoring is now applied to rote learning, basic literacy and numeracy skills, to curricular areas characterized by very complex information and to those involving high-order concept formation. Given ingenuity on the part of the teacher, the scope seems endless.

Peer tutoring must not suffer death by dilution. In particular, organization of projects must be and remain clear, precise and well thought through. Correspondingly, there must be no assumption that positive evaluation results reported for one method will necessarily apply to other methods or variants thereon. Every new development will need to be evaluated in its own right.

Lest this sounds too oppressively serious, it is as well to end with a reminder that children like peer tutoring because it's fun! It can also be fun, as well as richly rewarding professionally, for the teacher.

REFERENCES

Allen, V.L. (ed.) (1976) *Children as Teachers: Theory and Research on Tutoring.* New York: Academic Press.

Brierley, M., Hutchinson, P., Topping, K. and Walker, C. (1989) Reciprocal peer tutored cued spelling with ten year olds. *Paired Learning*, 5, 136-40.

Cicirelli, V.G. (1976) Siblings teach siblings. In V.L. Allen (ed.), *Children as Teachers: Theory and Research on Tutoring.* New York: Academic Press.

Cohen, P.A., Kulik, J.A. and Kulik, C.-L.C. (1982) Educational outcomes of tutoring: a meta-analysis of findings. *American Educational Research Journal*, **191**, 237-48.

Cook, S.B., Scruggs, T.E., Mastropieri, M.A. and Casto, G.C. (1986) Handicapped students as tutors. *Journal of Special Education*, **19**, 483-92.

Croft, S. and Topping, K. (1992) *Paired Science: A Resource Pack for Parents and Children.* Dundee: University of Dundee, Centre for Paired Learning.

Custer, J.D. and Osguthorpe, R.T. (1983) Improving social acceptance by training handicapped students to tutor their non-handicapped peers. *Exceptional Children*, **50**, 173-5.

Devin-Sheehan, L., Feldman, R.S. and Allen, V.L. (1976) Research on children tutoring children: a critical review. *Review of Educational Research*, **46**, 355-85.

Fantuzzo, J.W., Polite, K. and Grayson, N. (1990) An evaluation of reciprocal peer tutoring across elementary school settings. *Journal of School Psychology*, **28**, 309-23.

Fitz-Gibbon, C.T. and Reay, D.G. (1982) Peer tutoring: brightening up foreign language teaching in an urban comprehensive school. *British Journal of Language Teaching*, **20**, 39-44.

Foot, H.C., Morgan, M.J. and Shute, R.J. (eds) (1990) *Children Helping Children.* Chichester: Wiley.

France, L., Topping, K. and Revell, K. (1993) Parent tutored cued spelling. *Support for Learning*, **8**, 11-15.

Gartner, S., Kohler, M. and Riessman, F. (1971) *Children Teach Children: Learning by Teaching.* New York: Harper & Row.

Goodlad, S. and Hirst, B. (1989) *Peer Tutoring: A Guide to Learning by Teaching.* London: Kogan Page.

Karegianes, M.L., Pascarella, E.T. and Pflaum, S.W. (1980) The effects of peer editing on the writing proficiency of low-achieving tenth-grade students. *Journal of Educational Research*, **73**, 203-7.

Maher, C.A. (1984) Handicapped adolescents as cross-age tutors: programme description and evaluation. *Exceptional Children*, **51**, 56-63.

Osguthorpe, R.T. and Scruggs, T.E. (1990) Special education students as tutors: a review and analysis. In S. Goodlad and B. Hirst (eds), *Peer Tutoring: A Guide to Learning by Teaching.* London: Kogan Page.

Oxley, L. and Topping, K. (1990) Peer-tutored cued spelling with seven. *British Educational Research Journal*, **16**, 63-78.

Palincsar, A.S. and Brown, A.L. (1986) Interactive teaching to promote independent learning from text. *The Reading Teacher*, **39**, 771-7.

Pigott, H.E., Fantuzzo, J.W. and Clement, P.W. (1986) The effects of reciprocal peer tutoring and group contingencies on the academic performance of elementary school children. *Journal of Applied Behavior Analysis*, **19**, 93-8.

Posen, B. (1983) Peer tutoring among young offenders: two experiments. Unpublished M.Ed. thesis, University of Newcastle-upon-Tyne.

Sharpley, A.M. and Sharpley, C.F. (1981) Peer tutoring: a review of the literature. *Collected Original Resources in Education*, **5**, 7-C11.

Topping, K.J. (1988) *The Peer Tutoring Handbook: Promoting Co-operative Learning.* London: Croom Helm.

Topping, K. (1990) Peer tutored paired reading: outcome data from ten projects. In S. Goodlad and B. Hirst (eds), *Peer Tutoring: A Guide to Learning by Teaching.* London: Kogan Page.

Topping, K. and Lindsay, G.A. (1992) Paired reading: a review of literature. *Research Papers in Education*, **7**, 199-246.

Topping, K. and Whiteley, M. (1990) Participant evaluation of parent tutored and peer tutored projects in reading. *Educational Research*, **32**, 14-32.

Watt, J.M. and Topping, K.J. (1993) Cued spelling: a comparative study of parent and peer tutoring. *Educational Psychology in Practice*, **9**, 95-103.

Wheldall, K. and Colmar, S. (1990) Peer tutoring for low-progress readers using 'Pause, Prompt and Praise'. In H.C. Foot, M.J. Morgan and R.J. Shute (eds), *Children Helping Children.* Chichester: Wiley.

Chapter 8

The Social Relational Approach

Eric Hall

EDITORS' INTRODUCTION

The chapter by Eric Hall is distinct from other chapters in Part 2 – it presents an approach that should underlie the surrounding chapters. Most educators will understand Hall's basic argument at a 'gut level'. If the social relationships between pupils in the class and between teachers and pupils are sound, supportive and trusting then class members will interact more happily and successfully. Hall does not identify specific groupings and group sizes and does not make major claims for enhancing academic achievement. Yet, specific tasks (communication, circletime, etc.) do require pairs and larger groupings of pupils to work together, share information and solve problems. The reader should bear in mind that pedagogic relationships between group size, task assigned and group composition apply in the social as well as the intellectual field.

  The theoretical building blocks that characterize Hall's approach are mainly from humanistic and experiential psychology. Obviously, reference to specific learning tasks are not included here – for it is assumed that social and emotional development are the bases for intellectual development (a theme repeated in chapters 2, 4, 5, 6 and 7). Hall argues that social and emotional development is often related to personal and social education and is given only low stature within the National Curriculum. Certainly this chapter should raise key questions concerning this accorded stature. Hall amply demonstrates the importance of personal and social education by citing cases where the social relational approach has improved the behaviour of disruptive pupils and disruptive classes.

  Finally, this chapter is not simply a theoretical treatise that argues for a greater consideration and planning of social relationships in the classroom; it presents a number of useful techniques and cites many references for the practitioner to follow up. Hall also indicates that social relationships are developmental in nature; involving trust, communication and the ability to collaboratively resolve problems.

INTRODUCTION

A piece of advice I was given as a teacher in training was to start tough and then let things go a bit once a good relationship had been established with the class. The assumption behind this advice is that things can only get worse as the class learns how to take advantage of weakness and what they can get away with. This advice was probably appropriate in view of the lack of instruction in classroom management. Using this approach, the control of what is happening in the classroom remains entirely with the teacher and this control is maintained by fear.

In contrast, consider the possibility of having a set of skills and activities designed for working with a class which is difficult to control, in which there are poor relationships between the pupils and a general lack of involvement in the content of the lessons. By using these skills the class changes into a group of co-operative children, who listen and show caring for each other, who become more involved in their general classroom work and request repeats of the activities they have done. Here the pupils have a far greater control over what happens in the classroom and the students have become self-motivated.

This chapter explores ways in which this situation can be realized in schools by improving social relations and emotional development through effective group work. 'Effectiveness' in relation to educational processes is a notoriously elusive concept and definitions will vary according to the policy of the school or the personal philosophy of the individual teacher. For the purposes of this chapter, I will define effective as the accomplishment of the educational goals set by the class teacher on behalf of or with the co-operative pupil group. That children are often placed in groups in the primary classroom is well established as a means of organizing the post-Plowden (1968) primary school classroom and is increasingly and systematically used as a method-ological tool in the secondary school, although many researchers have challenged that pupils actually collaborate in groups. However, the sheer variety of different approaches to the organization of working in groups is reflected in the diversity of techniques outlined in this book.

Working in groups is often regarded as a convenient vehicle for pooling the intellectual abilities of pupils in order to investigate a topic or area of study (content) and although the teacher may be concerned about the relationships within the group, it is rare for the group to reflect directly on the ways in which they are working together (process). It is even rarer for the teacher to feel that she has the knowledge, skills or expertise to facilitate the processing. In this chapter we argue that effective working in groups requires the systematic and rigorous development of interpersonal skills; skills which pupils in schools appear to be expected to acquire by chance or simply as a result of being involved in groups. The necessary interpersonal skills for working in groups can be learned and the teacher plays a vital role in the initiation, monitoring and evaluation of these skills if it is to be systematic and coherent as opposed to haphazard and serendipitous learning 'despite' the teacher.

There is evidence from research carried out in primary schools (Galton and Williamson, 1992) that to simply put pupils into groups sitting around a table does not mean that the children involved are working as a group; they may be working individually. The product of the work group may turn out to be largely the result of the efforts of one of the more capable or dominant members. Research in the US (Hertz-Lazarowitz and Miller, 1992) indicates that there are necessary conditions for effective working in co-operative groups and it seems reasonable to assume that the same principles apply to all forms of group work in schools. Both Hertz-Lazarowitz (1992) and Johnson and Johnson (1992) regard the development of interpersonal skills as one of these necessary conditions.

The following are some of the interpersonal skills that could be introduced to pupils:

- Giving effective feedback
- Expression of feelings in the 'here and now'
- Listening, attending and turn-taking
- Responding, questioning, summarizing and clarifying
- Drawing out, encouraging and the use of humour
- Awareness of interpersonal style – aggressive, manipulative, passive
- Awareness of non-verbal communication

At the time of writing there is a move in primary schools, instigated by central government policy, away from working in groups towards more didactic approaches for individuals in streamed groups or classes, with an emphasis on basic academic skills such as reading, writing, spelling and number work. Few would deny the importance of these literacy and numeracy skills and it is unlikely that hitherto any primary schools actually or wilfully neglected them. Part of the argument for this so called 'return to the basics' is that the acquisition of such basic skills are a necessary preparation for 'life' and the world of work. However, it should be noted that the technological and managerial revolution of the past thirty years emphasizes 'interpersonal competence' as much as literacy and numeracy.

It is ironic that the current developments in organizational management theory (Morgan, 1986) stress the need to flatten hierarchies and to talk about differentiation by role, the importance of working in groups, the need for interpersonal skills and the ability to use personal authority in decision making. As the world of work changes, these relational skills are seen as important as the acquisition of knowledge, which can rapidly become out of date. It is significant that these personal and interpersonal skills are described as 'Lifeskills' (Hopson and Scally, 1981). If these are to be squeezed out of the curriculum, the extent to which education is a preparation for life is diminished.

The acknowledgement by classroom teachers and employers of the importance of 'Lifeskills' led to the development of a wide range of forms of personal and social education. The books and publications related to this development were largely concerned with secondary education (Ryder and Campbell, 1988), but a similar approach was also beginning to filter into the primary school, particularly with projects around the notion of enhancing the self-concept. These primary developments are reviewed by Lang (1988) and in evaluations such as Hall and Delaney (1992). The evaluations which are reviewed below indicate that the promotion of Lifeskills and personal and social education as part of the curriculum has a positive effect on the co-operative climate of the classroom group, which is bound to have a positive effect on smaller working groups.

Most of these activities emerged from developments in the United States out of the experiential learning structures which are derived from the tradition of humanistic psychology. The exercises have had a strong influence in the practical training of managers and helping professionals. One offshoot of these developments is humanistic education (Hamachek, 1977; Hall and Hall, 1988), which is similarly difficult to define, though five main characteristics are typical of a humanistic approach:

1. There is an emphasis on personal meanings, how individuals perceive themselves, their values, choices and meanings. Thus, the self-concept has a central role in humanistic education and the relation between the self and the subject-matter to be learned plays an important part in the learning process.
2. The relationship between the teacher and the pupil and amongst the pupils themselves also plays an important part in the learning process. This notion is explored eloquently in Carl Rogers' (1983) *Freedom to Learn for the 80s*, which provides substantial clinical and experimental evidence to support the primacy of the social relational perspective and consolidates the earlier reviews by Brophy and Good (1974).
3. Individuals and groups are considered integrated wholes rather than as a collection of parts. As it is proposed in general systems theory (Bertalanffy, 1950) and applied to education by Provis (1992), the individual or the group is more than the sum of its individual parts. The pattern of relationships adds to the identity of the group and if the pattern of relationships is changed, then the individual or group acquires a different personality, with different outcomes in terms of behaviour and quality of achievement.
4. Awareness of feelings is considered to be of equal importance as intellectual understanding when thinking about the process of learning. This is an essential aspect of an holistic approach to education and is an important element of self-image, values related to the subject matter and the quality of the relationships within the classroom groups. Humanistic educators are often criticized for laying undue emphasis on feelings rather than intellectual development. A more accurate position is that learning cannot be properly understood without a serious consideration of feelings.
5. Experiential learning is the cornerstone of humanistic education. Learning from experience has long played an important part in primary education in the United Kingdom and in areas such as Nuffield Science and the Humanities Project in the secondary curriculum. This is, however, given an added dimension in humanistic education as there is a strong emphasis on learning from experience about the self and the immediate relationships within the work group. Conscious and directed attention is paid to the process as well as the content of learning.

Although the emphasis of this chapter is on humanistic education, I am not suggesting that this approach should necessarily dominate the activities of the classroom. Other theoretical models such as behaviourism and psychodynamics provide useful explanations of what is happening for individuals and groups in the classroom and certainly in the case of behaviour modification can provide practical solutions that improve classroom management and discipline in the classroom for both pupils and teachers. Didactic teaching and rote learning may have a place in the repertoire of every teacher.

The use of experiential learning considered here is only one of many approaches to social learning. There are other related and overlapping models used in schools which in varying degrees take a more cognitive approach to social relations. Values clarification (Simon, 1972) involves the discussion of beliefs, attitudes and values related to all aspects of living and can be applied by the teachers to ongoing issues in the classroom. Pring (1984) discusses the use of hypothetical moral dilemmas based on the work of Kohlberg (1971) to stimulate discussion for moral development as part of a programme of personal and social education. This approach can result in a heated discussion which may touch on important ethical issues, but may still remain distanced from immediate classroom concerns. A recent development in secondary schools in the UK is to replace personal and social education with a form of citizenship education (Lynch, 1992), which again moves to a discussion of issues rather than an examination of what is happening in the immediate classroom situation.

The thrust of the argument in this chapter is that the introduction of humanistic approaches to social relations learning, which makes use of experiential learning and focuses the 'here and now' experience of the classroom group, can have a substantial effect on the quality of the relationships and learning in a classroom group and in its subgroups. The integration of the practical activities associated with humanistic education will have a positive effect on the lives of both teachers and pupils by improving relationships, increasing friendship within the class and reducing the incidence of disprutive behaviour.

There is an abundance of sources providing materials for working in a humanistic mode which helps to foster the social relations in groups of children. These include Canfield and Wells (1976), Castillo (1974), Ballard (1982), Hall *et al.* (1990), de Mille (1967), White (1991), Thacker *et al.* (1992), Galloway (1990). These sources offer a wide range of practical activities which provide pupils with an opportunity to become more aware of themselves and how they relate to each other. In the next section, a selected sample of these activities are presented, which are then illustated with some case histories of teachers working with groups of children.

COMMUNICATION AND SOCIAL SKILLS

Experiential exercises usually involve pupils talking to each other and this has the potential to have a positive influence on communication skills. The pupils are, of course, communicating a great deal with each other, particularly outside the classroom. These patterns of communication often involve the learning of habits which are not helpful in the long term, such as racism, sexism, stereotyping, name-calling, taunting and so on. Just as with learning to drive a car or ride a horse, it is possible to realize the act wthout doing it skilfully. Patterns of relationships among pupils appear to become fixed and the targets for acceptance and rejection may remain unchanged for long periods of time.

A number of exercises focus directly on what have been identified as important communication skills. Indeed most experiential learning situations relate to communication in some way. There is evidence (Rubin, 1980; Hartup, 1978; Foot *et al.*, 1980) that children learn social skills from their peers rather than from adults and that this appears to result from peers with similar cognitive and social abilities. The process of experiential learning in the classroom which directly involves communication provides a potent situation in which this peer group learning can take place, without necessarily involving the teacher directly in the learning process. In my view, the social relational approach advocated provides a broader mix of relationships in terms of level of social and cognitive skills. The development of friendship and the ability to join a group are important spin-offs from communication and social skills training.

Interpersonal and social skills do appear to be related to popularity and liking. Gottman *et al.* (1975) found that the more popular children in school were those who paid attention to other children, praised them, showed affection and went along with what the other pupils wanted to do. Those who frequently ignored others, refused to co-operate, ridiculed, blamed or threatened others tended to be disliked by their peers. Oden and Asher (1977) showed how a four-week programme in communication, non-verbal skills, co-operation, participation and helping significantly increased the children's popularity and the gains were still in evidence one year later.

A high proportion of the experiential activities presented in the books of exercises listed above provide exercises that are related to some aspects of communication and social skills. Here are some practical examples:

> 1. Listening. Pupils of all ages and abilities can be encouraged to learn the basic listening skills that are included in most forms of counselling skills training programmes by using the experiential model provided by Egan (1975). Pupils are divided into dyads to try out the skills which are recommended and have been demonstrated empirically (Ivey and Authier, 1978; Hargie, 1989) to contribute to more effective communication. These include: sitting with an open and attentive posture, encouraging the other person to talk by head-nodding and so on, reflecting content, reflecting feeling, self-disclosure and confrontation. In essence, pupils are being trained in generic counselling skills and it seems reasonable to assume that if they are becoming more empathic then they are more likely to get on with their peers, as is suggested in the Gottman *et al.* (1975) study described above.
>
> 2. Turn–taking. A small group of five to seven pupils can be invited to discuss a topic using the following rules. Only one person is to talk at one time and can only talk when he or she is holding an object provided by the teacher. If pupils want to say something, they have to ask for the object and are not allowed to contribute until it is in their hands. This is similar to passing the conch in William Golding's *Lord of the Flies*, and teachers have provided a conch-like shell for this purpose. A variation of this structure is to insist that the person who asks for the object repeats back to the speaker the gist of what has been said and gets the speaker's agreement before they can take over the object. This activity helps to develop the skill of reflection of content. At the end of the exercise, the pupils discuss what it felt like to engage in the exercise.

CIRCLETIME

This set of techniques, designed by Ballard (1982), aims to encourage pupils to participate in discussion sessions. It includes some of the communication skills described in the previous section, but it is described separately as it provides a neat package for working in the classroom. It is intended for groups of 6 to 12, but the same principles apply to sharing experience in the whole classroom group. The pupils sit in a circle with the teacher, possibly on the floor to reduce the teacher's perceived control over the situation. Then the groups are given topics to discuss which are bound to relate to the experience of all the members of the group, such as 'My favourite time of day', 'What was it like for you to change from primary to secondary school?' or 'What sort of things do you dream about?'. Every member of the group is invited to take a turn and the other group members are taught how to respond with reflection of feeling.

> You sound very excited about the chance of going on the trip.

> You seem to be upset about having to go out into the playground at lunch time.

This encourages an emphasis on statements of feeling in the group discussions. This in turn promotes a high level of self-disclosure and much supportive attention is paid to these disclosures involving participation from all members of the group. Ballard (1982) provides a long list of possible topics, which can be easily elaborated by the creative teacher. With a short period of training, a teacher could provide an extensive affective curriculum. Circletime can be used over an extended period of time or for a few minutes at the beginning of the day or in a tutor period (White, 1991).

It would be too much to expect a class of pupils to suddenly switch to this way of working if they are used to being taught didactically. The pupils have to learn how to contribute to the whole group and how to make supportive and helpful comments to pupils who have spoken. It is important not to give up if the first attempt does not appear to be successful. The opportunity to express feelings is invariably perceived as positive by the pupils, even though they may not appear to have been co-operating in the early stages of the activity.

USING FANTASY, IMAGERY AND DRAWING

A further set of related techniques is the use of aspects of fantasy, imagery and drawing. These are often described as right brain activities, based on the model which suggests that the processes such as logical reasoning and thinking in words are in some way mediated by the left side of the cortex of the brain and other processes such as thinking in images, experiencing feelings and relaxation are in some way mediated by the right side of the cortex. The physiology of this model might be open to question, but it does provide a useful image for the clear separation between these two sets of activities.

On the basis of the reports of a substantial number of classroom teachers (Hall *et al.*, 1990), there are several outcomes from introducing aspects of fantasy to classroom groups which make an important contribution to the social relations in the classroom. The pupils become more relaxed, speak more quietly, treat each other more caringly and become more co-operative with each other. Sometimes there have been reports from teachers who have taken over the class from the teacher who has conducted the fantasy exercise to the effect: 'What on earth have you done to this group, I have never known them to be so quiet and co-operative.' Pupils appear to be willing to listen to what their peers have to say and respect it. Since there are no 'right answers', any contribution is acceptable and it is not possible for a dominant member of the group to do most of the work towards completing the task. A common report from teachers is that a child in the group who had never spoken in front of the class before talks about their fantasy experience and has the reward of being listened to with respect.

This section will limit the discussion to a process described as scripted fantasy by Hall *et al.* (1990), though there is a rich array of techniques for using forms of imagery in the classroom. Scripted fantasy involves the classroom teacher settling the class down, inviting them to close their eyes and reading them a script which provides a stimulus for the generation of images from the children. Here is a practical example:

> The teacher asks the group to relax, close their eyes, take three deep breaths and then slowly reads the following script:

> 'I want you to imagine you are by the sea – it doesn't have to be a place you know. [pause] Have a good look around. What can you see? What does the sea look like? Are there other people around or are you alone? [pause] What can you hear? What sort of noise is the sea making? [pause] Can you smell the sea? [pause] What are you doing – lying – sitting – walking? [pause] Feel the wind blowing in from the sea – is it warm or cold? Try

and taste the sea in the air. [pause] Now try and get the sense that something is about to happen – that someone is coming along the shore to meet you – just let the pictures come – who comes? [pause] What do you do together – what do you say to each other – what happens? [long pause] When it is right for you, take a deeper breath and begin to come back to the room. Perhaps open your eyes and have a look around.'

Care has to be taken in choosing a script as, in this example, there may be pupils who have never been to the seaside. Generally, primary-age children come to enjoy working with imagery very quickly and invariably ask for more. Young children can experience visual imagery without closing their eyes and project pictures into the space in front of them. With infants it is possible to suggest that a mouse is running round the classroom (de Mille, 1967) and the pupils will follow the imaginary mouse around the room, often pointing and laughing at its antics. Some pupils have difficulty in closing their eyes in a public situation and there is no need to insist. Violet Oaklander (1978), who provides a moving account of the use of a range of media for generating forms of imagery, suggests using the phrase 'You can peep if you want to.' More pupils appear to co-operate simply because they have been given the choice. Alternatively children who do not wish to take part in the exercise can be invited to sit quietly at the back of the room so as not to disturb the others. Having sat at the back, the pupils invariably report having had a fantasy and from then on, tend to join in the general activities of the class in a more co-operative manner.

Pupils can be asked to draw a picture of their fantasy experience or write about it. If the children are invited to pin up their drawings to display to the whole group, there is a high level of motivation from the pupils to look at each other's drawings and a serious involved silence falls over the group as they do this. Writing generated by the imagery is reported to be of a high quality and to include a high proportion of feeling statements (Hall and Kirkland, 1984).

The use of scripted fantasy may appear to be an esoteric activity and far removed from the demands of basic skills and the National Curriculum and yet it can also be used to learn factual material and difficult abstract concepts in areas such as maths and science (Hall *et al.*, 1990). It has been used to generate empathy in history lessons and for the practice of skills in sport. Other applications include the mental rehearsal of social skills, anticipating future events and goal setting. Research into memory has always emphasized the superiority of learning using images over words and so there are strong academic arguments for developing skills at using imagery, apart from its use in personal and social education.

Clearly the teacher has to be sensitive to the specific needs of the group they are working with, but in my experience, nursery school children, experienced teachers and all stages in between can benefit from forms of the exercises which have been described above.

CASE HISTORIES

In order to illustrate these general principles and activities in action, a series of short case histories are offered of work with individual classes which also involve elements of evaluation.

The first project (Wooster and Carson, 1982) examined the effects of a programme of social and communication skills on a class of 26 8-year-olds. The pupils were described by their teacher: 'This is the most difficult group of children I have ever taught.' Their behaviour exhibited spitefulness, rejection, bickering, tale-telling, sulking, irresponsibility, isolation and a fear of new experiences. Measures of reading ability and self-concept revealed a pattern of low achievement and low self-esteem. Some parents had even threatened to withdraw their children from what was perceived to be a very destructive social climate. The group was described as coming from socially and economically deprived backgrounds. The class included six travellers' children and the social relations between them and the rest of the class were not good.

The class had several changes of teacher when they were taken over by one of the writers of the report. She had recently been influenced by a course which involved counselling and communication skills and ways of enhancing self-concept. Her aim was to pass on to the children the skills that she had learned, providing a form of what Alschuler *et al.* (1977) described as 'psychological education'. The class was chosen because the social relations had been so poor within the group.

Initially, brainstorming was used to deal with a number of organizational problems, such as leaving the classroom open at playtime, getting in and out of assembly quietly, and rearranging the furniture in the classroom. This permitted a high proportion of the children to take part in the decision-making and to express a point of view without it being judged.

The classroom discussions were formalized using 'Circletime' (Ballard, 1982) and the pupils were encouraged to listen carefully to what the others were saying and to respond supportively. The discussions were complemented by self-concept development exercises (Canfield and Wells, 1976) and exercises involving physical contact and sensitivity training (Castillo, 1974; Simon and O'Rourke, 1977; and Colwell, 1979). After two terms, there were dramatic and statistically significant gains in both reading and self-concept scores.

In this short space of time, the class moved to a more co-operative climate, taking more responsibility for the discipline and problem solving of the class. They provided a great deal of mutual support and they helped each other to maintain a positive view of themselves. No special effort had been made with their academic development, but this seemed to improve at the same time as their social skills.

A similar study involving a class of slow-learning pupils was set up by Wooster and Leech (1985). The class was given a course in social and personal education for one day a week for ten weeks. The activities involved are described in Leech and Wooster (1986) and included a range of experiential exercises involving self-concept enhancement, values clarification, interpersonal skills and the use of imagery. The researchers designed an interesting measure of friendship, which at the same time contributed to the personal and social education programme. In one of the sessions the children coloured a picture of an island. They wrote their own name in the centre, which represented the chief's hut. Around this they were to mark on the names of their classmates, deciding how far away their huts were to be. This might even be on a neighbouring island across shark-infested water. The exercise was repeated at the end of the course. This produced an activity that both had a value for the learning process and provided a quantitative measure of friendship to evaluate the programme. At the end of the ten-week period, the pupils were more friendly and attended better at a statistically significant level.

In an evaluation of the use of developmental group work in middle schools in Exeter, Thacker (1985) reported a number of positive gains on the basis of eleven one-and-a-quarter-hour sessions. The exercises used were based on the work of Button (1975) and are in line with the general approach discussed in this chapter. The teachers were perceived by their colleagues to become less forceful, calmer, more child-centred and viewed pupils in a more positive light. The pupils reported that they got on better with the teachers, who shouted less and allowed the pupils to join in discussion more. The report provided interesting case-history data of change in individual pupils.

A further small-scale study which used patterns of friendship as a measure of the success of a personal and social education programme in an infant class is provided by Hall and Delaney (1992). A class of 25 5- to 7-year-olds were given a version of the Island Test described above and the same test was also given to a parallel class as a control group. The school was situated on the edge of a large council estate and a high proportion of the pupils came from low-income families. The social problems in the area appeared to have an influence on the pupils' behaviour within the school. This was particularly obvious at playtime, when behaviour often consisted of aggressive play, with many disruptions and arguments. The children handled most confrontations by physical aggression – kicks, slaps and punches. Quite often this behaviour was brought back with them into the classroom, affecting their behaviour on collaborative tasks in a negative way.

The programme was carried out on one afternoon a week in the summer term and the exercises were planned so that they could be conducted by one teacher with the whole group, even though they would be dividing into subgroups for many of the activities. The programme included activities to examine self-esteem, to mix the established friendship patterns in the group, the use of fantasy with drawing, encouraging the expression of feelings and the use of touch between students. A simple example of a self-esteem enhancement exercise was the 'Magic Box' (Canfield and Wells, 1976) involving a real box, which the children were told contained the most important person in the world. Inside the box was a mirror. Many of the children loved the box and asked to look inside over and over again. Some of the exercises were repeated several times at the request of the children even though they did not seem to be particularly successful at the first attempt. Many personal and social education programmes involve a single attempt at an exercise which is then judged on the initial response from a group as to its effectiveness. Teachers are then faced with the task of devising or discovering new exercises to keep groups 'entertained'.

Scripted fantasy was found to be helpful in generating a great deal of sharing feelings and experiences among pupils and was used in combination with simple relaxation techniques. The first fantasy involved 'inventing your own favourite place'. The pupils were asked to imagine a calm, sunny, pleasant day, and to think of a place where they would really like to be. They might be on their own or with others who were kind and helpful. In spite of the fact that many of the children would not close their eyes and appeared restless, the class teacher who was observing commented on how well the pupils had 'got into it'. Later fantasies taken from de Mille (1967) involved inventing a mouse which scurried around the room and fantasies that included placing their mother or father in situations which became more and more bizarre. Several of the children would point during the fantasy and start to laugh, indicating the extent to which they were identifying with the images.

The art work that was generated by the fantasy and the discussion that emerged out of 'Circletime' sometimes included negative feelings about other members of the class. In previous work, the teacher had stopped these forms of discussion, feeling that they were doing more harm than good. This time she persevered. It is possible that denying or avoiding uncomfortable feelings is not conducive to promoting healthy relationships. What was provided was a means whereby pupils would have the vocabulary to express feelings and events which were uncomfortable. This might have the effect of preventing them being distorted into negative projections onto other pupils. This would suggest that the skills for dealing with conflict are just as necessary for maintaining friendship as those of trust and empathy.

At the end of the programme, the class and the control class were give the Island Test for the second time. A comparison of the residual scores indicated a significant improvement in the experimental class scores compared to the control class. Indeed, while the scores for the experimental class had improved, the scores for the control class had deteriorated. The deterioration could have been predicated at this time of year and the personal and social education programme appears to have reversed the tend for this particular class.

A similar outcome is reported by Wooster (1990), who provided a ten-day programme of social skills training for a class of first-year senior children with moderate learning difficulties in a special school. The typical behaviour of this group in conflict situations involved pushing, verbal aggression, hostile gestures and sulking. These behaviours and the need to ask the teacher to intervene in disputes indicated that the pupils could not cope with disagreements in socially acceptable ways.

The social skills training programme involved the pupils in activities that encouraged them: to talk and listen to one another, to work together, to show others they were valued, to consider the consequences of behaviour, to identify and carry out friendly actions, to find alternative solutions to problems, to consider what they valued, to identify feelings, to experience problem solving and to reflect on learning experiences. The programme consisted of one session a week for ten weeks. Each of the whole-day sessions involved a series of experiential activities including examples from each of four main areas: communication, co-operation, affirmation and problem solving. Because of the inter-relationship of these areas, activities aimed primarily at one area would be likely to generate elements of the other three areas. The discussion that followed the activities would also include things that happened in the group that had not been planned in advance.

Most of the activities were conducted in a circle to promote group feeling and the teacher involved was always part of the circle and took turns. The discussions of the exercises always took place in the circle. A range of techniques were used to set up random pairing rather than friendship groupings. At the end of each day of social skills training, a circle was used to review and close the day.

Examples of exercises from the four main areas listed above are:

Communication. Talking in Pairs. The children sat facing each other in pairs. A told B everything he or she remembered doing after school until bedtime. Two minutes were allowed and then the roles were reversed from B to A for two more minutes. Then the children formed a circle and reported on what their partner did. Discussion topics included: 'Which was it harder to do, talk or listen?' 'Was it easy to remember everything your partner said?' 'How did you show you were listening?'

Co-operation. The pupils organized themselves in groups of four. They were told to imagine that the four of them were going to live together on the island and they had to agree on the things they would want to be on the island. When they all agreed on something, then they could draw it. At the end of the activity each group brought their island to the circle and described it to the others.

Affirmation. The friendly box. This involved a box with a slit at one end and a pile of named cards kept at the side of the box. A new pile was used each time. When pupils noticed that a friendly act had been performed towards them it was recorded on their card and posted into the box. During the closing circle at the end of the day the box was opened and the cards were read out, providing affirmations for the children who had performed the friendly action and those who noticed them.

Problem Solving. Choose a fruit. Eight large pictures each showing a different fruit were displayed. The pupils sat in pairs and each child decided on a different fruit. When they had chosen, they were told that they could keep only one fruit between them, so they had to decide which one they would keep. Having decided, they then joined another pair and decided which of the two fruits they would keep.

The programme was partially planned ahead, but was changed intuitively to meet what appeared to be the changing needs of the group.

Significant differences were obtained between testing completed before the training and after the training on measures indicating reduced impulsivity, improved alternative thinking, a decline in unfriendly behaviour, friendlier feelings and a clearer concept of friendship. There were no corresponding changes in a comparison group. The group appeared to have learned the skills of friendly behaviour, which was still in evidence ten weeks after the course had ended.

The studies which have been described have all involved single classes taught by one teacher. It is inappropriate to generalize from any of them as the outcomes probably depend a great deal on the particular qualities of the teacher and unique nature of the social cultures of the classes involved. However, the outcomes have been consistent and are repeated in numerous similar studies carried out by teachers involved in small-scale studies. In spite of the differences in the pupils, their backgrounds and their teachers, the outcomes of these studies have always been in areas that are described as positive by both teachers and pupils. The pupils have become more friendly and co-operative: they listen to each other and show an interest in what the other pupils have to say; there is a reduction in what might be described as bad behaviour; the pupils make more constructive verbal contributions to the whole classroom group; and there are small improvements in academic achievement. Another consistent report is that the pupils invariably ask for more activities of this nature and there have been many reports of the relief experienced at the opportunity to express feelings and share personal experience with the peer group without being rubbished or put down.

In these studies, the direct attention paid to the social relations in the classroom group appears to have changed the social climate of the group. The development of friendship, improved communication skills and enhanced self-concept also appears to provide the children with an improved sense of control over their lives, which, Hall and Hall (1988) argue, provides the basis of self-discipline and the necessary conditions for social development.

It is accepted that children grow and learn through social interaction during the first five years of life. It seems unreasonable to think that this process ends when children begin school. It is my conviction that group work can make a contribution to academic and social learning which goes beyond life in school and makes a positive contribution to wider society.

All of this has to be considered in the light of the National Curriculum and the pressures that are being put on both teachers and pupils to get through prescribed programmes of work in a limited amount of time. In primary schools there is currently a call to spend more time on 'basics' and testing. In secondary schools the important developments in personal and social education are either being developed as cross-curricular activities, which means that there is a good chance they will be ignored, or changed to a more formally taught form of civics. If teachers are to continue to pay attention to the social and relational issues in the classroom, there will have to be ways of keeping these ideas in their consciousness through pre-service and in-service training.

REFERENCES

Alschuler, A.S., Ivey, A.E. and Hatcher, C. (1977) Psychological education. In C. Hatcher, B. Brooks and others (eds), *Innovations in Counselling Psychology*. San Francisco: Jossey-Bass.

Ballard, J. (1982) *Circlebook*. New York: Irvington.

Bertalanffy, L. von (1950) The theory of open systems in physics and biology. *Science*, **3**, 25-9.

Brophy, J.E. and Good, T.L. (1974) *Teacher–Student Relationships: Causes and Consequences*. New York: Holt, Rinehart & Winston.

Button, L. (1975) *Developmental Groupwork with Adolescents*. London: Hodder & Stoughton.

Canfield, J. and Wells, H.C. (1976) *100 Ways to Enhance Self-concept in the Classroom*. Englewood Cliffs, NJ: Prentice-Hall.

Castillo, G. (1974) *Left-handed Teaching*. New York: Praeger.

Colwell, L.C. (1979) *Jump to Learn: Teaching Motor Skills for Self-esteem*. San Diego: Pennant Educational Materials.

Egan, G. (1975) *The Skilled Helper*. Monterey: Brookes/Cole.

Foot, H.C., Chapman, A.J. and Smith, J.R. (1980) *Friendship and Social Relations in Children*. New York: Wiley.

Galloway, D. (1990) *Pupil Welfare and Counselling: An Approach to Personal and Social Education*. London: Longman.

Galton, M. and Williamson, J. (1992) *Groupwork in the Primary Classroom*. London: Routledge.

Gottman, J., Gonson, J. and Ramussen, B. (1975) Social interaction, social competence and friendship in children. *Child Development*, **46**, 709-18.

Hall, C. and Delaney, J. (1992) How a personal and social education programme can promote friendship in the infant class. *Research in Education*, **47**, 29-39.

Hall, E. and Hall, C. (1988) *Human Relations in Education*. London: Routledge.

Hall, E. and Kirkland, A. (1984) Drawings of trees and the expression of feelings in early adolescence. *British Journal of Guidance and Counselling*, **12**, 39-45.

Hall, E., Hall, C. and Leech, A. (1990) *Scripted Fantasy in the Classroom*. London: Routledge.

Hamachek, D.E. (1977) Humanistic psychology: theoretical–philosophical framework and implications for teaching. In J. Treffinger, J.K. Davis and R. Ripple (eds), *Handbook on Teaching Educational Psychology*. New York: Academic Press.

Hargie, O. (ed.) (1989) *A Handbook of Communication Skills*. London: Routledge.

Hartup, W.W. (1978) Children and their friends. In H. McGurk (ed.), *Issues in Childhood Social Development*. London: Methuen.

Hertz-Lazarowitz, R. (1992) Understanding interactive behaviours: looking at six mirrors of the classroom. In R. Hertz-Lazarowitz and N. Miller (eds), *Interaction in Co-operative Groups*. Cambridge: Cambridge University Press.

Hertz-Lazarowitz, R. and Miller, N. (1992) *Interaction in Co-operative Groups*. Cambridge: Cambridge University Press.

Hopson, B. and Scally, M. (1981) *Lifeskills Teaching*. London: McGraw Hill.

Ivey, A.E. and Authier, J. (1978) *Microcounselling*, 2nd ed. Springfield, Ill: Charles C. Thomas.

Johnson, D.W. and Johnson, R.T. (1992) Positive interdependence: key to effective cooperation. In R. Hertz-Lazarowitz and N. Miller (eds), *Interaction in Co-operative Groups.* Cambridge: Cambridge University Press.

Kohlberg, L. (1971) Stages of moral development as a basis for moral education. In C. Beck, B. Crittendon and E. Sullivan (eds), *Moral Education Interdisciplinary Approaches.* Toronto: University of Toronto Press.

Lang, P. (ed.) (1988) *Thinking about Personal and Social Education in the Primary School.* Oxford: Basil Blackwell.

Leech, N.A. and Wooster, A. (1986) *Personal and Social Skills: A Practical Approach for the Classroom.* Exeter: Religious and Moral Education Press.

Lynch, J. (1992) *Education for Citizenship in a Multi-cultural Society.* London: Cassell.

Mille, R. de (1967) *Put Your Mother on the Ceiling: Children's Imagination Games.* New York: Walter.

Morgan, G. (1986) *Images of Organization.* London: Sage.

Oaklander, V. (1978) *Windows to Our Children.* Moab, Utah: Real People Press.

Oden, S. and Asher, S.R. (1977) Coaching children in social skills and friendship making. *Child Development*, **48**, 495-506.

Plowden Report (1968) *Children and Their Primary Schools: A Report of the Central Advisory Council for Education.* London: HMSO.

Pring, R. (1984) *Personal and Social Education in the Curriculum.* London: Hodder & Stoughton.

Provis, M. (1992) *Dealing with Difficulty: A Systems Approach to Problem Behaviour.* London: Hodder & Stoughton.

Rogers, C.R. (1983) *Freedom to Learn for the 80s.* London: Charles E. Merrill.

Rubin, Z. (1980) *Children's Friendships.* Cambridge, Mass: Harvard University Press.

Ryder, J. and Campbell, L. (1988) *Balancing Acts in Personal and Social Education: A Practical Guide for Teachers.* London: Routledge.

Simon, S.B. and O'Rourke, R.D. (1977) *Developing Values with Exceptional Children.* Englewood Cliffs, NJ: Prentice-Hall.

Simon, S.B., Howe, L.W. and Kirschenbaum, H. (1972) *Values Clarification.* New York: Hart Publishing.

Thacker, J. (1985) Extending developmental groupwork to junior/middle schools: an Exeter project. *Pastoral Care*, **3**, 4-12.

Thacker, J., Stoate, P. and Feast, G. (1992) *Groupwork Skills: Using Groupwork in the Primary School.* Devon: Southgate Publishers.

White, M. (1991) *Self-esteem: Going for the Positive in Education.* Cambridge: Cambridge Resource Packs.

Wooster, A.D. and Carson, A. (1982) Improving reading and self-concept through communication and social skills training. *British Journal of Guidance and Counselling*, **10**, 83-7.

Wooster, A.D. and Leech, N. (1985) Personal and social education for slow learning children: a research and development project. Paper presented at the International Congress on Special Education, Nottingham, July 1985.

Wooster, R. (1990) Social skills training through classroom interaction. Unpublished M.Phil. thesis, University of Nottingham.

Chapter 9

A Common Basis for Success

Colin Rogers

EDITORS' INTRODUCTION

In many of the chapters in this volume the claim is made that group-based classroom learning is effective due, in part at least, to the way in which motivation is enhanced. Motivation is clearly a popular and potentially useful explanatory concept. In the following chapter, Rogers examines the concept of motivation itself and illustrates how it can be interpreted in a number of different ways. Drawing on work from North America as well as research recently conducted in the UK he argues that some of these interpretations are more useful than others in helping to promote a classroom ethos that is conducive to success.

Rogers also points out that many of the effects that may be attributed to group processes are not necessarily unique to groups. Pupil learning, and particularly pupil motivation, is seen to be influenced by the nature of the context within which that learning takes place. Group structures can be interpreted as being primarily a way of influencing key aspects of that classroom context.

In common with other chapters in this book, the argument here is that laissez-faire approaches to group work are unlikely to be effective. Indeed, they may well prove to be ineffective in relation to effective practices based upon individualized learning. As was argued in Chapter 2, there are a number of different classroom structures available to the teacher, only some of which, of course, can be recognized as being group-based. Each of these structures needs to be considered in terms of its own merits and, in respect to motivation, in terms of the degree to which it creates an effective motivational context.

INTRODUCTION

The aim of this chapter is to consider, from a social psychological perspective, some of the issues involved in the interplay between group work in the classroom and motivational enhancement. As can be seen from even a cursory glance through the other chapters in this volume, there exists a wide variety of types of group work in classrooms, and an equally wide, if not wider, array of approaches to the task of beginning to explain the effectiveness of group work. The present chapter does not, therefore, attempt to set out a complete view, but instead to selectively examine some of the more important aspects of group work that would seem to have a motivational spin-off.

A common assumption concerning the role of groups would be that pupils respond well to the experience of group work and therefore find their motivation enhanced. As a consequence, the adoption of group work in the classroom may be considered particularly when the work of pupils with some motivational problems or with more general learning difficulties is being considered. (It is important here, of course, to draw the distinction that has been made by virtually all the other contributors to this volume between group work and merely placing pupils into groups and then leaving them to work individually.) At the end of the day the act of learning remains an individual one. It is you, I or the individual pupil who grasps or fails to grasp a new idea. The role of a group, desirably, is to enhance this process of learning, to help to ensure that individuals learn more and are able to utilize that material more effectively. This is, then, essentially a concern with the nature of the environment within which the individual operates.

The environment provided by a group, however, is necessarily more complex than that provided by the physical environment of the classroom. The group environment is essentially an environment of relationships. These relationships, as argued by Berndt and Keefe (1992), can have either a positive or a negative effect upon the behaviour of an individual within the school context: an individual pupil will be affected not only by the characteristics of the others with whom they associate, but also by the quality of that relationship. The formation of groups within a classroom therefore can act to introduce pupils to desirable others (with 'desirable' clearly needing some definition) and they can also act to introduce more effective and positive relationships.

Berndt and Keefe's discussion is primarily concerned with the longer-term effects of friendships formed within the overall context of schooling. However, they themselves recognize that the grouping strategies adopted by teachers can have similar effects, either directly or by helping to influence the pattern of friendship formation itself. At the outset then it is clearly reasonable to suggest that group-based approaches to teaching need not necessarily lead to motivational enhancements. Just as the effects of friendship choices and the nature of those friendships can have either beneficial or detrimental effects upon a pupil's perceptions of, and attitudes towards, school and school work, so the decision to teach within a group context may have either beneficial or detrimental consequences upon a pupil's motivation. A similar point emerges from Galton and Williamson's (1992) discussion of primary pupils' responses to group work. In an interesting presentation of two case studies, Galton and Williamson begin to demonstrate how the benefits obtained by one teacher with group work are not always obtained by another. Their discussion of some of these differences will be returned to later but for the present it is important to note that they clearly see motivational factors as having a central role to play. Before looking more directly at the role of groups in determining motivational responses it is necessary to say something about the nature of motivation itself.

ASSUMPTIONS ABOUT MOTIVATION

Motivational research has developed at a fairly fast and furious pace over the past decade or so. The following section aims to give only a brief summary of some of this work. The interested reader is directed towards the following for a fuller account: Ames and Ames, 1989; Covington, 1992; Weiner, 1992; Schunk and Meece, 1992; and Galloway *et al.*, 1994. While the details of particular theoretical positions are of considerable importance, and while there are still many points of detail which require clarification, some important areas of agreement are now emerging clearly and it is becoming increasingly possible to see how these areas of agreement can give rise to the formation of points of principle which can serve as useful guides to the development of motivational enhancement programmes. Such principles can be equally well suited to the task of generating frameworks within which existing practices, including group work, may be analysed in terms of their motivational impact.

NOTIONS OF MOTIVATIONAL STYLE: QUANTITATIVE VERSUS QUALITATIVE APPROACHES

One clear central theme emerges from the literature, and that is the development of a *qualitative* view of motivation (Ames, 1984; Dweck, 1991). It is possible for motivation to be considered primarily in *quantitative* terms, that is assessed with respect to directly observable aspects of individual behaviour. Within such a framework the individual who is well motivated is seen to spend more time on task, is seen to work harder and with greater enthusiasm and is likely to make more effective use of the abilities which they possess (all other things being equal, therefore, the individual with more motivation will have the higher level of attainment).

Such descriptions of behaviour are likely to feature within almost any meaningful definition of motivation within the school context. The more significant aspects of quantitative approaches to the conceptualization of motivation are to be found in the assumed origins of these differences.

A quantitative view of the nature of motivation in a school context might also be described as an entity view, in which motivation is seen to be a property of the individual pupil which the child brings in with them to school. The nature of motivation, according to this view, is essentially the same from one pupil to the next. The significant differences between pupils are associated with the amount of this entity each of them have. In short, the better or more motivated pupils are literally seen to have more motivation. The development of motivation is something that takes place largely prior to the pupils' present engagement in school. The development of motivation is seen to be the responsibility of parents, previous teachers and the general social environment. The present school context is seen to play only a relatively minor role.

In contrast to this, a qualitative view of the nature of motivation places an emphasis upon the process by which an individual pupil comes to have a particular *current* orientation towards his or her work. Motivation is increasingly understood in terms of the particular perceptions which pupils have of their current circumstances and their own position within them. The nature of these perceptions, which crucially include self-perceptions, has been the focus of the great part of motivation research in recent years and the details of some of this will receive greater attention below. The current position (Ames, 1984; Dweck, 1991) places a substantial emphasis upon the individual pupil's perceptions of the goals to which they see themselves working at any one time, the nature of the abilities which they have which are relevant to the task in hand, and the level of confidence they have in their ability being sufficient to meet the demands of those tasks. As will be seen later, the nature of these perceptions can be influenced by the nature of the present learning context (i.e. goals can be changed, perceptions of the nature of the relevant abilities can alter) and with these changes will come changes in the nature of motivation. In one sense at least then, motivation comes to be seen as a product of the interactions that take place between the pupil and the current context. An immediate corollary of this is that schools can influence motivation.

It may have been noticed that in the preceding paragraph a reference was made to changes in the 'nature' of motivation, rather than changes in the level or strength of motivation. The second main aspect of the shift towards qualitative conceptions of motivation is that differences in motivation between people are not just differences in the degree to which each has the same amount of the same thing, but rather the degree to which each displays different motivational styles.

MOTIVATION AS A STRATEGY

The notion of motivational style is similar to notions of styles of dress, design styles of various kinds, particular styles developed in the worlds of art and literature. A style may be associated with a particular individual initially, in the sense that they are generally seen to be the originator, but becomes something that is recognizable separately from the characteristics of the individual currently displaying it. So one adopts a particular style of dress. An aspiring author may try out a number of styles of writing before establishing the one that suits. Individuals may adapt the style to their own circumstances and add their own embellishments, but the style remains recognizable nonetheless. Those who develop ways of dressing, writing, painting or whatever that are entirely unique to themselves would tend to be referred to as idiosyncratic in their style.

The other aspect of style in these various other situations is that people can adopt different styles on different occasions. In terms of dress style, one may generally adopt a casual one but sometimes change into a quite different style that better suits the particular occasion. There are two things to note here. Some styles can in a sense be said to be predetermined in that they are not the unique creation of one individual. Second, the style adopted is a response to the individual's understanding of the requirements of the situation. The same person may adopt (one would hope) quite different dress styles when attending weddings, funerals, walking trips, football matches and a night out in a pub. The person who doesn't may well be said to have 'no style'. Their dress is not adaptive.

So it is with motivational style. There will be some styles which are well recognized and established and which are 'adopted' (although the process is almost certainly not as deliberate as this implies) by different people on different occasions. Some individuals may be particularly disposed towards the adoption of one particular style over a range of circumstances. Certain styles may be more likely to be adopted by the majority of people under particular circumstances. Essentially the style taken up by any one person on any one occasion can be considered to be a strategic response to the perceived demands of that situation. The fact that it is the *perceived* demands to which the strategic responses are made indicates that different styles may well be adopted by different people in what may appear to the outsider to be the same circumstances. This notion of strategy is a familiar one to those engaged with educational research. Pollard has discussed the development of groups within classrooms referred to by him as goodies, jokers or gangs. These in many ways are seen as resulting from a process of negotiation between teacher and pupil in which each party seeks to develop their own 'interests at hand' (Pollard, 1985). There is a close and growing coincidence of interest between those researchers who have approached classroom processes from the essentially sociological tradition exemplified by the classic work of people such as Hargreaves and Woods (Hargreaves, 1972; Woods, 1980) and current work on the nature of classroom-based motivational processes. Both are increasingly concerned with the ways in which individual pupils negotiate their ways through a series of challenges both in the sense of threats and opportunities, thrown down to them by life in school. Against this general background, motivational processes clearly have to be seen as rooted in the context of the school classroom. Strategic responses to particular situations can only be properly understood when there is some understanding of the situation itself. Motivational processes and classroom processes need to be seen as component parts of an interlocking system. Motivational style then, rather than being seen as a property of the individual, is seen as the result of interaction between the individual and the situation. The important implication of this is that changes in situation may well give rise to changes in style.

SELF-WORTH, MASTERY ORIENTATION AND LEARNED HELPLESSNESS

Some of these aspects of motivational style can be briefly illustrated by making reference to the emerging results of an ESRC-funded research project based at Lancaster (Rogers *et al.*, 1993a and b; Galloway *et al*, 1994).[1] This project has been concerned with attempting to examine the prevalence of three major motivational styles in two secondary school populations. In addition the study takes on a developmental and longitudinal aspect by examining the distribution of these styles in the primary schools which 'feed' the secondaries. There is a further concern with exploring differences between children who may have special needs and those who may not.

The three motivational styles examined are those which have been most clearly identified in the motivational literature over the past decade: mastery orientation, self-worth motive and learned helplessness. Each of these has been reasonably well examined in terms of its own dynamics and processes and the references given below will allow the interested reader the opportunity of exploring these in greater detail than can be set out here.

Mastery orientation (Dweck, 1986, 1991; Elliott and Dweck, 1988) is the most positive of the three styles in the sense that the goals of the individual adopting this particular approach can be seen to most closely parallel those espoused by the school system. In strategic terms mastery-oriented children are aiming for improvements in their work. They are concerned with working towards mastery over a particular task or topic (although they will not necessarily obtain this). They will see a clear link between the effort they expend and the outcome obtained. This effort outcome co-variation applies not only to the absolute level of effort applied (how hard one works) but also the appropriateness of the working tactics adopted (how effectively the effort has been directed). This perceived link between effort, work habits and the eventual outcome makes the mastery-oriented pupil likely to reflect upon instances where success has not been obtained in order to attempt to determine what changes may be needed to work habits and effort expenditure to ensure future success. Help from others, such as teachers, is likely to be sought where it appears that this would aid the chances of obtaining success and attempts will be made to carefully reapply strategies that have been known to work in the past. This approach maintains a focus upon ultimate success. The mastery-oriented individual is, then, one who maintains relatively high levels of confidence in his or her ultimate success, maintains positive but generally realistic expectations for the future and is willing and able to confront learning difficulties in an open, honest and productive manner.

In contrast, the self-worth-motivated individual (Covington, 1992) has developed an overriding concern with their own level of ability. Covington's analysis starts with the assumption that ability (in the academic sense) is a culturally valued commodity. (It would follow then that where this form of ability is not so valued the self-worth motive may not be found. However, it also follows that where other abilities, e.g. ability in athletics, obtaining a regular stream of dates, stealing cars and not getting caught, are culturally valued the dynamics of the self-worth motive may apply in respect to these activities also.) Due to the value attached to ability, it becomes important for an individual's own sense of self-worth for them to be able to present themselves, and to be able to perceive themselves, as an able person. Now clearly the most straightforward way of doing this is to obtain success in highly difficult tasks where it is widely assumed that such success can only be obtained by persons with the highest level of ability. Given the normative definitions that would, necessarily, apply in these situations, it follows that such a route to unqualified and uncomplicated confirmation of ability is only open to a select few in any area of endeavour. For lesser mortals, if doubts about self-worth come to dominate, some other strategy needs to be developed.

It is here that Covington (1992) makes his most significant contribution to the motivation literature by setting out the nature of some of the strategies that the self-worth-motivated may adopt when self-worth is challenged. Simply to illustrate: one may protect a self-concept of relatively high ability in the face of possible failure by withholding or reducing effort (thus enabling any actual failures to be attributed to the lack of effort rather than the lack of ability); by selecting particularly difficult tasks where a choice exists (thus enabling any possible failure to be attributed to the difficulty of the task rather than a lack of ability); or by procrastinating (thus enabling any subsequent failure to be attributed to the late start rather than a lack of ability). Any middle-aged player of a competitive sport who has found themselves up against a much younger opponent will be familiar with this strategy of 'getting your excuses in first'.

Two things seem clear from the above descriptions of the nature of the strategies adopted by the self-worth-motivated. One, they are clearly strategies selected because they are appropriate to the objective at hand (namely, coming through a threatening experience with one's self-image of ability as little damaged as possible). In as much as these strategies are selected and put into operation with energy and determination the person adopting them is clearly motivated, often highly so. Two, the self-worth-motivated, although following highly motivated strategies, are not adopting strategies that will actually enhance their chances of learning and improving their overall performance. In two senses the strategies of the self-worth-motivated can be seen to be mal-adaptive. First, they are ultimately self-defeating in that the more they are applied the less likely will be the chances of academic success and so the more the defensive strategies will be needed. Second, the behaviour patterns adopted are unlikely to be well suited to the concerns of most schools and teachers. The well motivated pupil from the teacher's point of view is likely to be the one who selects appropriate tasks, makes a prompt start and increases effort when this would appear to increase the chances of overcoming difficulty. The self-worth motivated individual will often do the opposite.

The third style examined in our research is that of learned helplessness (Diener and Dweck, 1978, 1980; Dweck and Wortman, 1982; Covington, 1992; Seligman, 1975). In one sense this style is more difficult to see as strategic. While the mastery-oriented and self-worth-motivated pupil each directs behaviour towards particular goals, the learned helpless pupil seems to abandon all sense of strategic activity. In fact, if there is a strategy at all it is one of surrender, and often abject surrender at that. The learned helpless pupil is likely to be seen to give up relatively easily when confronted with difficulty. They will have low aspirations and are likely to frustrate their teachers' attempts to enhance their performance by refusing to believe that any increase of effort or change of work habits in their own part would result in improved outcomes. Learned helpless children see themselves as fundamentally lacking the level of ability required to obtain the level of success looked for. Furthermore, they believe that they are quite unable to do anything about altering this state of affairs. It is here, of course, that the strategic sense of the learned helpless plan of action can be seen. If success really is believed to be out of reach then there is nothing to be gained by seeking to strive for it. The only sensible strategy available is to give up.

THE LANCASTER STUDY

There is not sufficient space available here to describe the full details of the methods and measures used in the Lancaster study. However, some attention needs to be given to one aspect of the approach adopted. In setting out to determine the relative incidence of each of the above motivational styles we wished to make use of procedures which bore some similarity to the child's ordinary experience of school and which were not overly dependent upon self-report inventories or abstract psychological tests. Such an approach is fully in keeping with the view that motivational style represents a strategic response to a particular context. To this end a procedure developed by Craske (1988) was adopted. This technique involves presenting to pupils four consecutive tests, in this case over a period of about one week, each bearing a close resemblance to each other in terms of format. Let these tests be identified as A, B, C and D.

Test A provides a baseline measure of the child's performance capabilities. Test B is designed to be significantly more difficult and therefore produces a lower score, but is presented as being another test like A. Test C is presented in the same way and is actually (as shown by pilot work) of the same order of difficulty as Test A. Each pupil is presented with feedback giving their scores on the previous tests before they begin the next. Most pupils obtain a lower score on Test B than on Test A. The first question is to ask how this affects performance on C. The reasoning applied here suggests that the mastery-oriented pupil will not be affected adversely by the difficulty of B and will therefore perform at least as well as C as on A. The self-worth-motivated and the learned helpless pupil would each be likely, for different reasons, to be affected adversely by the experience of Test B and would therefore obtain a lower score on C than on A.

Test D is presented as being another more difficult test, but is actually again set at the same difficulty level as A. The argument now is that the self-worth and learned helpless pupils will show different responses to Test D. Both groups, recall, had shown a loss of performance on C relative to A. The learned helpless pupil, on being told that D was another difficult test, would be likely to reduce effort in keeping with their belief that B had already indicated that they lacked the ability required for the harder tests and that they could therefore expect to fail again here. The self-worth-motivated pupil, on the other hand, has had his or her self-worth concerns raised by the experience of B (the relative lack of success implied a possible lack of ability) which presumably leads to the commencement of defensive strategies which have the effect of reducing performance on C. However, on being told that D is 'difficult' the self-worth-motivated find that the excuse is already in place. Any disappointing result on D can now be attributed to the difficulty of the task and need not imply a lack of ability. This in turn reduces the need for the implementation of defensive strategies and therefore gives rise to an improvement in performance on D relative to C. In short, while the learned helpless and the self-worth-motivated show the same sequence of responses up to and including Test C, the learned helpless will continue to show a loss of performance on Test D while the self-worth-motivated will not. Craske has used this procedure to classify children into the learned helpless and self-worth-motivated styles and has then been able to demonstrate other differences between them that help to validate the procedure.

In the case of our current research two main sets of tests were constructed, one in English and one in Mathematics, so that the effects of these different tasks could be investigated. It was also necessary to produce somewhat different versions appropriate for the age group and ability level to which the test was presented.

Two main samples of pupils were included in the study. First, a longitudinal sample, which was first studied towards the end of year 6 (the final year of primary school) and then followed through into year 7 and on into year 8 (the second year of secondary school). Second, a cross-sectional sample was examined comprising pupils from years 9 and 11 (year 11 being the final year of compulsory schooling). In addition to this, pupils who were in our year 6 schools but were not going on to attend our secondary schools, and those who came into year 7 from primary schools other than the ones looked at in year 6 were also included but do not form part of the longitudinal sample.

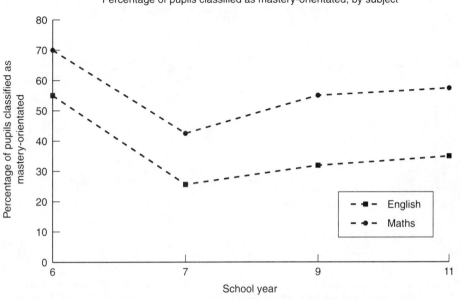

Figure 9.1   *Percentage of pupils classified as mastery-oriented in English and Mathematics.*

This study has yielded a large amount of interesting material. One small aspect of it will enable some basic points about the prevalence of motivational style to be made.

The main concern here is to demonstrate simply the ways in which motivational style seems to vary across various conditions. Consider first Figures 9.1 to 9.3 showing, for English and Mathematics, the percentage of pupils demonstrating each of the three main motivational styles as a function of year group.

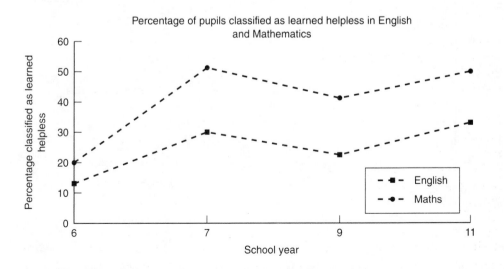

Figure 9.2   *Percentage of pupils classified as learned helpless in English and Mathematics.*

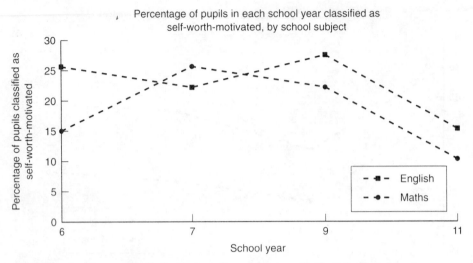

Figure 9.3   *Percentage of pupils classified as self-worth-motivated in English and Mathematics.*

Two general findings emerge from these figures. First, the proportion of children showing mastery orientation, in both subjects, decreases quite markedly following the transfer from year 6 to year 7 (primary to secondary school). Following this initial change there is some recovery of the proportion of children showing mastery orientation, again in both subjects, but not back to the levels of year 6. Not surprisingly, there is a corresponding increase in learned helplessness between years 6

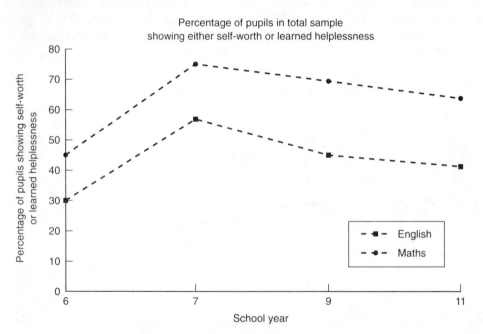

Figure 9.4   *Percentage of pupils showing either learned helplessness or self-worth motive in English and Mathematics across years 6 to 11 – whole sample.*

and 7 and, following a fall between years 7 and 9, a further increase between years 9 and 11. Changes in the self-worth motive are somewhat more complex but a clear view of the changes in mal-adaptive styles can be seen in Figure 9.4, where the data for both learned helplessness and self-worth motive are combined.

Second, while the pattern of *changes* across year groups is very much the same for the two subject areas, it is also clear that English as a subject produces a lower proportion of mastery-oriented pupils in all four age groups, and that there are more pupils with either of the two mal-adaptive styles in English than in Mathematics.

One or two other observations from the results of this study will be helpful here. It seems to be the case that there is relatively little stability across years at the level of the individual pupil. In other words if individual pupils are followed from year 6 to year 7 and their motivational style compared it is often the case that a different style is being displayed in the later year. Furthermore, the degree of stability or change that is observed varies according to subject and motivational style. To illustrate, 52 per cent of the pupils who demonstrated learned helplessness in English while in year 6 still did so in year 7. However, only 21 per cent of those who showed the self-worth motive in English while in year 6 still did so in year 7. In Mathematics greatest stability was found for the mastery-oriented style with 41 per cent showing the same style in years 6 and 7, while least stability was again in the self-worth motive (13 per cent showing this style in both years) but with only 19 per cent now showing learned helplessness in both years.

There are clearly some general effects related either to the age of the pupil or to the stage of schooling (or both) coupled with some effects that are related to the subject studied. Furthermore there is little evidence of consistency across the two subject areas in terms of style displayed. That is, it is not generally the case that pupils who display one style in, say English, will also display that same style in Mathematics. The main conclusion at present is that motivational style is clearly influenced by progress through the school system, by the actual work being undertaken and to some degree by the school attended and the teacher by whom one is taught.

EXPLANATIONS OF MOTIVATIONAL STYLE

In an earlier discussion of these results (Rogers *et al.*, 1993a) three different bases for the explanation of the processes involved in each motivational style were considered. Each of these was held to have different implications for the way in which motivational processes were to be understood, and more importantly, responded to.

Personality

Expressed in terms of personality, motivational style is seen as being essentially a product of the underlying personality traits of each individual pupil. With its origins in the work of people such as Atkinson (Atkinson and Raynor, 1974; Atkinson and Raynor, 1978; Weiner, 1992) there is a broad explanation here of a relatively high degree of similarity in response over varying situations and of relatively consistent differences between people.

Information processing

An information processing model is one derived most clearly from the work of Weiner drawing on attributional theory (Weiner, 1992). Individuals develop relatively stable and consistent ways of interpreting information concerning their successes and failures which broadly reflect culturally determined beliefs about the importance of effort, ability, task difficulty and so on in determining levels of success. The particular pattern of attributions made by any one person will depend largely on the pattern of success and failure they have enjoyed (or otherwise) in a specified area of endeavour. Under such a model one would anticipate a greater degree of motivational variability over contexts than with the personality model and a growing degree of stability within an individual as they develop a clearer and lengthier history of success and failure in specific domains.

Goals and self-beliefs

A model set on patterns of goals and beliefs is perhaps the one that is most likely to fit with our own data and also seems to be the model that is most favoured by other researchers (Ames and Ames, 1989; Elliott and Dweck, 1988). This model assumes that variations in motivation are a function of particular beliefs held by the individual in relation to their current context. As the context itself is subject to change over time and circumstances, so one would expect the motivational characteristics displayed to vary also. The goals and self-beliefs model predicts variability within individuals and also suggests that particular situations will have a general effect upon the motivational style demonstrated by the people involved in them.

What are the goals and self-beliefs that are of significance? The goals first of all relate to the individual's own view of the essential purpose of the exercise they are currently engaged in. Nicholls (1989) set out the differences between performance goals on the one hand and learning or mastery goals on the other. The goals adopted are in many respects a function of both the individual and the setting but in many cases the influence of the setting would seem to be very powerful. When working with a learning or mastery goal the pupil's concern is with increasing their own learning and working towards mastery of the topic under study. The point of the exercise is to attempt to emerge from the experience knowing more than one did at the start. Success and failure are likely to be measured against this criterion, rather than against normative criteria provided by other people's levels of performance. With a learning or mastery goal even the pupil with the absolute lowest level of performance can feel a sense of success and accomplishment if they can move forwards.

With performance goals the concerns are different. The purpose of the activity is now concerned with evaluation of the self, both by the self and by others. The essential goal is not necessarily to do with making progress, with enhancing one's own level of understanding, but instead is to do with trying to maximize the positive approval one might obtain from others. If positive approval is not available (or is judged to be unlikely) then the prime object of the exercise is to avoid negative judgements of oneself. Self-evidently, performance goals are more likely to be associated with mal-adaptive motivational styles.

The next major self-belief of concern is that to do with the perceptions one has of the nature of ability. It is important here to distinguish between beliefs associated with the nature of ability and those associated with level of ability. Nicholls (1984, 1989) has been associated most clearly with work concerned with the nature of these ability beliefs but other researchers have also made important contributions (Stipeck, 1984; Eccles and Midgley, 1989). A basic distinction can be made between entity and incremental views of the nature of ability. With an entity view of ability one is likely to see ability as being fixed and uncontrollable. It is necessary to learn to live with the levels of ability one has, because there isn't any way in which they can be increased. This is essentially the view of ability that seems to drive the self-worth-motivated person. It is of importance, simply because ability is fixed to avoid coming to the conclusion that one has reached the limits set by it.

The incremental image, however, presents a view of ability that is much more akin to the common conception of 'skill'. Under the incremental view ability can be added to and enhanced provided that one knows what steps to take. There is no reason to assume that a lack of ability sets a permanent ceiling on performance levels. Nicholls' (1984) earlier developmental work suggests that younger children may be more likely to have an understanding only of the incremental view of ability, as they have yet to fully differentiate ability from effort as possible causes of success and failure.

In addition to such beliefs (learning goals and the nature of ability) individual pupils can differ in terms of the level of confidence they have in their current level of ability (under either view of the nature of ability). Typically, confidence levels will range from high to low along a continuum. The important differences however are likely to be between those who see themselves as having a sufficient level of ability to complete successfully the task in hand and those who do not. Some individuals are likely to be more confident than others across a large range of tasks and activities, and others to have lower levels of confidence, while it will also be the case that levels of confidence will vary within an individual across different situations.

EFFECTS OF GROUPS ON MOTIVATIONAL STYLE

The key question to be addressed now is, how would the use of grouping strategies affect the degree to which differences in motivational style will be displayed? From what has gone before it is clear that variations in the school context can and do influence motivational style. The use or non-use of groups within the classroom is clearly a factor that will influence the nature of the classroom context. The impact of groups is addressed throughout this volume and it is not necessary therefore to consider the impact of groups upon pupil behaviour and performance in great detail here. Instead, use will be made of summaries presented elsewhere.

Brown (1988) has provided a very useful summary of the general social psychological processes involved with the use of groups in a wide variety of settings. Following Reicher's (1982, 1984) work Brown states that groups can have varying effects upon the behaviour of individuals. Mere membership of a group, or a crowd, does not itself ensure better or worse behaviour. The nature of the group, its purposes and intention are critical in determining outcomes (for examples, see Chapters 2, 4 and 5 in this volume).

Brown goes on to provide a useful review of the research that has examined the effects of groups on productivity. For many years social psychologists have been concerned with attempting to answer the question of whether people working in groups are more effective than they are as individuals. There is some evidence, indeed some of the earliest available, that suggests that people do not work more effectively in a group. Ringlemann's (1913) classic rope-pulling study demonstrates the simplest approach to this. Ringlemann assessed the strength of pull exerted by a number of individuals pulling on a rope one at a time. He then combined them into a group and asked them all to pull at once. The total pull exerted by the group was less than the statistically combined pull of the individuals. Naturally the nature of the task is important here and problems of managing the physical co-ordination of effort (ensuring that everyone pulls at the same time for example) are going to be relevant. However, Brown's review shows quite clearly that there are many other situations where individuals in a group do not operate more effectively than they do as a set of individuals. Even in brainstorming sessions a greater number of ideas are likely to be produced by a number of people generating ideas separately and then combining them than they will if they attempt to generate ideas together as a group (Brown, 1988).

However, it also emerges from Brown's review that the particular dynamics of the group are critical. Holt (1987) has demonstrated that Ringlemann's classic findings can be reversed (i.e. the group pulls harder than the sum total of individual pulls) when the group has a social reality outside of the task. In other words, groups created simply for the purpose of a laboratory-based study do not have the same dynamics and impact upon individual members as do groups that have developed some significant social history.

The classic studies of Asch (1956) on the effects of inter-group co-operation and competition on interpersonal relationships and the consequences of this for an understanding of race relations also demonstrate the importance of looking at the longer-term impact of group involvement on members. As groups develop a sense of common purpose and as individual members come to see their personal fates as being connected to those of the other group members, so the group increasingly comes to exercise an influence upon those members. These observations have formed the basis for the development of a number of approaches to co-operative group work within classrooms (Slavin, 1987, 1989, 1990; Sharan, 1989; Johnson and Johnson, 1985, 1987, Chapter 5 in this volume).

A further useful review is provided by Galton and Williamson in their discussion of their own investigations into the effectiveness of different implementations of group work within classrooms. A number of concluding points emerge from this. While there may be a very complex story to tell regarding the effectiveness of groups in terms of measured productivity, when the concern is with the learning that takes place it seems clear that co-operative and collaborative groups (the latter being particularly concerned with the joint production of some end product) can and do produce better outcomes than a classroom that works on individualistic lines, especially if it is the case that the individualistic classroom is also competitive (Ames, 1981, 1984).

However, Galton and Williamson also conclude that it is not the case that any group will produce benefits. If groups are to produce the most effective outcomes they ought to be of mixed ability (and it should be noted that Galton and Williamson are addressing themselves to primary school classrooms), and it is particularly important that members of the highest-ability bands are included. The groups need to have a clear sense of responsibility and ownership for the work they undertake and while some individual rewards may be appropriate it is also clear that rewarding of individual group members needs to be carried out carefully if the beneficial effects of group work are not to be reduced.

Galton and Williamson's own observations of more and less effective teachers (in respect of the teachers' ability to manage classroom groups) also reveal the importance of having tasks that are clear and unambiguous and in helping the pupils to develop the skills needed to enable them to be able to collaborate effectively. These observations are supported by work elsewhere. Slavin (1990) for example has shown how co-operative groups need to be carefully structured if they are to be successful in the objective of enhancing pupil learning. Slavin's work has consisted of examining in some detail the effects of structuring co-operative work groups in different ways. The details of the different structures need not concern us here, but it is important to note that there are some common effects to a number of different structures. First, the imposition of a structure on the group by the teacher is invariably accompanied by the imposition of some structure on the task to be worked at. This structuring helps to ensure that Galton and Williamson's concern with having relatively unambiguous tasks is likely to have been met. Second, the concern with setting up a structure and with ensuring that each pupil has a particular role to play and understands the nature of that role and its relationship to the roles of others, also helps to ensure that pupils are encouraged, indeed sometimes required, to reflect upon the process of collaboration.

Slavin himself has drawn attention to three seemingly necessary conditions the presence of which helps to ensure the success of co-operative group teaching methods (Rogers and Kutnick, 1990). These can be summarized as: having a group goal; having clear individual accountability; having a reward system which enables each individual within the group to have an equal opportunity to succeed. The presence of the group goal, the requirement for the group to produce something between them, ensures that they will have to work together as a group and that they will need to attend to the interdependencies that this creates. The group goal helps to bring about the particular interdependent relationships which both help to promote more positive self-esteem amongst the pupils and also to reduce their dependency upon the teacher (Kutnick, 1988). Individual accountability helps to ensure that particular members of the group cannot simply let others get on with the work, while the 'equal opportunity scoring systems' help to ensure that each member of the group can see themselves as being able to make a valid and valued contribution to the group's activities.

We can now move on to show how these summary points coincide with those presented by Epstein (1989) in relation to considering the ways in which environments in general can be assessed for their motivational effectiveness.

CONTEXT EFFECTS ON MOTIVATION

Epstein (1988, 1989) has drawn attention to six key areas of school, and indeed home, environments which can be seen to have a critical impact upon the nature of the motivation displayed by pupils in that context. In examining these six areas within this final section of this chapter, I hope to be able to demonstrate how the use of groups in itself cannot be regarded as a panacea for all motivational problems. Rather, it will be the case that groups can be employed both effectively and ineffectively with respect to motivational enhancements and that in many cases of effective employment the group is being used to create conditions that might have been produced in some other way. In other words, teachers should not take the view that groups *have* to be used in order to enhance pupil motivation, and they should certainly take the view that the adoption of group-based work in itself does not and will not ensure motivational enhancement.

Epstein's six areas are covered by the acronym TARGET standing for: Task; Authority; Recognition; Grouping; Evaluation; and Time. Each of these will be examined briefly below. In addition to the work published by Epstein herself another application of the TARGET format can be seen in Ames (1992).

Task

The task dimension includes the degree to which pupils are prepared to approach the task in a mastery-oriented way as well as the details of the task design itself. The Lancaster project, referred to above, is showing very clear task effects in that our Mathematics tasks generally seemed to produce more mastery-oriented approaches to the work than those employed in English. It is recognized that these differences are not necessarily indicative of the subjects as a whole but in our discussions of these findings with the teachers of the pupils involved a common theme emerged which relates to the degree to which the pupils are likely to have received clear and unambiguous feedback in the subject area in the past. Mathematics was generally understood to be more likely to provide such clear feedback and hence more likely to develop mastery approaches. The work of Schunk (1990, 1992) mentioned above has also demonstrated how clear feedback and a concern with developing strategic approaches to learning (which require the pupil to be able to judge readily their progress) helps to develop a positive sense of self-efficacy. A good level of self-efficacy (a belief that one can effect change) is an important component of mastery orientation. In addition to these concerns the task itself can be designed so as to make it more or less interesting and motivating. Lepper (Lepper and Malone, 1987; Lepper and Hodell, 1989) has demonstrated how tasks can be motivationally 'tweaked' in this way. It is clear that none of these task-related factors are going to be uniquely associated with the use of groups. Group work with tasks that are poorly defined, provide little in the way of clear and informative feedback, provide goals which are seen to be unattainable and lack any inherent interest, are likely to reduce mastery approaches to learning. However, it is likely that, in following the relatively tight prescriptions found in schemes such as those developed by Slavin (1990) for the use of co-operative groups, teachers will need to give attention to the structuring of the task along the lines discussed above. It is also likely that teachers who *begin* to adopt group work will give greater attention to the design of materials. (Readers familiar with the Hawthorne effect will know that novelty can act as a powerful motivator for both pupils and teachers alike. The lack of truly long-term research into the use of groups or almost any other technique always makes it very difficult to know the degree to which enhancements might be maintained over a pupil's school career.)

Authority

Here there is a very close coincidence of the concerns set out by Epstein in relation to motivational enhancement and Galton and Williamson's observations of what makes group work effective. The authority dimension is essentially concerned with the degree to which pupils see themselves in control of the learning situation. A considerable debt is owed here to the work of Deci and Ryan (1985) and their colleagues who have studied in some detail the ways in which a sense of *control* over the learning situation helps to encourage a more positive approach to motivation. Galton and Williamson again make some useful observations here when they demonstrate how pupils seem to feel a reduced sense of control and ownership over group tasks when those tasks are not clearly defined (showing a link with the task dimension) and when the teacher encroaches on the group's own decision-making processes. Their observations of two teachers, selected as representatives of more and less successful operators of learning groups, reveal how successful practice is often associated with an ability to observe the pupil groups in action without intruding into the group. The teacher's body language (how close to a group she sits, the degree to which she communicates that she does *not* want to comment on what the pupils are doing) all help to determine a sense of pupil control. Deci and Ryan have also drawn attention to the importance of goal setting. A greater sense of control is likely to be developed if the pupils can set their own goals, particularly if this is done within a framework where normative assessment systems are not employed (see Evaluation below). As Galton and Williamson's work makes abundantly clear, the use of groups in and of itself again does not ensure that the authority dimension will be employed in a manner that will lead to motivational enhancement. However, the evidence so far gathered clearly indicates that good examples of collaborative group work can considerably increase the sense of ownership pupils feel over the work they do.

Recognition

This dimension is centrally concerned with the use of rewards, incentives and other forms of praise. It again will have a close similarity with many of the concerns discussed under Evaluation below. Recent work (Graham, 1990; Graham and Folkes, 1990) on the use of praise in the classroom context illustrates some of the issues involved here. An attributional approach to motivation (Weiner, 1986, 1992) highlights the importance of pupils seeing effort, rather than ability, as a cause of success and failure. In respect to failure particularly, pupils who see ability as the cause are more likely to develop learned helpless responses than are those who see lack of effort as being responsible. Analysis of pupils' responses to praise indicates some quite complex effects in which it is possible that praise for effort delivered in the context of failure may actually be taken as implying a low level of ability ('If I tried hard and still failed I must be stupid!'). Again groups in themselves do not ensure an appropriate use of recognition.

Grouping

Here it is possible to claim a unique effect for group work, for Epstein concludes that the use of groups, particularly those employing co-operative approaches, is likely to enhance positive motivational styles. Slavin's work is again important here in drawing attention to the conditions (referred to above) under which the benefits of group work will be obtained. Co-operative groups would seem to benefit motivation largely because they help to remove a perceived absolute link between ability and success (Ames, 1984). Groups that bring together pupils of a range of abilities, and that are structured in such a way that success requires realistic contributions from all pupils, help to ensure that the group develops a concern with maximizing the performance of each pupil and that relative failure by one pupil does not equate to relative success by another ('I have performed better than you so I am a better pupil').

Evaluation

The effects of evaluation systems, the means by which pupil performance is assessed and monitored, can have very clear and powerful effects upon pupil motivational style. A number of researchers (including Covington, 1992; Jagacinski, 1992) have shown how evaluation systems which are normative and public can readily undermine the motivation of those who do not unambiguously succeed. One of the key aspects of the performance goals discussed above is their concern with one's performance *vis-à-vis* others. Clearly highly normative evaluation systems, particularly when these are operated publicly, will tend to encourage the adoption of performance goals and thereby reduce the tendency for mastery orientation to develop. The use of groups is of benefit here in that they tend to reduce the degree to which pupils perceive the class as being highly differentiated in terms of pupils' ability and success. The work of Weinstein and her colleagues (Marshall and Weinstein, 1984; Weinstein *et al.*, 1987; Wigfield and Harold, 1992) shows how pupils who work in classrooms which are seen to be highly differentiated (i.e. where the teacher is seen to treat the more and less successful pupils most clearly differently) are the ones most prone to the harmful effects of teacher expectations (Rogers, 1982; Dusek, 1985). When group work encourages pupils across the ability range represented in the class to work together on a joint project the degree of differentiation is necessarily reduced. It can also be noted again that Slavin has identified equal opportunity scoring as one of the essential elements in good group work practice. In other words, it again seems to be the case that it is not always the use of the group *per se* which may help enhance motivation. It is instead the case that appropriate use of groups is one way, perhaps a particularly effective one, of creating conditions which enhance motivation, conditions which can equally be created in classrooms that do not employ groups as such.

Time

Closely related to concerns with the task dimension, the concern here is again with the degree to which pupils are able to effectively plan their work within a framework of deadlines that enables progress to be maintained and a sense of control and self-efficacy developed. A sense of working under pressure to meet deadlines imposed by others can reduce motivation (Deci and Ryan, 1985) but it is not clear that the adoption of group work will necessarily help here unless attention is given to the management of the group by the pupils themselves. This emerges as an important point. One important aspect of mastery orientation is the sense a pupil has of having a relevant and effective strategy at their disposal. Pupils placed in a group-work setting without any such strategies for managing the group itself are likely to find themselves disadvantaged in respect to the time dimension as well as in other respects. Ames (1993, personal communication) has argued that very little attention is given in school to encouraging pupil (or parental) reflection upon the actual process of learning. In attempting to develop more positive motivational climates she argues that teachers need to devote more attention to discussing with pupils the nature of the learning process in relation to the work at hand. In setting up learning groups, teachers need similarly to attend to the ways in which pupils can be directed to thinking about what it is they are setting out to achieve and how they can help to achieve it. In many group settings (Galton and Williamson, 1992) the purpose of the activity is not made clear to the pupils. Under such circumstances it is almost impossible for them to develop effective time and task management strategies.

CONCLUSION

I am conscious of the relatively little direct discussion of motivation in group settings that has taken place in this chapter. This has been quite deliberate. As our understanding of the processes involved in developing effective motivational styles progresses, so it becomes clearer that there is no 'royal road' to the enhancement of motivation. A positively motivated pupil is characterized by a particular orientation to their work and by a particular set of goals and self-beliefs. In a sense it doesn't matter how these goals and beliefs are created as long as they are there. It is hoped that the above discussion has helped to demonstrate that the adoption of group work can help to create circumstances under which positive motivational gains can be made. However, by the same token it should also be clear that the adoption of group work by no means guarantees this. Teachers who use, or are considering the use of, group work strategies in their classrooms need to consider very carefully how and why they hope to be able to enhance pupil performance or behaviour. One clear advantage of pupils working in and as a group is that each pupil is less likely to see their outcomes as being totally dependent upon ability and more likely to be able to see how the development of effective working practices will increase their own chances of gaining success. This should not be interpreted as meaning that teachers can simply hand over responsibility for learning to the groups themselves. Certainly, groups that are effective in motivational terms will be ones which encourage a clear sense of control among the pupils. However, creating the right conditions for the development of these positive effects is no straightforward matter. What is clear is that ineffective group work will be motivationally damaging in comparison to an effective individual learning context.

NOTE

1. Learned Helplessness and Self-Worth Motivation in Pupils with Special Needs. Financed by the Economic and Social Research Council (Grant No. R000232296). Directed by Professor D. Galloway (now at Durham University) and Dr C. Rogers. The assistance of the ESRC is gratefully acknowledged. Others involved in the project include Derrick Armstrong, Carolyn Jackson and Elizabeth Leo. Responsibility for the comments made here lies with the author.

REFERENCES

Ames, C. (1981) Competitive versus co-operative reward structures: the influence of individual and group performance factors on achievement attributions and affect. *American Educational Research Journal*, **18**, 273-87.

Ames, C. (1984) Competitive, co-operative and individualistic goal structures: a cognitive–motivational analysis. In R. Ames and C. Ames, *Research on Motivation in Education, Vol. 1, Student Motivation*. London: Academic Press.

Ames, C. (1985) Effective motivation: the contribution of the learning environment. In R.S. Feldman (ed.), *The Social Psychology of Education: Current Research and Theory*. Cambridge: Cambridge University Press.

Ames, C. (1992) Achievement goals and the classroom motivational climate. In D.H. Schunk and J.L. Meece (eds), *Student Perceptions in the Classroom*. Hove: Lawrence Erlbaum Associates.

Ames, C. and Ames, R.E. (1989) *Research on Motivation in Education, Vol. 3, Goals and Cognitions*. London: Academic Press.

Asch, S.E. (1956) Studies of independence and conformity, 1. A minority of one against a unanimous majority. *Psychological Monographs*, **70(a)**, 1-70.

Atkinson, J. and Raynor, J. (1974) *Motivation and Achievement*. Washington, DC: Winston.

Atkinson, J. and Raynor, J. (1978) *Personality, Motivation and Achievement*. Washington, DC: Hemisphere.

Berndt, T.J. and Keefe, K. (1992) Friends' influence on adolescents' perceptions of themselves at school. In D. Schunk and J. Meece (eds), *Student Perceptions in the Classroom*. Hove: Lawrence Erlbaum Associates.

Brown, R. (1988) *Group Processes: Dynamics Within and Between Groups*. Oxford: Basil Blackwell.

Covington, M.V. (1992) *Making the Grade: A Self-worth Perspective on Motivation and School Reform*. Cambridge: Cambridge University Press.

Craske, M.-L. (1988) Learned helplessness, self-worth motivation and attribution retraining for primary school children. *British Journal of Educational Psychology*, **58**, 152-64.

Deci, E.L. and Ryan, R.M. (1985) *Intrinsic Motivation and Self-determination in Human Behavior*. New York: Plenum.

Diener, C.S. and Dweck, C. (1978) An analysis of learned helplessness: continuous changes in performance, strategy and achievement cognitions following failure. *Journal of Personality and Social Psychology*, **36**, 451-62.

Diener, C.I. and Dweck, C.S. (1980) An analysis of learned helplessness: 2. The processing of success. *Journal of Personality and Social Psychology*, **39**, 940-52.

Dusek, J.B. (ed.) (1985) *Teacher Expectancies*. London: Lawrence Erlbaum.

Dweck, C.S. (1986) Motivational processes affecting learning. *American Psychologist*, **41**, 1040-48.

Dweck, C.S. (1991) Self-theories and goals: their role in motivation, personality and development. *Nebraska Symposium on Motivation 1990. Volume 38*. Lincoln: University of Nebraska Press.

Dweck, C.S. and Wortman, C.B. (1982) Learned helplessness, anxiety and achievement motivation. In H.W. Krohne and L. Laux (eds), *Achievement, Stress and Anxiety*. Washington, DC: Hemisphere.

Eccles, J.S. and Midgley, C. (1989) Stage-environment fit: developmentally appropriate classrooms for young adolescents. In C. Ames and R. Ames (eds), *Research on Motivation in Education, Vol. 3, Goals and Cognitions*. London: Academic Press.

Elliott, E.S. and Dweck, C.S. (1988) Goals: an approach to motivation and achievement. *Journal of Personality and Social Psychology*, **54**, 5-12.

Epstein, J. (1988) Effective schools or effective students: dealing with diversity. In R. Haskins and D. MacRae (eds), *Policies for America's Public Schools: Teachers, Equity, Indicators*. Norwood, NJ: Ablex.

Epstein, J. (1989) Family structures and student motivation: a developmental perspective. In C. Ames and R. Ames (eds), *Research on Motivation in Education, Vol. 3, Goals and Cognitions*. London: Academic Press.

Galloway, D., Rogers, C., Armstrong, D., Leo, E. and Jackson, C. (1994) *Motivating the Difficult to Teach*. London: Longman.

Galton, M. and Williamson, J. (1992) *Groupwork in the Primary Classroom*. London: Routledge.

Graham, S. and Barker, G. (1990) The downside of help: an attributional–developmental analysis of helping behaviour as a low ability cue. *Journal of Educational Psychology*, **82**, 7-14.

Graham, S. and Folkes, V. (1990) *Attribution Theory: Applications to Achievement. Mental Health and Interpersonal Conflict*. Hove: Lawrence Erlbaum Associates.

Hargreaves, D.H. (1972) *Interpersonal Relations in Education*. London: Routledge & Kegan Paul.

Holt, J.H. (1987) The social labouring effect: a study of the effect of social identity on group productivity in real and notional groups using Ringlemann's method. Unpublished manuscript, University of Kent (cited in Brown, R., 1988).

Jagacinski, C.M. (1992) The effects of task involvement and ego involvement on achievement related cognition and behavior. In D.H. Schunk and J.H. Meece (eds), *Student Perceptions in the Classroom*. Hove: Lawrence Erlbaum Associates.

Johnson, D.W. and Johnson, R.T. (1985) Motivational processes in co-operative, competitive and individualistic learning situations. In C. Ames and R. Ames (eds), *Research on Motivation in Education, Vol. 2, The Classroom Milieu*. London: Academic Press.

Johnson, D.W. and Johnson, R.T. (1987) *Learning Together and Alone* (2nd ed.). Englewood Cliffs, NJ: Prentice-Hall.

Kutnick, P. (1988) *Relationships in the Primary School Classroom*. London: Paul Chapman.

Lepper, M.R. and Hodell, M. (1989) Intrinsic motivation in the classroom. In C. Ames and R. Ames (eds), *Research on Motivation in the Classroom, Vol. 3, Goals and Cognitions*. London: Academic Press.

Lepper, M.R. and Malone, T.W. (1987) Intrinsic motivation and instructional effectiveness in computer-based education. In R.E. Snow and M.J. Farr (eds), *Aptitude, Learning and Instruction, Vol. 3, Conative and Affective Process Analysis*. Hillsdale, NJ: Lawrence Erlbaum Associates.

Marshall, H.H. and Weinstein, R.S. (1984) Classroom factors affecting students' self-evaluations: an interactional model. *Review of Educational Research*, **54**, 301-25.

Nicholls, J.G. (ed.) (1984) *Advances in Motivation and Achievement, Vol. 3, The Development of Achievement Motivation*. London: JAI Press.

Nicholls, J.G. (1989) *The Competitive Ethos and Democratic Education*. London: Harvard University Press.

Pollard, A. (1985) *The Social World of the Primary School*. London: Holt.

Reicher, S.D. (1982) The determination of collective behaviour. In H. Tajfel (ed.), *Social Identity and Intergroup Relations*. Cambridge: Cambridge University Press.

Reicher, S.D. (1984) The St Pauls riot: an explanation of the limits of crowd action in terms of a social identity model. *European Journal of Social Psychology*, **14**, 1-21.

Ringlemann, M. (1913) Recherches sur les moteurs animés: travail de l'homme. *Annales de l'Institut National Agronomique*, 2nd series, **12**, 1-40.

Rogers, C.G. (1982) *A Social Psychology of Schooling*. London: Routledge & Kegan Paul.

Rogers, C. and Kutnick, P. (1990) *The Social Psychology of the Primary School*. London: Routledge.

Rogers, C.G., Armstrong, D., Jackson, C., Galloway, D. and Leo, E. (1993a) The transfer from primary to secondary school and the incidence of different motivational styles. Paper presented at the annual conference of the American Educational Research Association, Atlanta, Georgia, USA.

Rogers, C.G., Armstrong, D., Jackson, C., Galloway, D. and Leo, E. (1993b) The transfer from primary to secondary school, attainment differences and the incidence of different motivational styles. Paper presented at the annual conference of the British Educational Research Association, Liverpool.

Schunk, D.H. (1990) Self-concept and school achievement. In C. Rogers and P. Kutnick (eds), *The Social Psychology of the Primary School*. London: Routledge.

Schunk, D.H. and Meece, J. (eds) (1992) *Student Perceptions in the Classroom*. Hove: Lawrence Erlbaum Associates.

Seligman, M.P. (1975) *Learned Helplessness: On Depression, Development and Death*. San Francisco: Freeman.

Sharan, S. (1989) *Co-operative Learning: Theory and Research*. New York: Praeger.

Slavin, R. (1987) Developmental and motivational perspectives on co-operative learning: a reconciliation. *Child Development*, **58**, 1161-7.

Slavin, R. (ed.) (1989) *School and Classroom Organization*. London: Lawrence Erlbaum.

Slavin, R. (1990) Co-operative learning. In C. Rogers and P. Kutnick (eds), *The Social Psychology of the Primary School*. London: Routledge.

Stipek, D.J. (1984) Young children's performance expectations: logical analysis or wishful thinking. In J. Nicholls (ed.), *Advances in Motivation and Achievement, Vol. 3, The Development of Achievement Motivation*. London: JAI Press.

Weiner, B. (1986) *An Attributional Theory of Motivation and Emotion*. New York: Springer-Verlag.

Weiner, B. (1992) *Human Motivation: Metaphors, Theories and Research*. London: Sage.

Weinstein, R.S., Marshall, H.H., Sharp, L. and Botkin, M. (1987) Pygmalion and the student: age and classroom differences in children's awareness of teacher expectations. *Child Development*, **58**, 1079-93.

Wigfield, A. and Harold, R.D. (1992) Teachers' beliefs and children's achievement self perceptions: a developmental perspective. In D.H. Schunk and J.L. Meece (eds), *Student Perceptions in the Classroom*. Hove: Lawrence Erlbaum Associates.

Woods, P. (1980) *Teacher Strategies*. Beckenham: Croom Helm.

Chapter 10

Evaluating Group Work

Colin Rogers and Peter Kutnick

EDITORS' INTRODUCTION

In the concluding chapter to this section, Rogers and Kutnick consider some of
the issues that would need to be borne in mind if one were to set out to evaluate
group work in a classroom context. This is not intended as a complete account of
how to do an evaluation. Rather, the chapter serves a summarizing function for
those that have preceded it before we move on to the two applications of group
work to be discussed in the chapers which follow.

INTRODUCTION

> These approaches demonstrate that co-operative group work is not a single, specific form
> of classroom organization but encompasses different approaches, different types of task
> and different demands for co-operation.
> (Bennett, Chapter 4, this volume)

The above quote helps to illustrate some of the problems that one might face in setting
out a framework within which the evaluation of group work might take place. In
talking about group work, as Bennett amongst others has made clear, we are not
talking about a single, unitary activity in relation to which we can produce a single set
of evaluative criteria.

This chapter seeks to set out a relatively brief consideration of some of the factors
that would need to be considered if one was to undertake an evaluation of group work
practices and in the process draws together the main themes that have emerged
throughout this volume.

The latter aspect of this task is a difficult one, largely due to the approach that we
ourselves have adopted to the editorial task involved in constructing this volume. It
was not our intention at the outset to provide a volume that promoted a view of the
nature of group work. Rather it has been our intention to demonstrate the variety of
approaches and practices that can legitimately claim to be able to inform the nature of
group work practice. In doing this we have encouraged the authors of the individual
chapters that precede this one (and indeed the authors of the two which follow) to
adopt their own particular line and to tell their own particular story regarding the
operation of groups in educational contexts. Naturally this gives rise to many points of
contrast. For example, the approach adopted by Light and Littleton in their discussion

of the cognitive approach to group work is markedly different in its style and general assumptions to the chapter by Hall concerning the interpersonal relational aspects of group working.

However, while it may be useful and desirable to draw attention to the differences that exist between the broad approaches adopted by our various contributors, there is a clear sense of emerging themes which can forcefully cut across the various differences in emphasis and approach.

The most striking of these is the repeated observation that conceptions of the learner have changed enormously over the last decade or so and that these changes not only point to the desirability of group work, they actually seem to make it a necessary condition for effective learning to take place.

Many of our writers have referred to the change in conception from the individual learner operating as the 'lone scientist' towards the learner functioning as a social being in the midst of a particular social context. What becomes increasingly apparent from this view is that the social context is not simply something that can be considered alongside the learning process, it is something that has to be considered as an integral part of the learning process. It becomes difficult to see how learning can always be considered as an individualistic activity, with a social dimension tacked on when it appears that it might be useful to do so. Instead learning needs to be addressed within the social context that will necessarily be a part of it. The options for the teacher, given this broad approach, are therefore not to do with *whether* a social dimension needs to be considered, but instead, *how* is the social dimension to be considered.

The question of how group work may relate to broader curriculum issues is one that will be addressed in detail by Anne Edwards in the following chapter. The present chapter will attempt to develop a concern with evaluation and the issues associated with this in a broader context where the implications can be considered to be more general in nature. However, before beginning to discuss the evaluation of group work it will be necessary to make a few opening comments about evaluation itself.

OBJECTIVES AND PURPOSES OF EVALUATION

It is easy for evaluation to get a bad press. All too often teachers tend to see evaluation as something that is done to them by other people. These other people will more often than not be people who have power and the ability to exercise control over resources. Evaluation is used as a tool of management, but the tool is understood to be a relatively blunt one with which people may be beaten, rather than a delicate one with which some fine tuning may be usefully carried out. This is unfortunate, and perhaps has more to do with the presentation of government policy in the media than anything else, but it would be particularly unfortunate if such a view were to be taken of the nature of evaluation here.

General approaches to evaluation

The process of evaluation can best be considered as a systematic approach to the gathering of information. The precise purposes lying behind this will vary, depending on the exact context and the intentions of the evaluator, but generally speaking the information is being gathered in order to allow judgements to be made about the effects or the effectiveness of a particular process. There are many techniques which may be used individually or in combination and it is not the intention here to give an account of all or even some of these. Rather the purpose is to set out some of the very broad concerns of any evaluation programme and then to look at the particular considerations that might be necessary in setting out to evaluate the effects of group work.

Summative or formative

One of the most basic distinctions, and in many ways one of the most important for present purposes, is that which can be made between summative and formative forms of evaluation. Summative evaluation is primarily concerned with establishing a view about the outcome of a particular activity once the activity has reached a natural breakpoint. The outcome of the summative evaluation may well be used to determine whether or not the activity resumes after the break has taken place. It will frequently be the case that a number of objectives will have been established at the outset of the activity being evaluated and these are then assessed during the evaluative period. It is possible then to make decisions regarding the degree to which objectives have been realized and targets met. Summative evaluation can take place when there is no particular commitment to the continuation of the activity. Indeed its use may be thought to be particularly appropriate under those circumstances where decisions as to whether or not to continue with the activity are contingent upon certain conditions, generally specified in the form of goals, objectives or targets, being met.

Formative evaluation on the other hand is generally carried out in parallel to the activity itself and is concerned with its ongoing development. It would more often be the case here that a commitment to the continuation of the activity has been made, at least for a minimum period of time, and that the continuation within that period is not dependent upon the outcome of the evaluation process. As its name suggests, formative evaluation is more concerned with aiding the development of a particular activity, helping with its formation, and should always therefore be seen as a positive tool to be used to the advantage of those who wish the project well.

It seems clear that the teacher setting up group work in a school context may well be interested in either or both forms of evaluation. Summative evaluation can be useful in aiding final decisions as to whether the effort has been rewarded with the anticipated or hoped for gains. Equally clearly, if the results of a summative evaluation are certainly positive then those results can be a powerful force behind arguments for the project's continuation or further development.

The assumption here is that it will be formative evaluation which the classroom teacher will be concerned with. The objective is to develop a clearer understanding of the processes involved in the implementation and enactment of a group work plan and then to begin to attempt to determine the effects of that plan. What follows is not intended to be a handbook of evaluation practice, (to do justice to all of the concerns that such a handbook would need to cover would take more than the single chapter available here), rather it seeks to set out some of the core concerns which a teacher wishing to undertake such an evaluation would wish to consider.

SPECIFIC CONCERNS WITH GROUP WORK

The introduction of any new practice, or any attempt to redefine the nature of an existing practice, needs to be preceded by the setting out of the expectations that the initiators might reasonably have for their endeavours. From the various chapters in this volume what are the areas where change might be anticipated?

The first area refers back to the chapter by Bennett. Here the point was made that researchers interested in group work have tended to form two different camps. First there have been those who are primarily concerned with using group work as a means of changing the fundamental nature of the teaching in use within a school or classroom. Group work is not conducive to a highly didactic style of teaching. In cases where current teaching styles are considered to be inappropriately didactic group work may be introduced in order to fundamentally change the style of teaching typically found within the school or classroom. The introduction of group work would be judged to be successful to the extent that teaching methods generally became less didactic and more participatory.

In other contexts the style of teaching may already be considered appropriate and the focus of attention is to be much more clearly on the effectiveness of the particular practices which are to be employed. Such a distinction is not intended to suggest that there will be cases where a concern with the effectiveness of teaching will not be relevant, it is assumed that this should always be the case. Rather, the point is made that it will be important to be clear as to whether the object is to bring about broad changes in approach, or detailed changes in the implementation of an approach.

The lack of such a distinction where it is needed can be a source of difficulty. It may well be inappropriate for teachers to become embroiled in discussions about the detailed aspects of a procedure when they have not yet developed a broad set of agreed assumptions about the general style to be developed and adopted.

A similar point emerges when consideration is given to the other fundamental distinction that needs to be made. Here the concern is not with the nature of the pedagogic strategy to be used, but with the degree to which group work is to be concerned with actual pedagogy or with the management of the classroom. The distinction between the two is, of course, a fine one. Effective pedagogic practices will not be developed in the absence of effective classroom management. To this extent there is a necessary relationship between the two sets of concerns. However, effective classroom management does not imply successful pedagogy. The class may be perfectly under control but learning very little.

As has again been stated in some earlier chapters (e.g. Kutnick and Rogers, Kutnick, and Merrett) groups have typically been identified as part of the collection of classroom management tools available to the teacher. A similar observation can be made (King, 1978) in relation to the teacher's deliberate use of gender as a grouping

principle. Placing boys and girls in separate learning groups may or may not give rise
to more effective teaching and learning but it may well make the classroom easier to
manage. It is not suggested here that group work ought not to be used as a
management tool, nor even that this is a less desirable objective or purpose than ones
which are more directly concerned with pedagogy. The main point again is that one
has to be clear about the purposes lying behind the introduction of group work before
any sensible attempt can be made to evaluate those outcomes.

The relationship between classroom management and pedagogy is well illustrated
by Merrett (Chapter 3). Different seating arrangements can be shown to have a clear
impact upon time on task. As Merrett makes clear, time on task itself is well
established as a variable which can influence the nature of, and the effectiveness of,
the learning that takes place. The careful use of different seating arrangements,
therefore, can help to influence learning. However, as Merrett argues in his chapter,
the relationship between seating arrangements, learning and the particular task in
hand might not always be entirely straightforward. The teacher will need to give
careful consideration to the interactions between task and seating plans. Merrett
himself makes the point that his approach to the management of groups in order to
improve pedagogy is more complex than it may at first appear and that it will require
particular skills on the part of the teacher. These skills, he suggests, are probably
under-developed in most teachers and training is therefore required. The authors of
this chapter share his pessimism with respect to the chances of appropriate training in
the pedagogic use of groups being available. If self-instruction is to be the order of the
day then self-evaluation becomes even more necessary.

However, it is also the case that the introduction of the time on task measure
provides a relatively simple means of evaluating the effectiveness of group work
procedures. The important point to emerge from Bennett, Merrett, and Johnson and
Johnson in particular is that groups operating without a clear structure and without an
established framework will be likely to engage in a relatively high level of off task or
low level talk. As we complete this text it is clear that present government thinking on
the nature of good practice within schools is likely to lead to teachers assuming that it
is desirable to return to whole class methods of teaching. As stated above, the one
point addressed by most of our contributors is that the typical classroom of the 1970s,
1980s and into the 1990s has not been characterized by group work, merely by
grouping. The evidence reviewed throughout this volume makes it clear that in order
to establish effective group practice and to gain the attendant benefits in terms of
more time on task and a higher level of pupil input it is essential that the structure of
the group is attended to.

DEVELOPMENTAL GAINS

In Chapter 6 Light and Littleton reviewed the results of a number of studies, many
conducted outside of the school classroom, which indicate that the social context
provided by group work can enable developmental progress to be made at a greater
rate than would be the case if each child operated individually.

A number of important points emerge from this discussion which are worth drawing
attention to here. The first is that there needs to be an emphasis on the developmental

change that takes place in the level of thinking displayed by the child. It seems clear from Light and Littleton's contribution (Chapter 6) that while many teachers will be familiar with their descriptions of some of the classic Piagetian studies, it will not always be the case that teachers, or others, will be familiar with the meaning of the results that have been obtained from these studies. The theoretical perspectives to be found in the writings of Piaget and Vygotsky have proven inspirational to many educationists who are concerned with the development of group work. The application of each of these perspectives, in their different ways, draws our attention to the developmental changes that group work may encourage in the individual child. This is the appropriate focus. Much group work practice, particularly co-operative and collaborative approaches, will lead to the production of a group product. The quality of this group product will often be of interest in its own right and will frequently be a powerful indicator as to the benefits likely to accrue to the individual participant. However, it is the advances in understanding, knowledge and ability to handle different types of information and concepts made by the individual child that will need to be the focus of attention in any ongoing evaluation.

Paradoxically, Light and Littleton point out how one particular teaching strategy, hailed initially as offering great advances in the instruction of the individual pupil, has helped to foster the use of group work in the ordinary primary classroom. The reference here of course is to the use of the classroom computer. The device intended to foster individual learning through the application of modes of instruction that could be more tightly linked to the progress made by an individual pupil has increasingly come to be seen to offer possibly greater potential as a device for facilitating the social milieu which many developmental theorists now regard as essential to effective development and teaching. This reminds us of the importance of auditing the use to which the classroom and its contents are put. Facilities are not always used in accordance with their initial intentions and constant monitoring of what is actually taking place continues to be of critical importance.

LONGER-TERM EFFECTS ON THE ORIENTATIONS OF PUPILS

The conclusion of Chapter 6 draws our attention to another important strand in considering the general effects of the adoption of group work. They point to research by Monteil (1992) which demonstrates that public and private performance of a task can have different effects depending on the self-perceptions of the individual. A person who is initially confident in their ability to perform the task well will have their performance enhanced in the public context while those who lack such confidence are likely to suffer reduced performance. The distinction between public and private performance is not the same as the distinction between group and individual performance. It is important to consider the nature of these differences before turning to look at the changes that might be expected in the perspective of the pupil consequent upon the adoption of group work.

This concern shown by Light and Littleton helps to provide a link with the work reported here by Rogers. Bennett, in Chapter 4, draws attention to the distinction that has been more fully addressed by Slavin (1987) between developmental and motivational approaches to understanding the effects of group work. Light and

Littleton's concluding comments make it clear that they would support an approach to the evaluation of group work which sought to explore the impact on both cognitive development and motivational processes. Given the current emphasis on cognitive approaches to motivation (see Galloway *et al.*, 1994) there seems to be little reason why a joint concern with both of these aspects would not be appropriate for the teacher looking at the impact of group work.

The initial point made by Light and Littleton was that performance in a public setting will have different effects upon people depending on their level of confidence in the task at hand. An individual with a relatively high level of confidence benefits from a public performance while those with a relatively low level perform better in private. In considering the expected impact of groups on performance it is worth considering a little further the nature of the distinctions that are being made here.

It is not the public *vs* private distinction which is problematic, it is rather the implicit distinction made by Light and Littleton between performance and other kinds of activity. Motivational theorists (e.g. Ames and Ames, 1989; Dweck, 1991) have made important distinctions between those settings which encourage learning goals and those which encourage performance goals. With performance goals in operation one is concerned, naturally enough, with the quality of the performance that one is displaying. Other people's assessments of that performance will be important and one is more likely to develop anxieties related to the adequacy of one's own performance. Performance goals can therefore give rise to fearful and defensive approaches to learning, where the pupil will be likely to attempt to cover up what they do not know. This, along with other strategies, is designed to try to ensure that any evaluations made of the performance are as positive as possible. However, while such a strategy may well be suited to the purpose of maintaining an acceptable public image, it will not necessarily enhance learning and thereby developmental progress. With contexts which encourage learning goals, however, this type of defensive behaviour is less likely to occur. An individual will be more willing to admit to their weaknesses and lack of understanding and is thereby likely to adopt strategies which will enhance the learning opportunities available to them.

From the point of view of the teacher setting up group work and concerned to determine what may or may not result from this, this distinction would be an important one to consider. It would be wrong to infer from Light and Littleton's chapter that group work would necessarily lead to pupils adopting performance goals as they were working in a more public setting. There are two main reasons why this would not necessarily be the case. It is not the simple presence of other people which gives rise to performance goals, but the roles and positions assumed to be held by those that are present by the pupil which count. The single figure of the teacher (Galton and Williamson, 1992) observing the work of a pupil with a critically observant eye will do far more to produce a performance orientation, than the presence of many other pupils who hold a non-judgemental role. The second reason is amply demonstrated by the work of Ames (e.g. Ames and Ames, 1989). Ames has argued that it is competition that encourages a performance orientation. Co-operative or collaborative approaches to learning through group work ought not to encourage performance orientations. Indeed, the opposite ought to be the case. The more pupils are engaged in working with their peers in order to produce a product the less likely they are to adopt performance goals. The less likely they are to adopt performance goals the more likely they are to develop positive motivational approaches.

In some respects we are drawing attention here to the longer term changes in the general orientations of pupils towards learning that the adoption of group work might establish. Effects which take place over the long term will only be picked out by evaluations which take an equally long-term perspective. Maintaining an evaluative stance over a protracted period of time can be demanding in terms of the resources it requires and it is generally the case, therefore, that evaluations are short-term exercises.

However, this does not mean that the motivational aspects of group work can only be assessed by teachers who are willing to make a relatively long-term commitment to evaluation. Indeed, the work reported by Rogers in Chapter 9 suggests that the motivational responses of pupils will be subject to variation over contexts and that it may be better to consider motivational style as an outcome of interactions between aspects of the pupil and aspects of the *current* work context. Given this, it not only becomes plausible to suggest that teachers might wish to monitor the effectiveness of group work in motivational terms, it begins to appear as a particularly important area to look at.

There is, then, a possibly important difference between the assessments that teachers might wish to make in respect to the cognitive development taking place within their pupils given the introduction of group work and the assessments that they might wish to make regarding the motivational and attitudinal components. The developmental gains need to be assessed over a relatively long period. Teachers need to ask whether the introduction of group work leaves pupils at, say, the end of year 5 further ahead in terms of their work progress than they might have been prior to the introduction of group work. This will necessarily involve the monitoring of pupil performance over a relatively extensive period so that year-on-year comparisons might be made. Motivational and attitudinal evaluations, however, would seem to be more appropriately made in the short term so that teachers can assess the impact that current arrangements seem to be having upon pupils.

The motivational gains that are believed to be possible given the introduction of group work are generally recognized as owing much to the changed relationships between pupils within the class. Hall in Chapter 8 and Topping in Chapter 7 have both drawn attention to the importance of directly considering the inter-pupil relationships which will emerge as the result of the introduction of group work. Hall, of course, has argued that improved social relationships ought not to be assumed as a desirable by-product of the introduction of group work. Instead he argues for a more directly interventionist approach. This in turn helps to make it clear that the teacher ought to have changes in social relationships as one of the objectives lying behind the introduction of group work methods. It would be consistent with a general concern with the evaluation of work designed to meet objectives to then evaluate the degree to which improvements in social relationships are actually obtained. It would seem appropriate to conclude that changes in social relations would need to be evaluated on a more or less continuous basis. Much in the same way as motivational states can be understood as the product, at least in part, of a current context, so too can the relationships between pupils be seen as the product of current forms of social organization.

In summary then, the evaluation of group work needs to be undertaken on an essentially continuous basis. The responses of pupils to their learning environments are themselves subject to change as the environment itself changes. Pupils' responses to group work both in terms of developmental progress and in terms of motivation and attitudes to school and learning cannot be assumed to be steady and easily predictable. It is hoped that the messages from elsewhere in this volume are sufficient to persuade the teacher that the effort will be worthwhile.

REFERENCES

Ames, C. and Ames, R.E. (1989) *Research on Motivation in Education, Vol. 3, Goals and Cognitions*. London: Academic Press.

Dweck, C.S. (1991) Self-theories and goals: their role in motivation, personality and development. In *Nebraska Symposium on Motivation 1990. Volume 38*. Lincoln: University of Nebraska Press.

Galloway, D., Rogers, C., Armstrong, D., Leo, E. and Jackson, C. (1994) *Motivating the Difficult to Teach*. London: Longman.

Galton, M. and Wiliamson, J. (1992) *Groupwork in the Primary Classroom*. London: Routledge.

King, R. (1978) *All Things Bright and Beautiful*. Chichester: Wiley.

Monteil, J.-M. (1992) Towards a social psychology of cognitive functioning. In M. von Granach, W. Doise and G. Mugny (eds), *Social Representation and the Social Bases of Knowledge*. Berne: Hubert.

Slavin, R.E. (1987) Developmental and motivational perspectives on co-operative learning: a reconciliation. *Child Development*, **58**, 1161-7.

Part 3

Practical Applications

Chapter 11

The Curricular Applications of Classroom Groups

Anne Edwards

EDITORS' INTRODUCTION

'Most teachers are secure in their grasp of curricular issues. The tricky part of teaching is getting the pupils to learn.' These sentences form part of the final paragraph in this chapter by Anne Edwards, which seeks to address the broad range of issues which a teacher will need to consider in developing applications of groups to particular curricular concerns. The point is clear and well made. The key problem for a teacher who is secure in her or his understanding of their own subject is how to engage pupils in the type of activities which will develop *their* understanding of that subject.

In many respects we will see that a consideration of the use of groups is no different from any other considerations that a teacher will have to make. As was argued earlier by Rogers in Chapter 9 in his consideration of motivational issues in the use of groups, many of the processes and issues involved are common to classroom practice.

However, Edwards is able to demonstrate in this chapter how teachers will need to give consideration to decisions regarding the use of groups alongside the other factors that have to be judged. For this reason, the ways in which groups are employed, and the circumstances under which such practices will be carried out, will vary between, say, the English and the physics teacher. Groups are not necessarily more or less relevant to either of the two disciplines just referred to, but the precise ways in which they are employed will vary.

Effective teaching, getting the pupils to learn what is wanted, is no easy matter. Edwards, in providing one of the two concluding chapters for this volume, shows us that thinking in terms of group work provides no simple panaceas. However, when given appropriate consideration alongside other matters relating to the curriculum and the pupils that teachers will always need to work with, groups provide another and potentially powerful tool.

THE WORTHWHILENESS OF GROUPS

Current concerns of classroom teachers include the constant problems of the management of children's learning, their own time and classroom resources. To these classroom management issues, in the UK at least, recently have been added problems of curriculum coverage and entitlement and the difficulties of continuous pupil assessment.

The current additions to teaching do not widen the agenda for teachers, but do intensify elements as external pressure is heaped upon the hapless practitioner. This context of public accountability does not encourage teachers to take risks. If the use of groups is to become more extensive, or even sustained, it has to be proved a worthwhile step. To borrow the language of accountability and quality control: the use of groups has to demonstrate fitness for purpose. Fitness for purpose in this context means the enhancement of pupil learning.

For thinking practitioners there are two elements to the notion of fitness for the purpose of improving pupil learning. The first is the power of the explanatory framework or theory that supports the particular use of groups. In other words, 'Does it make sense in terms of my understanding of how children best think and learn in classrooms?' The second element is its feasibility: 'Will I be able to manage the processes in my classroom and get the outcomes I want?'

Several contributors to this volume have presented evidence to suggest that a variety of the forms of peer and pupil–teacher interactions we call groups might enhance pupil learning. It may therefore be useful to consider how the two elements of theoretical framework and feasible practice may be integrated. The key connection between theories of pupil learning and the practicalities of classroom management is an understanding of task demand and its implications for matching task to learner (Galloway and Edwards, 1991).

Developing Norman's (1978) analysis of classroom tasks, Bennett *et al.* (1984) moved teachers' understanding of match from the neo-Piagetian view of providing novelty sufficient to stimulate accommodation processes. Their work took a view more in tune with neo-Vygotskian views of the learning process. The Norman–Bennett *et al.* analyses of task allow us to categorize a three- or four-stage learning process. In summary these stages are: introduction to the new information, opportunities to make sense of the information, opportunities to fine tune new understandings and to build them into an individual's repertoire of performance and responses. These stages have relevance for an understanding of the fitness for purpose of groupings as each may demand different criteria for the success of group work. For example, you would not expect a teacher-led introductory group session to produce deep levels of understanding in the learners, equally you may also be tolerant of the stumbling towards understanding occurring in an interactive group session at the second or 'making sense' stage.

The Norman–Bennett *et al.* breakdown of match finds a useful parallel in the neo-Vygotskian framework of supported learning across the zone of proximal development (ZPD) already discussed in this volume. Implicit in such frameworks is the notion of assisted performance (Tharp and Gallimore, 1988). This requires that the teacher engages in careful initial diagnosis and goal-setting and provides often considerable support at the early stages of learning but gradually manages a reduction in that support to the extent that the learner is able to demonstrate independent mastery of the new information. Both this model and the analysis of task demand provided by Norman and Bennett *et al.* recognize that progress does not occur in a simple linear way. For example, a learner may need to retreat from semi-independence to seek

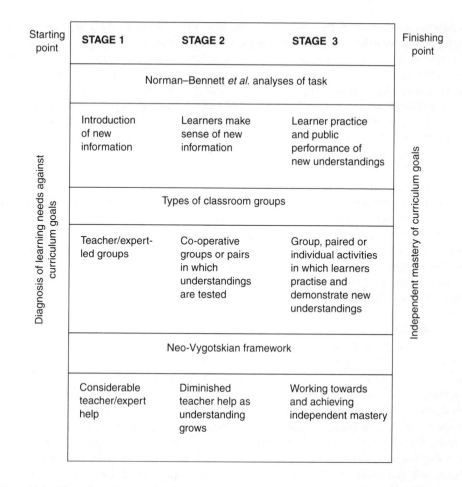

Starting point | Finishing point

Diagnosis of learning needs against curriculum goals

Independent mastery of curriculum goals

STAGE 1	STAGE 2	STAGE 3
Norman–Bennett *et al.* analyses of task		
Introduction of new information	Learners make sense of new information	Learner practice and public performance of new understandings
Types of classroom groups		
Teacher/expert-led groups	Co-operative groups or pairs in which understandings are tested	Group, paired or individual activities in which learners practise and demonstrate new understandings
Neo-Vygotskian framework		
Considerable teacher/expert help	Diminished teacher help as understanding grows	Working towards and achieving independent mastery

Figure 11.1   *The pedagogic purposes of groups.*

increased teacher support before moving on to individual mastery. Nevertheless it may be useful to consider a simplified version of these two frameworks as they do have some utility for an understanding of how groups may be used in classrooms (see Figure 11.1).

Each stage in the learning process, therefore, has different expectations of the effects of classroom grouping. At Stage 1 the concern may simply be that the teacher or more expert peer provides experience of a new skill or the introduction to a new piece of information. At Stage 2 tentative use of newfound language and concepts in a non-threatening context may be a paramount purpose. At Stage 3 the expectation may be that skills and information are used to prove mastery. If this analysis is accepted, the criteria for fitness for purpose is not uniform for all groupings.

The feasibility element of fitness for purpose should not be lost in a concern for learning. Does the understanding of the purpose of groups in classrooms actually assist teachers in managing classrooms? If we take as axiomatic that appropriate match of learner and task is a prerequisite for a well-managed classroom we are already halfway towards an affirmative response. But we do need to relate this framework to the most important commodity in the classroom: teacher time. In Figure 11.1 we can see that Stage 1 makes considerable demands on teacher (or more expert pupil) time, Stage 2 demands a low intervention, monitorial, watchful role and Stage 3 requires low teacher presence. Teacher time becomes a resource to be managed through the allocation of tasks to groups for a range of learning purposes.

So far the discussion has been in terms of broad frameworks which, though often useful starting points, have little utility for those concerned with the detail of practice. We need, therefore, to examine what happens at each stage and what optimum interactions might look like.

Stage 1 Alongside the 'teacher'
At this point in the learning process the concern is introduction to the field of experience. It may involve immersion in a bath of new language as the learner takes the first steps in a process of induction into the discourse used by experts in the field. Teacher or expert talk may dominate as the learner is oriented to the new field. An example of this might be a teacher-led whole class or group session, or the mixed groups of able and less able children who performed so well in the Bennett and Cass (1988) study of children's groupings and interactive teaching.

Stage 2 Making sense
This is the stage at which group work would appear to have most to offer. Well monitored but teacherless groups provide semi-private, often supportive contexts for learners' first gropings towards understanding or making sense of new information. The language of the expert discourse can tentatively be tried out, hypotheses warily tested and misakes made. This is the stage at which existing knowledge structures have to adapt to new understandings. It is a crucial stage in the management of pupils' learning for without it deep learning is unlikely to occur. To ignore this stage is to press the learner too rapidly from 'I hear' to 'I perform' without the time to do, reflect, talk and understand provided by this second stage of the learning process. It is also probably the most difficult stage to manage and for that reason above all warrants the attention it will receive later in this chapter when we look at co-operative learning groups.

Stage 3 Demonstrating mastery
This is the performance stage at which the learner practises and uses with ease the new skills and understandings acquired in the process of progressing through Stages 1 and 2. The language evident here should be appropriately competent pupil use of the expert discourse. Of course it is itself only a stage in the learning process and provides diagnostic opportunities for teachers who are planning pupils' subsequent learning.

Practice and mastery may also occur through individual activity. It is the stage that may, for example, lend itself to individual responsibility to a group or team in an inter-group competitive setting. Aronson's Jigsaw activities would be one example of this (Aronson *et al.*, 1978).

USING INTERACTIVE GROUPS TO ENHANCE LEARNING

Current understandings of pupils' learning in schools emphasize that academic subjects whether taught in primary or secondary schools consist not only of key knowledge concepts but also of ways of organizing and of acquiring the knowledge that may be unique to one subject and certainly integral to it (Bruner, 1960; Driver, 1983). Examples of the integrity of subjects can be seen as the basic concepts without which these subjects may not be understood, whether addition in mathematics or exchange in economics, and in the modes of enquiry which are subject-specific. In a primary school context there are, for example, important differences between the relatively closed nature of a scientific investigation and some of the more open-ended aspects of investigations using mathematics. The use of subject-specific language plays an important part in the acquisition of expertise. Mastery of a subject discourse is often one indication of mastery of a subject. Language use needs to be exercised and linguistic ambiguities clarified as expertise is developed. Some simple examples allow us to see the importance of the context of specific subjects. For example, 'state' in chemistry is not the same as 'State' in history, 'media' in English differs in substance from 'media' in biology.

If we take a view of teaching as a process of inducting a novice into what are held to be current notions of expertise we need to find ways of enabling the learner to acquire, use and understand the discourse of their subject. This is the case whether it be the language of literary analysis and concepts of Renaissance drama used when examining the work of Shakespeare or an understanding of colour mixing and the use of light and dark colours when starting to produce an expressive painting.

Learning to use the language or discourse of a domain is part of the induction into that domain. Language use empowers the learner by enabling him or her to hypothesize, extrapolate and extend personal understanding of a curriculum area. Language develops in use and so enhances learning. Writing about the social contexts of learning, Light and Perret-Clermont (1989) summarize the process so that we see 'pragmatic, intersubjective agreements in meaning . . . lying at the heart of the developmental process'. Ideally, interactive groups, whether pairs, small groups or whole-class, provide opportunities for 'intersubjective agreements-in-meaning' to be developed, explored, shaped and checked against the expert knowledge covered in school curricula.

This emphasis on language and learning in a curriculum area was clearly exemplified in the early 1980s in the United Kingdom in Open University material designed to help teachers develop pupils' mathematical thinking. Using the keywords Do Talk and Record (Floyd, 1981), the course team encouraged teachers to talk with children while they introduced new mathematical strategies; to give children the opportunity to assume increasing responsibility for strategy use; to provide activities for children to do; and to encourage talk in groups. A final record or evidence of mastery was to be required only after considerable pupil–pupil talk and 'rough' calculations had taken place. Language use, from initial immersion to final production, was the linking feature of each stage and the opportunities for tentative use of the discourse were built into the process.

The crucial stage in the process just outlined is the equivalent to Stage 2 in Figure 11.1. It is here that the sensitive management of learning is most clearly demanded.

Teachers know only too well that you can take a child to language but you can't make him or her use it.

The experiences of teachers of 5-year-olds illustrate how paired activities in classrooms may be set up in order to enable children to use the language associated with the conceptual understandings introduced at Stage 1 in Figure 11.1. In a small-scale study of twenty-four 5-year-old children, Molly examined the extent to which the carefully designed mathematical tasks she set for pairs of children actually gave them the opportunity to try out and use the new mathematical language and ideas she had introduced to them. The pairs were of unequal ability and were tape-recorded on task for a total of 600 minutes for the group of twenty-four pupils. After content analysis of the tape-recordings she noted that 79 per cent of the talk was related to the task and could mainly be categorized as giving or asking instructions and giving information (including self-directing talk). The only exception to this high level of on-task talk was during a money-sorting activity, when the children carried out the task demands but, familiar with the coins they were using, gossiped while sorting them. A clear lesson here was that match of task and child is the crucial ingredient.

Recordings of the other paired activities demonstated that well matched tasks could encourage children's thinking, but that watchful monitoring is necessary. Helen and Tracy were set a sequencing task (colour sequencing blocks) after working with Molly on sequencing activities. What Molly hoped to hear was the children's use of colour names, some counting and the use of sequencing language, e.g. first, second, next, last. An examination of a conversation between Tracy and Helen while on task illustrates what can be gained from this kind of activity.

Tracy: I'm, I'm going to do yellow. We got . . .
Helen: You, you've got to have green, I think. Haven't you?
Tracy: Red.
Helen: Two blue's. Innit?
Tracy: No, two reds.
Helen: Oops! . . . Two red . . . two reds . . . Two blues innit? Two greens?
Tracy: *No!* Like this. Two blues, two greens, two reds . . . Right? Then two blues again, t . . two greens, *two*-um-two greens and another green (watching Helen).
Helen: Two greens?
Tracy: Another green?
Helen: Another green. Yeh. I've got another green.
Tracy: Put it down there . . . so there . . . There we are. Now, now.
Helen: Yours is longer than mine. I must put . . . put a yellow there? Musn't I. Must I put –
Tracy: Oh! How many was there?
Helen: Two blues . . . two greens . . . two reds . . .
Tracy: Now two y . . yellows.
Helen: Two yellows.
Tracy: Two of everything, right?
Helen: But not these?
Tracy: But not those. After.
Helen: One . . . One there . . . I needs two, I needs two greens.

Tracy: *No!*
Helen: Two blues?
Tracy: Two blue . . . and starting all again after you've got-um-thing, after you've done-um-yellow. Right? Starting all over again.
Helen: I want yellows don't I?
Tracy: No.
Helen: Greens?
Tracy: Two greens, t . . two reds, two yellow. Then start all again – at the end 'til you gets up to the table.
[At task – no speech.]
Tracy: I'm doing that one.
Helen: I'm doing this one.
Tracy: I'm doing blue, red, blue, red, blue, red.
Helen: I'm doing green, red, green, green, red, green, green, red, green, (green) green, red, green.
Tracy: Green, red, green.
Helen: Must I do another yellow? [referring to another pattern]
Tracy: That's not it, like that, straight – like a line.
Helen: Oh –
Tracy: Like *that*
Helen: (intrans) . . .
Tracy: Don't get it wrong. Right?
Helen: Don't get it wrong.

Quite clearly the children were thinking hard. Tracy was using the counting and colour vocabulary, physically sequencing and giving support to Helen. Helen was also using some of the target language and was benefitting from the support Tracy provided as she physically completed the task. The language of sequencing was, however, not explicitly used. It may be a weakness in the task that words such as first and next were not evident. These words would be more likely to be needed by the children in perhaps a game which involved asking each other to select items according to their position in a row of items. Molly's watchful monitoring ensured that these weaknesses were identified and an additional task inserted in the learning programme.

Each child was gaining something different from the colour sequencing task. Tracy was testing and confirming her understanding. Helen was more tentatively groping towards the concept of sequencing and was using the context of a dialogue with Tracy to allow herself to direct her own thinking. She responded well to Tracy's instructions as the conversational tone dominated.

Helen: I want yellows don't I?
Tracy: No.
Helen: Greens?
Tracy: Two greens . . .

The pairing was a safe place for Helen who remained actively involved in the task throughout the session despite her, so far, weak grasp of the concepts she was using.

What this small study indicates is that induction into the expert discourse implies literally 'leading in'. That it is not enough to simply provide the language bath and expect absorption, understanding and use. Opportunities for the process of conceptual change have to be provided and, if used, groups should have distinctive pedagogic purposes which are planned and controlled by teachers and for which pupils are prepared. We return, therefore, to our earlier concern with the fitness for purpose of groups in classrooms.

CREATING A CLIMATE FOR LEARNING

Real learning is a risky business. It involves loss of current, sometimes comfortable, understandings without guaranteeing similar intellectual certainty and security. Resultant new connections made to previously securely-held ideas threaten established ways of seeing the world. And, above all, you may be *wrong* in your initial attempts at grasping or modifying conceptual understanding. As you operate as a learner at Stage 2 of the learning process you may use the new language inappropriately, or may not have worked out the ramifications of your new knowledge for your existing knowledge structures and may find yourself confronted by your own embarrassing illogicality. Yet successful learning, which in the end increases the predictability of our world, is rewarding. Success in learning is motivating. Co-operative groupings can be used to achieve the twofold aim of providing a non-threatening environment in which experimentation can take place and in which motivation-inducing success can occur.

Overt adult intervention, as opposed to responsive monitoring, of learners at Stage 2 would seem to have motivational effects as uncertainty occurs and active experimentation ceases. Prisk (1987) in her study of 6- and 7-year-olds noted pupil dependency behaviour once she joined groups which had, until her arrival, been engaged in well structured and task-focused discussion. She observed that as soon as she joined the group 'their behaviour changed and they appeared to hand over control of the discussion'.

A similar effect was noted in Molly's study where the following interchange occurred when a teacher's aide joined a pair of 5-year-olds engaged on a capacity task. The aim of this task was the use of the language of counting and of capacity words which included full, empty, holds more, holds less. Again the children worked in mixed-ability pairs on a task which built on previous language experience alongside the teacher. The two children, James and Winston, were each engaged in filling a large container with water carried in smaller beakers.

James: 11-12
Winston: Mine's already filled up.
James: -13
Winston: Right up to the top. Miss? Miss?
James: -14
Winston: Miss? Miss?
James: -15-16-17
TA (teacher's aide):   Wait a minute James. What's happening? Put another one in. What's happening? Look what's happening?
James: That.
TA: So why do you think that's happening? Put some more in and have a look. Eighteen – you said. What's happening? Why is it doing that?

James: I don't know.

TA: Put some more in. See what will happen again? Then what's happening?

James: It's all dripping down the back.

TA: Why is that happening Winston?

Winston: Because it's too much.

TA: Too much. Too much. Yes. So it didn't take eighteen did it? Do you think you'd better check that again?

James: Yes.

TA: I think you'd better watch what's happening to the water this time, and make sure it's full . . . And how many did yours take (-W)

Winston: A hundred.

TA: A hundred – Gosh! [TA goes away.]

Winston: Mine is nearly going up to the top.

James: Look at mine. Mine's high.

Winston: Mine's higher than yours.

James: Mine's high.

Winston: Mine's higher – mine's about a . . . a . . . hundred [mls] . . .

James: Mine's about a . . . fifty [mls]

Winston: Mine's about a hundred too. We've finished, we've finished Mrs Thing.

In this case the intervening adult was the teacher's aide, who was not fully aware of the narrow purpose of the task. She interpreted it to require accurate measurement and not a grasp of the more general concept of capacity. The intervention did not clarify anything for the children, it did not actually take them back through the activity and it broke momentarily into the rhythm of an enthusiastic response to the task in hand.

Adult intervention in Stage 2 activities is, of course, necessary in order to provide learning support and guidance. But it requires immense skill and a clear sense of the purpose of the task. Above all, the give and take of the children's exploration of meanings needs to be sustained. Few teachers have ever claimed their job to be an easy one!

One lesson from both Prisk's and Molly's studies would seem to be that teacher time is a commodity that has to be used appropriately and that when low-risk sense-making groups are required, responsive teacher monitoring and light intervention may be the most appropriate action. Task structuring and planned time for feedback provide alternative opportunities for checking 'intersubjective agreements-in-meaning' of pupils against the public discourse of the more expert.

In their discussion of a non-threatening learning environment and its conduciveness to conceptual change in teenage science pupils, Watts and Bentley (1987) conclude that an atmosphere of 'warmth and trust' is an essential prerequisite for pupil exposure of personal constructions and uncertainties. One purpose of co-operative groupings in classrooms can be for the testing out of freshly acquired and partial understandings in non-judgemental contexts. Pairs of children engaged in the drafting of stories, small-group problem solving in design and technology and the paired use of Logo Turtle in the acquisition of computing skills would be examples of activities in which risk and error will be an essential part of the learning process. These activities, which are at Stage 2 in Figure 11.1, demand careful task structuring, watchful monitoring from the teacher and children's ability to support one another.

Establishing a relatively low-risk opportunity for learning, however, may not be enough. Hughes (1990) noted a gender difference in the responses to failure of his groups of 6- and 7-year-olds working with Logo Turtle. The girls-only pairings performed less well than the boys-only and mixed pairs, both on paired and subsequent individual tasks. He found that analysis of performance revealed that the all-girl pairings were more disturbed by task failure. They criticized and blamed themselves and each other rather than reflectively analysing events. This evidence seems to indicate the need for teacher intervention in the preparation of pupils for group work. Groups can be places where risk and failure is OK. Maximizing the benefits of teacherless experiences demands considerable awareness of the purpose of groups on the part of pupils as well as careful task structuring on the part of teachers.

One way of assisting pupils in their learning in lower-risk teacherless contexts is to provide support facilities through computer-assisted learning (CAL). While practice in some classrooms might suggest that teachers see computers as resources for individualized learning of a simple drill and practice form, this may be far too narrow a perception of their uses. In a review of recent research on CAL and the socio-cognitive activities of pupils Light and Blaye (1990) conclude that CAL programmes can stimulate group work and do themselves influence the processes and outcomes of pupil–pupil interactions. For example, pupils are less likely to use computer help facilities than to turn to their peers when help is required. In their concluding speculations they wonder whether classroom computers will in future be used more to support and sustain learning interactions among pupils.

Clearly, learning interactions centred around CAL are happening to an extent. Pairs of children engaged in computer drafting of joint narratives or the use of mapping skills are witness to this use of the computer. But Light and Blaye are going further with their speculation, in the expectation that new technologies will produce more rather than fewer pupil–pupil interactions and that task-oriented CAL will help to create contexts in which children's understandings are exercised, tested and used in ways which enable learners to share and explore meanings. Far from inhibiting the social elements of learning, CAL has the potential to sustain contexts in which they are enhanced.

The Spoken Language and New Technology (SLANT) Project (Mercer *et al.*, 1991) indicates that computers can be used in classrooms to stimulate exploratory talk and reasoned argument between pupils. They suggest that the screen provides a common source of information around which discussions can take place. In addition, the speed and ease with which screen presentations can be modified or tested facilitates exploration and challenging discussion in a way that written texts cannot.

Jones and Mercer (1993) draw on the experience of the SLANT project to distinguish between the use of computers in individualized learning and their use in learning situations which are planned with notion of the ZPD and the social interactive context of learning at the fore. When the latter perspective is taken teachers become 'orchestrators' of computer-based activities and use computers in a variety of ways to support pupil learning. These methods may range from drill and practice to simulations and micro-world games selected appropriately to support learners as they progress through their ZPDs. Jones and Mercer emphasize that there is currently a dearth of educational software specifically designed to enable teachers and pupils, or pupils and pupils, to use computers as a basis for talk and joint activity. Nevertheless, they argue that the more interactive model of teaching and learning provided by a Vygotskian perspective does more clearly than any other model of learning pick up on the reality of British classroom life, where despite the lack of appropriate software pupils work in pairs or groups on one computer.

But as both Hughes (1990) and Jones and Mercer (1993) have indicated, mere exposure to CAL is insufficient to promote pupil learning. Learning experiences need to be structured by teachers and it is with this in mind that we consider ways in which teachers may prepare to maximize the potential for enhancing pupil learning offered by groups.

PREPARING PUPILS FOR GROUP WORK

It has been indicated several times already in this chapter that careful resourcing is not enough and that if pupils are to make best use of group work they need to develop strategies that facilitate their learning in groups. Phillips (1985), in a study of the language used in classroom groups by children aged between 10 and 12, identified what he described as five modes of interaction used by the children. Some modes were more conducive to developing children's thinking than others.

The styles that he identified were the *hypothetical* mode, in which children used statements such as 'what about' and 'if'. The second mode was *experiential*, marked by use of statements like 'I remember' or 'once'. An *argumentative but co-operative* mode was evident in the use of 'yes but' and 'yes well'. The *operational* mode supported activities and often used pronouns and accompanied pointing with the words 'those' and 'that' or involved instructions. The final mode he described as *expositional* and found it rarely used in teacherless groups. In this mode children gave explanations and information.

Phillips' study allowed him to relate modes to mental processes and to observe that the hypothetical and experiential modes provided more opportunities for higher-order thinking than did the others. He found that the hypothetical and experiential styles directed pupils to a review of the interaction so far, to jointly re-examine what had been said and to open up for further contemplation what is to be said.

These conventional or interactional strategies provide the opportunities for the continuous process of acting and reflecting considered by many to be a prerequisite to learning. Donaldson (1978) emphasizes the importance of reflection in the acquisition of abstract thought. To be able to exercise choice, to be conscious of the possibilities available, was for Donaldson a critical aspect to the development of disembedded thinking in children.

At a more practical level, Moore and Tweddle (1992) in their examination of language, learning and information technology emphasize that teachers need to provide opportunities for reflection to occur and to encourage pupils to be constructively critical of their own and each other's work as they engage with new technologies. While I would not wish to dispute Moore and Tweddle's advice, it is probably necessary to go beyond encouragement in order to ensure that reflection occurs in interactive group settings.

The modes identified by Phillips (1985) provide a useful starting place for practitioners who wish to develop pupils' use of reflective strategies in interactive group work. One small-scale study with 14-year-old pupils is typical of several carried out by teachers of primary and secondary age pupils who have been stimulated by Phillips' findings.

In this case the teacher, Ann, wanted to improve the quality of the thinking about poetry that occurred in the small classroom discussion groupings she used in her streamed English classes. Her first step was to help the pupils in one class to tape-record their own group discussions. Each group then listened to its own recordings in order to identify those interactions which moved the discussion on and those which inhibited it. The whole class shared their analyses and identified markers of productive and non-productive language and behaviour in groups. Ann's understanding of task demand shown in Figure 11.1 enabled her to develop the whole-class discussion to ensure that the pupils became clear that the smaller groupings were safe places for trying out ideas (Figure 11.1, Stage 2). Her readings of Phillips' study also meant that she was able to encourage pupils to highlight hypothetical and experiential language and to find opportunities for reflection.

The pupils identified those strategies that they felt were conducive to good group work in literature lessons and agreed to monitor themselves and each other in their use. Subsequent recordings revealed that this monitoring occurred and the use of hypothetical and experiential learning increased. Comparisons of written work made with other similar classes which had not analysed their group-work skills indicated that the self-monitored groups had a better grasp of the key concepts of the analysis of poetry they were meant to be acquiring than did groups which did not examine their own interactions.

In a similar study with 10- and 11-year-old pupils in technology sessions Ray's observations of his pupils when they were engaged in problem-solving group tasks led him to a different organizational technique. Once the class had, through an analysis of one activity, identified the interactive skills and group strategies that had been the most productive, Ray designated a number of his pupils' 'group facilitators' for the next exercise. One facilitator was allocated to each small task group with the single function of ensuring that the group worked together, all participated and the task was completed. Ray's role became that of monitor of participation and the level of pupil understanding of the task. Pupil on-task behaviour increased, task-completion rose to 100 per cent and Ray felt more informed about the actual performance and understanding of individual pupils.

What this and other similar studies have done is to indicate the usefulness of addressing the strategy or metacognitive level of pupils' classroom activities. Nisbet and Shucksmith (1986), in their helpful guidelines for teachers, isolate a set of strategies that successful learners apply to tasks and argue that these can and should be taught. The strategies outlined by Nisbet and Shucksmith (p. 28) are:

> *Asking questions*: defining hypotheses, establishing aims and parameters of a task, discovering audience, relating task to previous work, etc.
> *Planning*: deciding on tactics and timetables, reduction of task or problem into components and the skills required.
> *Monitoring*: continuous attempt to match efforts, answers and discoveries and initial questions or purposes.
> *Checking*: preliminary assessment of performance and results.
> *Revising*: redrafting plans or revising goals.
> *Self-checking*: final self-assessment of results and performance on task.

These strategies can also be described as tasks analysis, self-monitoring, checking against task goals and self-evaluation. Nisbet and Shucksmith usefully subsume them under the more generic notion of planfulness.

It would appear from Nisbet and Shucksmith's work that training in these strategies helps to create effective independent learners who are clear about goal setting, able to continuously evaluate (reflect upon) progress towards that goal and engage in considered evaluation of the final product. If group work is to meet the multiple aims of improving pupils' learning through opportunity for reflection and hypothesis testing, provide motivating opportunities for success and assist the teacher in the management of children and time, it would seem that the guidelines offered by Nisbet and Shucksmith (1986) are a useful starting point for the preparation of pupils.

For many teachers what is being suggested is little more than a systematic extension of a form of good practice which emphasizes enhancing pupil responsibility for reflection and evaluation. Action research work carried out by primary school teachers on developing pupil self-evaluation indicates that the most surprising effect is the extent to which children from the age of 7 are able to engage in evaluatory self- and peer-appraisal and the impact that reflective evaluation discussion has on their command of the subject discourse. This appears to be the case whether the focus be design and technology, science, geography, writing or practical mathematics. Reflective evaluation, it seems, needs to be built into the process. Valued in its own right it quite easily appears to become part of everyday classroom practice.

MANAGING GROUP WORK

Work in British secondary schools on the use of flexible learning strategies (Waterhouse, 1988) provides an interesting parallel to research on learning strategies in primary schools. Though aimed primarily at offering learning pathways which match the optimal learning styles of pupils, the cycles of teaching and learning offered help us to see how group work may be used in a variety of forms. Like the work of Nisbet and Shucksmith (1986), the frameworks offered in flexible learning are subject-free to the extent that they are being adopted across all subjects at all levels in some British high schools and indeed are being systematically introduced into both vocational and non-vocational courses in further and higher education in the UK.

Supported self study is a commonly used framework in flexible learning and illustrates the potential and the limitations of group work in the teaching and learning process.

Points 1 and 2 in Figure 11.2 correspond with Stage 1 in Figure 11.1 as learners work alongside the more expert. Points 3, 4, 5 and 6 equate with Stage 2 in Figure 11.1 as learners work, often in pairs or groups, on tasks that are designed to enhance learning. At points 7 and 8 public performance and assessment occur and a parallel with Stage 3 in Figure 11.1 is evident.

Clearly there are different groupings at different stages in the cycle. At 1 the group may be the whole class led by the teacher. At 2 it may be, for example, two pupils or a group of ten or more with the teacher. In 3, 4, 5 and 6 the group may be a pair of children creating an electrical circuit, or using a computer database; a group of four writing a piece of music which they will later perform; or a group of eight identifying the key features of a scene in a play they have just watched or read. In each case these are co-operative groups faced with clear task demands and the expectations that they can evaluate against these demands as they proceed and that they will draw upon both old and new knowledge. At points 7 and 8 the group may be the work group, equally it could be the whole class and at point 8 of the model of teaching and learning, it may also involve the teacher in individual work with pupils.

The teacherless interactive groupings found at 3, 4, 5 and 6 therefore have an important but limited part to play in a cycle of learning. Their limitation arises from their location in the private domain of low threat. While this is necessary for tentative accommodation of new ideas to occur it is essential that the value of such groups is seen in relation to input and final evaluation in the domain of publicly accepted expert knowledge.

The link between the public and private domains is made through careful task analysis and resourcing. If pupils are to self-evaluate while they are on-task, the goals that are set for them have to be clear and unambiguous. The task goal may be clearly open-ended as in a problem-solving task. But even here pupils need to know the purpose of the task, for example, whether it is designed to enable them to practise a recently acquired skill or to demonstrate an understanding of some key subject concepts, or both. Expert teachers who work in this way with pupils attend to task resourcing as one way of scaffolding or supporting learners. Careful resourcing can limit the number of tangential options and any ambiguity in interpreting the task. For example, if a group activity is aimed at allowing children to explore the weight-bearing quality of different shapes, resources (which include only one strength of card, measuring instruments, scissors, a timer and weights together with guidelines for recording) provide a structure for the activity which enable learners to acquire the skills and knowledge valued in the public domain.

An advantage of this model is the time that the teacher is left free for quality time to spend at points 1, 2, 7 and 8 with other pupils. As Bennett and Dunne (1992) noted, several of the primary school teachers they had encouraged to use co-operative group work 'were astonished at the decline in pupil demands on them'. This point returns us to the feasibility concern raised at the beginning of the chapter.

Evidence from action research studies with practising teachers seems to suggest that learners need to be prepared for working in groups. That preparation apparently needs to include an understanding of strategies of behaviour and of self-monitoring or reflection on task. The preparation may take class time which might otherwise be spent more directly on curriculum issues. Nevertheless, once pupils have acquired interactive group skills, whether as pairs, in small work groups or as whole-class peer assessment groups, the learning that occurs is worth the effort.

The worthwhileness is fortified, not only because it seems that understanding is both enhanced and evinced, but also because teachers are eventually released to deploy themselves, as the high-quality expert resources they are in classrooms, with children at other stages of the learning cycle. Most teacher time is freed specifically for pupil assessment and introducing new knowledge and skills. Figure 11.3 indicates how this might work in practice.

Figure 11.3 is an example of a primary school teacher's planning in which individual activities, paired work, group and whole-class tasks are used in one session. The class has been divided into groups for the management of pupil learning. Activities and

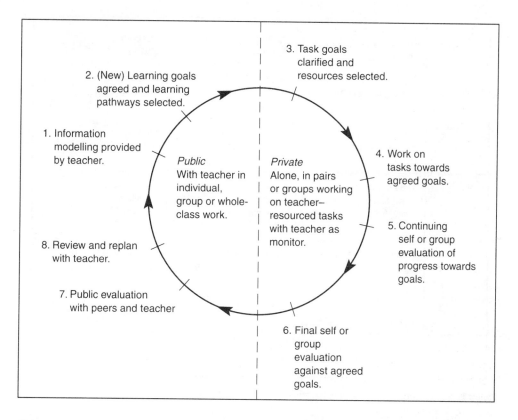

Figure 11.2 *A model of supported self study.*

deployment of teacher time are driven by pupil learning needs. Each learning need can be categorized according to the stages outlined in Figure 11.1. Different stages seem to require different groupings. Group A starts as an homogeneous group requiring the introduction of 'new' information but as it moves on to Stage 2, pairs are employed to maximize opportunities for immediate language use. It may seem appropriate to use mixed-ability pairings so that the quicker learners can give the less competent the support they need in the initial stages or provide the socio-cognitive conflict described by Light and Perret-Clermont (1989). Group B is clearly at Stage 2 and working in small task groups on co-operative problem-solving tasks that may involve some inter-group competition. Group C is largely at Stage 3 of the learning cycle and starts by working in homogeneous pairs or even as individuals on a task that allows the teacher to assess for mastery. Later in the session the group moves on to a Stage 1 activity at the start of a new learning cycle and works as a whole group with the teacher. The session concludes with whole-class feedback which allows Group C to revise and revisit earlier learning and groups A and B to begin to become familiar with future learning opportunities. Above all the feedback element allows pupils to listen to and use publicly the mathematical language they are acquiring in their group tasks.

The lesson plan just outlined appears to be indicating that homogeneous groups with a single-subject class focus is the way forward. Homogeneity would seem to be appropriate for this particular session. However, the case has been made in this

Group	Learning need	Activity/ resources	Teacher action
A	Introduction to measuring with cms Initial attempts at measuring with cms	Work with chalkboard, tape and objects Work in pairs on measuring tasks and record sheets	Introduce ideas and work with group Monitor with care
B	Develop competence in measuring with cms	Group problem solving in 3s and 4s. Task cards, tapes, paper, card, markers	Initial resourcing monitoring
C	Practice in use of cms Introduction to metres	'Estimate' task card, tapes, record sheets, in pairs Tapes, rulers, objects	Monitor very lightly Introduce ideas and work with group
ABC	Consolidation of activities	Feedback from each group to whole class	Lead and facilitate feedback

Figure 11.3   *A primary school teacher's session plans.*

chapter that decisions about group composition need to be driven by pupils' learning needs, and heterogeneous groups may be effective in other circumstances. The premise also applies to decisions about class focus. A recent study of London primary schools indicated that having limited focus in a session by keeping all the children engaged on one subject area tended to enhance pupil learning (Mortimore *et al.*, 1988).

My own experiences as a teacher suggested, however, that there are occasions when a mixed-class focus can be advantageous. A pattern of single-focus sessions can lead to the difficulties for slower learners so stunningly identified by Bennett *et al.* (1984) in their study of the match of task and child. Their findings revealed that teachers of 7- and 8-year-olds frequently did not provide the slower learning children with sufficient time for consolidation and practice at the learning stages equivalent to Stages 2 and 3 in Figure 11.1. Consequently the very children who needed most time for consolidation were denied it and set on a spiral of misconceptions. It would seem yet again that attention to the learning needs of the child should set in motion the classroom management strategies.

Some checkpoints, developed with teachers, may be useful in the evaluation of the appropriateness of groupings in teachers' planning. In order to ensure that groups are being used to manage learning and not simply to manage learners, teachers contemplating building group work into any session should be able to answer yes to each statement on the following checklist.

I know what learning outcome(s) I would like to see from this activity.

I am convinced that this form of group work is the best way of ensuring that the pupils develop their understanding.

I have constructed and resourced a task which will lead to or allow the pupils to demonstrate the learning outcome(s) I want to see.

The pupils will be clear about what is expected of them and have or are beginning to acquire the skills and understandings required to complete the task.

I am satisfied that the group composition is appropriate (mixed ability? pairing? grouping? same sex?)

The opportunity for pupil reflection and self-evaluation is built into the task.

I have sufficient time to set up the task with the group, the opportunity to monitor the group while they are on task and time for feedback and reflection when the activity has been completed.

My use of grouping is flexible and any learning sequence may require change in size of groups to enhance pedagogic purposes.

CONCLUDING POINTS

The contribution of this chapter to the collection has been to examine curricular application of group work. The very focus of the chapter eliminates activities that may be deemed non-curricular. Of these the more creative activities of the brainstorming small group is the most obvious omission in a chapter which deals with groups and pedagogy. Quite clearly, despite addressing curricular concerns, there has been no attempt to suggest that each curriculum subject will make intrinsically different uses of groups. On the contrary, the case has been made that groups of whatever kind have to justify their use as classroom management strategies on criteria drawn from an understanding of how learning occurs and the relationship between learning and task-setting. Any justification which is driven by a concern with the processes, both internal and contextual, associated with an individual's learning will necessarily highlight similarities in learning across curricula rather than differences in curricular usage of groups.

Of course teachers of English will differ from teachers of physics in their expectations of the curriculum outcomes of groups. They will use groups in ways that fit with their understanding of how novices become experts in their subject. Most teachers are secure in their grasp of curricular issues. The tricky part of teaching is getting the pupils to learn. Hopefully this chapter has acknowledged just how tricky that is but has held out some strategies for using groups to assist pupils in their acquisition of expertise in any of the subjects they might study.

NOTE

I would like to express my thanks to all those teachers, named and unnamed, whose classroom research has enabled me to develop these ideas in the context of the practice of teaching.

REFERENCES

Aronson, E., Blaney, N., Stephan, C., Sikes, J. and Snapp, M. (1978) *The Jigsaw Classroom*. Beverly Hills, CA: Sage.

Bennett, N. and Cass, A. (1988) The effects of group composition on group interactive processes and pupil understanding. *British Educational Research Journal*, **15**, 19-32.

Bennett, N. and Dunne, E. (1992) *Managing Classroom Groups*. Hemel Hempstead: Simon & Schuster.

Bennett, N., Desforges, C., Cockburn, A. and Wilkinson, B. (1984) *The Quality of Pupil Learning Experiences*. London: Lawrence Erlbaum.

Bruner, J.S. (1960) *The Process of Education*. Cambridge, MA: Harvard University Press.

Donaldson, M. (1978) *Children's Minds*. London: Fontana.

Driver, R. (1983) *The Pupil as Scientist*. Milton Keynes: Open University Press.

Floyd, A. (1981) *Developing Mathematical Thinking*. London: Addison Wesley for the Open University Press.

Galloway, D. and Edwards, A. (1991) *Primary School Teaching and Educational Psychology*. London: Longman.

Hughes, M. (1990) Children's computation. In R. Griere and M. Hughes (eds), *Understanding Children*. Oxford: Blackwell.

Jones, A. and Mercer, N. (1993) Theories of learning and information technology. In P. Scrimshaw (ed.), *Language Classrooms and Computers*. London: Routledge.

Light, P. and Blaye, A. (1990) Computer-based learning: the social dimensions. In H.C. Foot, M.J. Morgan and R.H. Shute (eds), *Children Helping Children*. Chichester: John Wiley.

Light, P. and Perret-Clermont, A.-N. (1989) Social context effects in learning and testing. In A. Gellatly, D. Rogers and J. Sloboda (eds), *Cognition and Social Worlds*. Oxford: Clarendon Press.

Mercer, N., Phillips, T. and Somekh, B. (1991) Spoken language and new technology. Research Note, *Journal of Computer-Assisted Learning*, **7**, 195-202.

Moore, P. and Tweddle, S. (1992) *The Integrated Classroom: Language Learning and IT*. London: Hodder & Stoughton.

Mortimore, P., Sammons, P., Stoll, L., Lewis, D. and Ecob, R. (1988) *School Matters*. Wells: Open Books.

Nisbet, J. and Shucksmith, J. (1986) *Learning Strategies*. London: Routledge & Kegan Paul.

Norman, D.A. (1978) Notes towards a complex theory of learning. In A.M. Lesgold, J.W. Pellegrino, S.D. Fokkema and R. Glaser (eds), *Cognitive Psychology and Instruction*. New York: Plenum.

Phillips, T. (1985). Beyond lip-service: discourse development after the age of nine. In G. Wells and J. Nicholls (eds), *Language and Learning: An Interactional Perspective*. Lewes: Falmer.

Prisk, T. (1987) Letting them get on with it: a study of unsupervised group talk in an infant school. In A. Pollard (ed.), *Children and Their Primary Schools*. Lewes: Falmer.

Tharp, R. and Gallimore, R. (1988) *Rousing Minds to Life: Teaching Learning and Schooling in Social Context*. New York: Cambridge University Press.

Waterhourse, P. (1988) *Supported Self Study: An Introduction for Teachers*. Coventry: NCET.

Watts, M. and Bentley, D. (1987) Constructivism in the classroom: enabling conceptual changes by words and deeds. *British Educational Research Journal*, **17**, 121-35.

Chapter 12

Co-operation and Bullying

Peter K. Smith, Helen Cowie and Lucia Berdondini

EDITORS' INTRODUCTION

One recurring theme of this volume is that pupils must be able to work together if they are to maximize their classroom experience. Working together draws upon particular social skills (discussion, joint problem-solving, trust) to enhance co-operation and collaboration. Effects within the classroom of this working together are seen in the promotion of social development (with regard to self-concept and inclusion within the classroom group) and intellectual growth.

Peter Smith and colleagues apply their thoughts, energy and social psychological approach to the school and classroom problem of bullying. The chapter does not draw upon a singular theoretical perspective but acknowledges how development, social interaction and social facilitation can be combined in the formation of a 'co-operative group work' (CGW) programme. Bullying is identified within the social situation of the class, taking place between all types of pupil – including classically defined bullies and victims, and more recently defined bully/victims, rejected and controversial pupils. The chapter expands and qualifies information expressed in previous chapters. For example: the variety of attitudes to working in small groups held by pupils and teachers introduced in Chapter 1 is given a real focus in Smith's two case studies, in which the liking of CGW varies with regard to popularity and aggressiveness in pupils. And the success of the CGW programme is, in part, due to teachers' willingness to take on this new responsibility with enthusiasm. Friendship (see Chapter 2) has positive and negative benefits in CGW. Assumptions that pupils will co-operate and that co-operative programmes are easy to construct and bring to fruition in class are quickly dispelled (also discussed in Chapters 4 and 5).

This chapter is written with a remarkable degree of honesty and reminds both teachers and researchers that experimental classroom developments are not clear and simple applications of theory. Bullying is a major cause of poor classroom social climate and poor interpersonal relations that inhibit social and intellectual development. Co-operative group work is a useful approach to help overcome a number of the problems caused by bullying. Readers are shown that this intervention can be effective, but the intervention will not affect all pupils in the same way. Teachers will need to make a strong commitment to make it work.

INTRODUCTION

What are the first things you remember about your time in the school classroom? The teacher? Perhaps. The things you learnt? Mmm. The other children – the class bully, the most popular child, the scapegoat – very probably. It's a fair bet that the peer group, the relationships amongst classmates and between you and other age-mates, will be something that has stayed with you longer than many of the formal 'lessons' learnt at school.

Educators who are committed to group work, of course, acknowledge the influence of peers. Much more than either the traditional whole-class 'talk and chalk' model, or the possibly Piagetian model of the solo learner encountering the problems posed by the world (or the teacher) in relative isolation, group work demonstrates that learning has a social context. However, in the field of group work in education there are a number of distinct theoretical traditions which underpin practice. These reflect different value systems, some of which overlap and some of which are in opposition to one another. There seems to be some divergence of emphasis in educators' perceptions of the value of group work (Cowie, 1994).

Some educators view the social context of group work primarily in terms of its direct instructional impact. Following a Vygotskian lead, the influence of the more expert or knowledgeable child on the less expert is hypothesized to be beneficial. When the structure of learning groups is considered, it may be in terms of more, or less, skilled children – same- and mixed-ability groupings, as for example in Bennett and Dunne (1992); or perhaps the sex composition of groups will be the focus. If characteristics of individual children are described, they are usually in terms of cognitive or learning characteristics. For example, in discussing group work individual children may be 'hard grinders', 'attention getters', 'easy riders', 'intermittent workers' and so forth (Galton and Williamson, 1992).

Other researchers are more interested in the socially facilitative aspects of group work. At its most basic level, group work can promote the flow of communication among participants by encouraging group members to share experience or ideas in a friendly and supportive peer group. It can be used to enhance peer relationships within the group by creating a social context in which it is safe to explore hopes, fears, anxieties and aspirations. Where children are experiencing personal difficulties, group work offers a setting where conflicts can be examined and possibly resolved with the help of peers and a facilitative adult (Silveira and Trafford, 1988). In British schools this kind of group work, based on methods developed by counsellors, is most commonly found in lessons which are about personal and social education. The teacher does not dominate but models qualities of empathy and active listening in a non-judgemental way.

Traditionally, schools did not encourage pupils to express emotions in the classroom, and until around twenty years ago it was virtually unknown for pupils to sit in a circle with their teacher as facilitator exploring experiences and perceptions with one another. The view of educators then was that personal feelings and interpersonal relationships are best taken care of within the family. More recently, educators have taken on board the view that positive self-esteem is a basis for development as a person and that this should be catered for within a balanced curriculum (Brandes and Phillips, 1979; Hopson and Scally, 1981; Pike and Selby, 1988). Their underlying philosophy states that personal and interpersonal experience forms a basis for individual growth and for learning. If the characteristics of individual children are described it is usually in personal terms ('a confident child', 'a shy person', 'one who takes risks in the group') or in terms of roles ('the challenger', 'the peace-maker', 'the joker'), describing children who may be at different levels of personal development, but who are thought of as benefiting from interactions within the group.

But the social structure of groups, and the characteristics of individuals within the group, can be analysed in other ways too – ways drawn from psychological research in child development which, we will argue in this chapter, may also be very relevant to the pedagogical process and to the success or failure of group work itself.

An early and influential way of looking at group structure in this psychological tradition, in a classroom as in other semi-permanent, recurring groups, has been the sociogram. Asking, or observing, who likes whom (or plays with whom, or chooses to sit next to whom) provides a vivid, diagrammable portrayal of classroom structure. Sociograms date back to the work of Moreno in the 1930s; as an example, Clark *et al.* (1969) show the relative popularity of children by means of concentric circles, indicating the number of best friends each child has. Such figures are useful in showing, at a glance, such aspects as: who is a 'star' in the class? who is an isolate? what cliques are there? how strong is sex segregation in friendships? As we shall see, this will be of relevance when we look at which children like co-operating with others, and which do not.

Another example of a sociogram, from our current research, is shown in Figure 12.1. We shall refer to this figure again later.

SOCIOMETRIC STATUS TYPES

Notwithstanding the utility of this kind of sociometry, it has a drawback. The drawback stems ultimately to the neglect of *disliking* in social groups; and the fact that this *is* a drawback has emerged over the last decade of psychological research. There is an ethical issue here in the researchers' concern that the experience of categorizing peers in terms of disliking them might be distressing or hurtful for some members of the class, or might rebound to the detriment of disliked peers. However, studies so far (Hayvren and Hymel, 1984) have failed to find any adverse consequences of using the techniques.

A key study in initiating this approach is that by Coie *et al.* (1982). These researchers, studying 8- to 14-year-olds in North Carolina, USA, asked children both whom they liked most in the class and whom they liked least. They found that liking and disliking were not polar opposites, at least as far as the class consensus was concerned. Admittedly, some *popular* children were liked and not disliked, and some *rejected* children were disliked and not liked. But, in addition, there were *controversial* children, liked by some and disliked by others; and there were *neglected* children, whom no one picks out either to like or dislike. Together with *average* (and sometimes *other*) categories, these form five (or six) *sociometric status types*. This more detailed breakdown of classroom social structure suggests that the simple popular–unpopular axis of a sociogram is only a partial, incomplete look at classroom social dynamics. In our study we have explored sociometric status in greater depth by also interviewing the children about how they came to make their choices and why.

But, how useful are these categories? A substantial body of research suggests that the different sociometric status types do indeed delineate particular kinds of pupil, and yield different expectations for social and also perhaps academic behaviour. The study by Coie *et al.* (1982) showed that popular children were seen by classmates as leaders, but also as children who co-operate and are not aggressive or disruptive. Controversial children are also leaders, but they are high on aggression. These two types of leaders have of course been highlighted in previous studies of leadership. Rejected children are aggressive, but do not have the leadership skills to compensate. Neglected children are neither leaders, nor co-operative, nor aggressive.

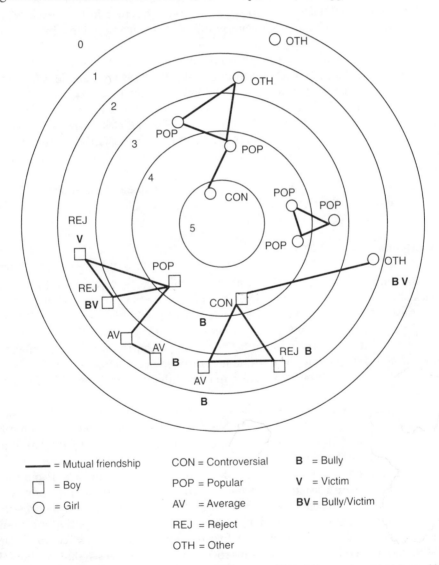

Figure 12.1 *Sociogram of one class of children, indicating mutual friendships, sociometric status and bully/victim status.*

Further studies have fleshed out these distinctions. For example, Ladd (1983), observing 8- and 9-year-olds in playgrounds, found that rejected children (compared to popular and average children) spent less time in co-operative play and social conversation, and more time in arguing and fighting. They tended to play in smaller groups. Thus, the peer perceptions do seem to be based in actual, observable behaviour.

In Figure 12.1, we have combined features of the traditional sociogram with labels of sociometric status. In this figure, circles represent girls, and squares, boys, in a class of 17 children. Each child was asked to name 3 children they liked most and 3 they liked least, in the class. The position of a child in the concentric circles shows the number of other children who included them in their 'liked most' nominations. For example, the child in the centre received such a nomination from 5 classmates; the others, from 4, 3, 2 or only 1 classmate. The connecting lines show those children who reciprocated 'like most' nominations and can be thought of as being mutual friends. All but one child in this class have at least one mutual friend, though in some classes this proportion is much higher.

So far this shows positive liking; we have also indicated the sociometric status types, which additionally take account of the 'liked least' nominations. Thus, of the 6 children in or near the centre, 4 are popular, but 2 are controversial indicating that they also received several 'liked least' nominations.

BULLIES AND VICTIMS

Sociometric status provides one way of analysing, or dissecting, social structure. But of course, it is only one way. There are many ways of doing this. Another dimension, very important in children's perceptions, is that of bullying and victimization. Although there are developmental trends in children's understanding of the terms 'bully' and 'victim' (Madsen and Smith, 1993), children generally respond to these terms readily and have a basic understanding that a bully is repeatedly nasty or hurtful to someone else (often smaller or weaker), and that the victim is the recipient of this. When obtaining 'bully' and 'victim' nominations, we generally clarify or provide such short definitions to avoid misunderstanding. Children can usually identify or nominate the bullies and victims in their class quite easily, and different children in a class show considerable consistency in their nominations.

It is clear that children who receive many 'bully' nominations from classmates – say, over 50 per cent – might be thought of as 'bullies', and those with say over 50 per cent 'victim' nominations might be thought of as 'victims' in the class. However, we have found that a substantial minority of children may collect quite a lot of *both* 'bully' and 'victim' nominations. Those who get at least 33 per cent of both nominations from classmates, we have called 'bully/victims'. Such children have been recognized in other work on bullying. Stephenson and Smith (1989), using teacher nominations, described both 'bully/victims' and also 'provocative victims', i.e. victims who by their provocative or disruptive/aggressive actions can be said to have brought some bullying on themselves in a way which is not true of most victims (who may just have the wrong hair colour, or skin colour, or who may just deal with a bully unassertively). Again, Pikas (1989) distinguishes the provocative victim from the 'ordinary' victim.

We feel that, so far, the distinction between a provocative victim and a bully/victim is tenuous and that there is major overlap between these categories. From our analyses, bully/victims are seen as aggressive and disruptive, like bullies, but they are also recipients of bullying.

How do these categories relate to sociometric status? One study found that in junior/middle schools bullies are often seen as controversial, or rejected; victims are often seen as rejected, or neglected (Boulton and Smith, in press). This study did not examine bully/victims as a separate category. However, related research suggests that bully/victims tend to have different family constellations and characteristics from either bullies or victims (Bowers *et al.*, 1992; Smith *et al.*, in press).

In Figure 12.1, we have indicated those children who were bullies (B), victims (V), or bully/victims (BV); in this class, by the criteria above, there were 4 bullies, 1 victim and 2 bully/victims. Three of these 7 children have rejected status.

GROUP WORK WITH DIFFERENT TYPES OF CHILDREN

One problem for the classroom teacher is to curb the bully and help the victim; to prevent a rejected child from disrupting the classroom atmosphere, and encourage the neglected child to participate more fully. Group work might help in this.

Group work brings children together; depending on the type of group work, it may bring children together to co-operate, or collaborate, towards a common goal. This *might* assist in improving social relationships amongst the working group. The group members could find that the sharing of information, mutual assistance and joint pleasure in a common achievement foster respect for others with whom they might otherwise seldom interact. If teachers form groups outside friendship groups, improvements in general social relationships in the classroom could follow. Indeed, such forms of group work might help break down barriers of race and gender. Ideally, a classroom climate of trust and co-operation would develop. In fact it is claimed in many experimental studies of co-operative learning (Sharan, 1980; Slavin, 1987; Hertz-Lazarowitz *et al.*, 1989) that a direct outcome of co-operative learning interventions is that peer relationships are enhanced, prejudice reduced and tolerance for peers with learning or social disabilities increased.

However, forming groups outside normal friendship groups has dangers. Some children (especially rejected and controversial children) are seen by peers as not very co-operative. A rejected child may be placed with others who do not like him or her, and the group may function poorly as a consequence. A bully/victim may refuse to co-operate and be disruptive. A neglected child, or a victim (especially if in a group with one or more bullies) may simply feel intimidated. In such circumstances, group work might even be counterproductive.

The role of the teacher is clearly important here. First, the teacher would need to consider carefully the composition of groups in the above terms; and, in addition, watch for and work with the inevitable interpersonal difficulties which will arise with any group work. Second, the teacher's own motivation to employ group work, and their ability to cope with the difficulties introduced by certain pupil relationships, will be likely to influence the effectiveness of any co-operative programme.

Nevertheless, on an optimistic view group work could help solve many of the problems of classroom social structure – problems which are scarcely tackled by conventional pedagogic techniques. Neglected children could be helped to participate effectively. Bullies could be helped to understand the viewpoints and feelings of others, and to give and take more generously. The interpersonal difficulties experienced by many children and diagnosed by our labels could be tackled at source, in the successes and failures of co-operative endeavour. Co-operative or collaborative group work could both highlight the difficulties in relationships some children experience, and, if targeted and used optimally, help work through and overcome these difficulties.

How feasible is this? Experimental studies of group processes and group work have suggested that it can increase liking and reduce aggression (see Galton and Williamson, 1992, for a review). But many of these are somewhat artificial studies, often carried out with newly formed groups in laboratory settings, rather than in normal classrooms. Typically the intervention is done by an experimenter (not by the teacher) over a short period of time and evaluated immediately. Furthermore, there is seldom evidence that the outcomes are long-lasting. Such limitations are not true of all studies, but when studies are done in actual classrooms (e.g. Slavin, 1983) the outcomes for intergroup relationships, while perhaps encouraging, are not uniformly positive.

In the school context, Olweus (1991) on the basis of Norwegian research mentions co-operative group work as one means of reducing school bullying; though not as what he considers a 'core' component. He does not describe the research evidence for this, however. On the whole, research on the *social* consequences of group work, let alone on the influence of social structure on success of group work, in naturally functioning classrooms and over a reasonable timespan, remains somewhat meagre.

SOCIAL CONSEQUENCES OF GROUP WORK

Our first study of the impact of group work on social relationships actually focused on ethnic relationships (Smith *et al.*, in press). We introduced training in co-operative group work (CGW; see Appendix for explanation) for three teachers, each in a different middle school with an ethnically mixed intake. In each school, the class with the CGW-trained teacher was paired with a same-age class experiencing the normal curriculum (NC) (which only included about half as much group work as that used in the CGW classes). The CGW sessions typically involved trust-building exercises, problem-solving tasks, brainstorming, co-operative games, role-play activities and discussion groups; with groups reporting back to the whole class, followed by teacher 'debriefing'.

Assessments of social relationships were made at the beginning, middle and end of the school year. The results were reasonably encouraging. In particular, liking of classmates increased in the CGW classes relative to the NC classes. Also, different race peers were rated as more co-operative, in the CGW classes. Children reported that they enjoyed the CGW activities, and the three teachers were positive about the experience.

In this project, two of the three teachers had already been experienced in using many co-operative techniques, and had taken part in a world studies programme (Pike and Selby, 1988). The third teacher was relatively inexperienced, but shared the values of the other two teachers in her commitment to anti-racist practices and her wish to create a co-operative climate in her class. The three teachers were certainly not a random sample of junior/middle school teachers, but were selected for their experience or interest in CGW techniques. Thus, it remained an open question whether the gains (only found for some indicators) could be found in a wider sample of teachers. Also, we felt it would be interesting explicitly to include measures of bullying and victimization. This led to a second study (both funded by the ESRC, Swindon).

THE SECOND CGW INTERVENTION STUDY

This research was carried out over two years in three racially mixed middle schools, the children's ages ranging from 7 to 12 years. In two schools, some classes took part in the co-operative group work intervention, and others were matched controls carrying on with their normal curriculum. In a third school, three classes used the CGW training and there were no controls. Some children took part only in the first year, some only in the second year and some children were participants for both years. Altogether, 11 classes experienced an enhanced CGW curriculum, and 5 experienced the NC curriculum (see Cowie *et al.*, 1994b, for further details).

The teachers taking part in the CGW training in this study were not specially selected, although obviously they were willing to take part. Indeed, some of the CGW teachers were somewhat sceptical or ambivalent about the approach. Some of them became more enthusiastic during the project, but one school did drop out after the first year, in part because they felt that the perceived gains from being in the project were outweighed by the time needed for training and pressure on staff at a period of financial retrenchment and legislated curriculum change.

The CGW techniques covered a variety of methods, including trust-building exercises (e.g. self-introduction in pairs), group discussion (e.g. preparing issues for a reporting-back session), role play and simulation (e.g. the Trading Game, a role-play exercise designed for children which demonstrate power inequalities in world trading), co-operative games (e.g. circle games, parachute games) and debriefing (e.g. telegrams, smiley faces, sentence completion). The aim was to enable children to express their own point of view and to recognize that of others in a shared task. Debriefing sessions were important opportunities for the teachers and children to discuss difficulties or conflicts and try to resolve them. Three people were involved in the training: Helen Cowie, a member of the project team, who had designed the in-service training for the first study; and John Allen and Jim Lewis, teachers from the first study who were both very experienced in using CGW methods with their primary classes.

Characteristics of the children in the classes

Children were given individual assessments at the beginning and end of each academic year. Data was obtained from 108 children in the first year (55 boys, 53 girls) and from

100 children in the second year (59 boys, 41 girls). These assessments included ratings of liking of classmates, nominations of classmates as bullies or victims, as well as a stereotypes test to measure children's view of different ethnic groups (white, Asian and African-Caribbean) which was used operationally to define a prejudiced child. Using peer nominations of children liked most and liked least within each class, each child had been classified into the six sociometric status types (average, popular, controversial, neglected, rejected and other) and one of five bully/victim status categories (bully, victim, bully/victim, control and other).

As in our first study, it was apparent from the initial assessments that an appreciable number of children were experiencing bullying, or some degree of social exclusion, rejection or neglect by classmates. Others were clearly bullies. Figure 12.1 in fact illustrates one of these classes. In a typical class of around 25 children, it was not hard to identify several bullies, and several victims. Table 12.1 (showing data for the boys only) indicates that over a third of the boys were scored as either controversial or rejected, and an appreciable proportion were nominated as bullies or bully/victims (characteristically, these figures are considerably less for girls, so the overall class incidence is correspondingly reduced). These assessments were generally confirmed by in-depth interviews carried out with selected children in the middle of each year.

Table 12.1 *Percentage of boys falling in different bully/victim categories, by sociometric status type.*

Year 1	n	Bully/victim	Bully	Victim	Other	Control
popular	14	0	7	7	29	57
average + other	21	29	10	14	33	14
rejected + controversial	20	55	35	0	10	0

Year 2	n	Bully/victim	Bully	Victim	Other	Control
popular	13	8	0	15	31	46
average + other	23	26	17	9	30	17
rejected + controversial	23	30	43	17	9	0

We were interested to see if, for each child, there was a relationship between their sociometric status and the bully/victim category they were in. The two years were analysed separately, as some children were common to both; also, the two years provided an inbuilt replication such that consistent findings would have greater internal validity (Lykken, 1968).

An association was found in both years; rejected and controversial children generally were bullies or bully/victims, whereas peopular children were generally neither involved in bullying nor being bullied. This finding was strongest for boys, though girls showed the same trend. The overall figures for boys are shown in Table 12.1. As can be seen, the boys involved in bullying are seldom popular – though some may be controversial (disliked strongly by some children, but having their own 'gang' of friends who like them). These associations are highly significant statistically (p<.0001 in the first year; p<.005 in the second year; chi-square tests).

How effective was the group work intervention?

Altogether, a considerable number of comparisons were possible to judge the relative effectiveness of CGW, compared to NC, in improving social relationships. However, the general picture obtained was one of no real difference between the CGW and NC classes. There were indeed one or two encouraging findings, but these were balanced by one or two discouraging findings in the opposite direction! This was true of most of our indicators of social relationships. There was one encouraging finding; on some of our analyses, nominations of children as victims fell more in the CGW classes than the NC classes. Thus, CGW may have encouraged some of the children susceptible to victimization to become more confident and skilful in their social interactions (Smith *et al.*, 1993). However, this positive result was not obtained in every analysis, and it was not found for the similar analyses for nominations of bullies. CGW did not seem to have reached them; a point we will return to.

This study, at least on the basis of most of the quantitative assessments, failed to replicate or extend the promising findings of our first study. With the one possible exception of reports of victims, social relations and prejudice had not convincingly been improved by CGW.

We believe a number of factors may be responsible for this. One, very probably, is that the CGW teachers were not specially selected at the start, and varied both in their commitment and in the amount of time actually using CGW techniques. Typical comments were:

> My problem is now wondering how much they have learned and how much they are going to do when they take the tests in a fortnight.

> I want the children to be nice but at the same time I want them to learn through working – not through playing a nice game.

Also, they did not always proceed through to debriefing as thoroughly as was desirable – as we have seen, CGW may bring up interpersonal problems and these need to be actively worked through. More fundamentally, some of the teachers revealed that they were ambivalent about co-operative group work; they expressed a tension between their desire to implement CGW methods and their need to maintain control of children who might be disruptive:

> When it started there were loads and loads of conflicts.

> In the end it's lift the lid and then put it down again and lift the lid for a bit, put it back down again.

> After twenty odd years your patterns are pretty firmly established and to change anything fundamentally is very difficult.

Interacting with this, in addition, was the challenging nature of the classes which most of the teachers were working with. These were difficult classes, each with a small number of quite disturbed children. Many of these children might not have appreciated being asked to work in groups outside friendship groups. This would make the issue of working through and debriefing very salient and demanding. This, coupled with some teacher inexperience, apathy, or simply pressure of time, could render the hoped-for benefits of CGW non-existent.

WHO LIKES CO-OPERATIVE GROUP WORK?

The apparent failure of this second study to show many clear social benefits of co-operative group work led us to look further at children's liking of co-operative group work in the classroom and its relationship with bully or victim status and sociometric status.

Most of the children in the CGW classes were interviewed at the end of each year about their liking of co-operative work. We elicited themes and patterns in the content of what they said. In addition, their answers were related on a 5-point scale from 1 (dislike a lot) through 3 (neutral) to 5 (like a lot). For this analysis we had in the first year a sample of 88 children (45 boys, 43 girls) and in the second year one of 93 children (55 boys, 38 girls). Again, the two years were analysed separately. As Table 12.2 shows, most children like CGW (65 per cent in total for the first year and 60 per cent for the second year). But there is a clear minority who strongly dislike it.

Table 12.2 *Percentage of bully (B) and bully/victim (B/V) children (those who bully others) compared to the rest (those who do not bully others) by different degrees of expressed liking for CGW.*

Year 1	Bully others	The rest	Total
n	26	59	85
dislike a lot	23	2	8
dislike a bit/neutral	15	32	27
like/like a lot	62	66	65

Year 2	Bully others	The rest	Total
n	39	54	93
dislike a lot	33	17	24
dislike a bit/neutral	21	13	16
like/like a lot	46	70	60

We then looked to see if there was an association between each child's score for liking CGW and the bully or victim category they were in. We found a consistent result for both years when we combined children who bully others a lot ('bullies' and 'bully/victims') and compared them with the rest (children not often involved in bullying). Whereas most children like CGW, some bully and bully/victim children dislike it strongly (see Table 12.2). This was statistically significant (or near-significant) (for the first year $p<.005$; for the second year $p<.06$; chi-squared tests). In Figure 12.1, for example, there are 3 boys, all nominated as bullies, who form a triangular cluster of mutual friendship at the bottom of the sociogram; all three disliked CGW a lot (score of 1). One, Winston, was also sociometrically rejected, being nominated by 9 classmates as someone they 'like least'. He said of CGW:

When you've got other people it gets on your nerves.

and

When teacher picks groups *we* can't pick groups. *She* picks groups . . . She always puts me with other people I don't like but she won't put me with my best friend . . . I think we should pick who we want to sit with.

Most children were adamant that they disliked having domineering children in their group; and when the domineering children were interviewed, it emerged that the feeling of dislike was mutual.

Marcia, a bully, had nothing good to say about CGW except that she disliked it and that she did not think that her teacher should use it in the following year. Her peers in the group found it a trial to cope with her because 'she always fights with everybody and she thumps'.

Hussein pointed out that CGW was a good way of working except when you had Sean, a bully, in your group. 'He is bad in a group. He kicks you under the table. Everybody's scared of Sean because he beats them up.' Sean was even more critical of fellow members of his group. 'They smell! This kid Angus that I work with, he spoils the ozone layer. He don't brush his teeth. I don't like him. Wee Angus Mackay [in a mock Scottish accent]'.

Kamran, a bully, was described by members of his group as 'an honorary friend' but a very acrimonious argument broke out during the interview during which it became clear that he was really an outsider, only to be tolerated if he was pleasant – which he found it very hard to be. For most of the interview he adopted a jeering attitude towards the others. For example, he showed total lack of empathy for the feelings of Marcus, when Marcus described what it was like when his mum left home. This contrasted markedly with the supportive way in which the others dealt with Marcus's sadness. The other members of the group noticed, and finally described Kamran to his face as 'horrible', 'nothing good about him' and 'sexist'.

Wayne, a bully, had little to say about CGW except that 'it stinks!' When asked to clarify he said that he had this view because 'all the poofs go first!' Members of his group could find little which was positive to say about Wayne though David allowed that 'he helps a bit'.

Here is what some bully/victims have to say about CGW:

I don't like it. You can't concentrate and people don't always listen. I hate girls and I don't like mixing.

I don't like CGW. I like working with my friends.

CGW causes fights when girls are in the group.

When I'm doing something they take it off me.

In Figure 12.1, Mark was a bully/victim, sociometrically rejected, who did not like group work (score of 2). According to his teacher:

Mark finds it very hard in groups. He thinks he's not going to be able to do the work. He never wants to be with the other people in the group . . . He believes he's being picked on. This afternoon he was trying very hard not to retaliate because it's all going down in a report he has to take home every day so he was saying to me, 'Look! I'm not retaliating. All these terrible things are happening to me and look how good I'm being!' Mark himself admitted that he is not always a very good group member and that 'sometimes I fight and argue'.

This contrasted with the views of victims who, depending on the group which they were placed in, reported positive feelings about CGW:

It's better because you get further with your work and more brainy people are there to help you.

You learn a lot.

In Figure 12.1, the one victim reported liking CGW a lot (score of 5).

We also looked at how sociometric status related to liking CGW. We found a relevant difference between boys and girls: girls generally like CGW, independent of their sociometric status, and more than boys. Especially in the second-year data, popular boys like CGW (whereas rejected boys disliked it). (There were only two neglected boys; they all liked CGW strongly.)

Popular children were much more likely to make statements like the following:

> It doesn't matter what colour children are. They all play together otherwise some would be left out and would be on their own.

> You get on with each other.

> We work well as a team.

> It's important to make new friends and to learn about other people.

Since the classes were of mixed ethnic origin children, we related each child's sociometric status, bully/victim status, and liking of co-operative group work to ethnicity (white/Asian/African-Caribbean), but no significant associations were found. We also analysed each child's sociometric status, bully/victim status and liking of co-operative group work with their prejudice scores, but again there were no significant associations.

CONCLUSIONS

In our study, most children liked co-operative group work, especially girls; but some boys, especially rejected boys, disliked it. These rejected boys overlapped considerably with the categories of bully and bully/victim; and it is these categories – children who are seen by peers as bullying others – which seem most to capture the majority of children who strongly dislike group work. Clearly, these children create difficulties in classrooms and schools. Many other children dislike them, and teachers will find them disruptive. (Often, of course, home or other circumstances may also be difficult for these children themselves.) This rejection of co-operative or collaborative group work by sociometrically rejected children has also been found in laboratory studies in this age range (Menesini and Fonzi, 1991); and a similar phenomenon in subgroups of secondary school children is described by Salmon (1992; Salmon and Claire, 1984).

But there are many 'false positives' in this categorization, too – many children who bully also say that they like group work (see Table 12.2). Although some may say that they like CGW, they are not always able to put its ideas into practice, as the testimony of their peers indicates. Nevertheless, it may well be that bullies who are able to articulate some of the principles of CGW are children who could be worked with to overcome their pattern of misusing power in their relationships with others. Joseph, a noted bully in the class, was visibly shaken when he was interviewed in the company of two other bullies and chose to distance himself from their attitudes. He said:

> I want to grow up with a nice attitude. I want people to like me and I want them to know me better.

Clearly, there is a danger of 'labelling' certain children as beyond help. Some children will be very difficult to work with, but the challenge remains as how best to support teachers not only to contain their disruptiveness, but also to try to improve their behaviour. We believe that forms of group work do have potential here, but it is very clear that using group work to develop co-operation in many of such children is difficult, since they will not like it, and other children will not like working with them. We are currently exploring the potential of IPR (interpersonal process recall; Kagan and Kagan, 1991) in group-work contexts to facilitate debriefing and to enable children mutually to examine and share feelings and cognitions in peer group situations (Cowie *et al.*, 1994a).

In summary, we believe that the social *relationships* in the classroom are a vital factor to consider when looking at the effectiveness of co-operative groups in real classroom situations. Co-operative groups have potential to help intergroup processes; and indeed we did find evidence that some children who were shy and victimized did gain confidence in the CGW programme. But other children may show resistance and even hostility to being grouped away from their friends or their 'gang'. It will not be impossible to work with these children – and indeed it may be thought essential to do so, since many of these latter children are rejected by peers and are likely to bully others. Teachers need to try to change such behaviour, and CGW will certainly bring these problems out into the open. Some classes, of course, will manifest these problems very much more than others.

But can teachers cope with the resulting challenge? First, they need to know something about the social dynamics of their class. Second, they need to know ways of coping with children who bully others. Third, they need a commitment to, and direct experience of, co-operative group work, both as facilitators in their own classroom and as participants in co-operative activities with their own peers. The values of the teacher are another important factor in the successful use of CGW (Lewis and Cowie, 1993).

CGW means putting pupils and teachers with very different values and perspectives into close interaction. This can be a strength when using CGW as an intervention, since these issues can be grappled with; but it can be a difficulty too, as we have tried to illustrate in this chapter. Both knowledge and values lie at the heart of a successful implementation of group-work procedures.

APPENDIX
Co-operative group work

In our view, the central feature of co-operative group work is the opportunity to learn through the expression and exploration of diverse ideas and experiences in co-operative company. Group work is co-operative in the sense that no one in any one working group is trying to get the best out of the situation; it is not about competing and winning, but about using the resources available in a group to deepen understanding, to sharpen judgement, to share ideas and support one another.

Groups which are working effectively will have the following characteristics:

- group members are, between then, putting forward more than one point of view or contribution in relation to the task they face;
- group members are disposed to be responsive to and be appreciative of the different contributions which group members make;
- the interaction assists with the development of group members' knowledge, understanding and sensitivity to others;

- the task is an appropriate one which allows or requires these things to happen.
- teachers frame the tasks to support the distinctive potential of learning through group work.

Group work takes many forms:

Discussion: groups of children work to share ideas and understanding. The focus may be on the interpretation of a poem or a picture, the sharing of an experience, the pooling of ideas or the eliciting of opinions. Discussions may lead to enhanced individual understanding, or they may lead to negotiation in the process of reaching group consensus.

Problem-solving tasks: the same task may be set simultaneously to small groups of 3 to 5 pupils and there may be a final review with mutual criticism. Alternatively (as in the Jigsaw method), groups of pupils may work on different aspects of the task and the different contributions are brought together and reviewed.

Role-play activities: each child is given a character within the framework of an event or situation. The characters interact according to their interpretation of the role. Children are free to contribute from their own strengths or perspectives, although they may be assigned a specific role.

Co-operative games: within a playful context children explore different aspects of working together, including co-operation, acceptance of one another, creative processes in the group, fun and involvement in working on a shared theme. Children experience warm-up exercises and games from many cultures; they also have the opportunity to design their own co-operative games.

Debriefing: it is important to encourage children to feed back to the teacher their feelings and thoughts about what they are doing and how they are experiencing it. Regularly, children are given the opportunity to reflect on an activity, to analyse what happened and how they feel about it. They are encouraged to think about themselves and how they relate to others. Strategies include 'sitting in the circle', 'passing the stone', 'speaking to the magic microphone'; these aim to help the children feel accustomed to feedback, peer-evaluation and self-evaluation as an integral part of learning.

NOTE

We are grateful to the participating pupils and teachers in the schools (all quoted under pseudonyms); also to Michael Boulton, Louise Bowers and Rema Laver for help in data analysis. The research reported here was supported by grants X204252003 and R000232318 from the ESRC, Swindon. Lucia Berdondini was supported by a grant from the University of Florence.

REFERENCES

Bennett, N. and Dunne, E. (1992) *Managing Groups*. Hemel Hempstead: Simon & Schuster Education.
Boulton, M.J. and Smith, P.K. (in press) Bully/victim problems in middle school children: stability, self-perceived competence, peer perceptions, and peer acceptance. *British Journal of Developmental Psychology*.
Bowers, L., Smith, P.K. and Binney, V. (1993) Cohesion and power in the families of children involved in bully/victim problems at school. *Journal of Family Therapy*, **14**, 371-87.
Brandes, D. and Phillips, H. (1979) *Gamesters' Handbook*. London: Hutchinson.

Clark, A., Wyon, S. and Richards, M.P.M. (1969) Free-play in nursery school children. *Journal of Child Psychology and Psychiatry*, **10**, 205-16.

Coie, J.D., Dodge, K.A. and Coppotelli, H. (1982) Dimensions and types of social status: a cross-age perspective. *Developmental Psychology*, **18**, 557-70.

Cowie, H. (1994) Co-operative group work: a perspective from the UK. *International Journal of Educational Research* [special issue on co-operative learning in social contexts].

Cowie, H., Lewis, J., Berdondini, L. and Rivers, I. (1994a) Interpersonal process recall in classroom groups. International Conference on Peer Relations, University of South Australia.

Cowie, H., Smith, P.K., Laver, R. and Boulton, M. (1994b) *Co-operation in the Multi-ethnic Classroom*. London: David Fulton.

Galton, M. and Williamson, J. (1992) *Groupwork in the Primary Classroom*. London: Routledge.

Hayvren, M. and Hymel, S. (1984) Ethical issues in sociometric testing: the impact of sociometric measures on interactive behaviour. *Developmental Psychology*, **20**, 844-9.

Hertz-Lazarowitz, R., Fuchs, I., Sharabany, R. and Eisenberg, N. (1989). Students' interactive and non-interactive behaviours in the classroom: a comparison between two types of classroom in the city and the kibbutz in Israel. *Contemporary Educational Psychology*, **14**, 22-32.

Hopson, B. and Scally, M. (1981) *Lifeskills Teaching*. London: McGraw-Hill.

Kagan, N. and Kagan, H. (1991) IPR: a research training model. In P.N. Dowrick (ed)., *Practical Guide to Using Video in the Behavioral Sciences*. Chichester: Wiley.

Ladd, G. (1983) Social networks of popular, average and rejected children in school settings. *Merrill-Palmer Quarterly*, **29**, 283-307.

Lewis, J. and Cowie, H. (1993) CGW, promises and limitations: a study of teachers' values. *BPS Education Section Review*, **17**, 77-84.

Lykken, D.T. (1968) Statistical significance in psychological research. *Psychological Bulletin*, **70**, 151-9.

Madsen, K. and Smith, P.K (1993) Age and sex differences in definitions of bullying. Paper presented at the European Development Psychology Conference, Bonn.

Menesini, E. and Fonzi, A. (1991) Azione ed interazione nello sviluppo dei comportamenti cooperativi. In A. Fonzi (ed.), *Cooperare e competere tra bambini*. Florence: Giunti.

Olweus, D. (1991) Bully/victim problems among schoolchildren: basic facts and effects of a school-based intervention program. In D. Pepler and K. Rubin (eds), *The Development and Treatment of Childhood Aggression*. Hillsdale, NJ: Lawrence Erlbaum.

Pikas, A. (1989) The common concern method for the treatment of mobbing. In E. Roland and E. Munthe (eds), *Bullying: An International Perspective*. London: David Fulton.

Pike, G. and Selby, D. (1988) *Global Teacher, Global Learner*. London: Hodder & Stoughton.

Salmon, P. (1992) The peer group. In J.C. Coleman (ed.), *The School Years*. London: Routledge.

Salmon, P. and Claire, H. (1984) *Classroom Collaboration*. London: Routledge & Kegan Paul.

Sharan, S. (1980) Co-operative learning in small groups: recent methods and effects on achievement, attitudes and ethnic relations. *Review of Educational Research*, **50**, 241-71.

Silveira, W.R. and Trafford, G. (1988) *Children Need Groups*. Aberdeen: Aberdeen University Press.

Slavin, R. (1984) *Co-operative Learning*. New York: Longman.

Slavin, R. (1987) Developmental and motivational perspectives on co-operative learning: a reconciliation. *Child Development*, **58**, 1161-7.

Smith, P.K., Boulton, M. and Cowie, H. (1993) The impact of co-operative groupwork on ethnic relations in middle school. *Schools Psychology International*, **14**, 21-42.

Smith, P.K., Bowers, L., Binney, V. and Cowie, H. (1993) Relationships of children involved in bully/victim problems at schools. In S. Duck (ed.), *Understanding Relationship Processes, Vol. 2, Learning about Relationships*. Newbury Park, CA: Sage Publications.

Smith, P.K., Cowie, H. and Laver, R. (in press) How co-operative groupwork affects social relationships in school: a question of values.

Stephenson, P. and Smith, D. (1989) Bullying in the junior school. In D. Tattum and D. Lane (eds), *Bullying in Schools*. Stoke-on-Trent: Trentham Books.

Name Index

Subject Index